THE
ZEBRA
MURDERS

THE
ZEBRA
MURDERS

A SEASON OF KILLING, RACIAL MADNESS, AND CIVIL RIGHTS

PRENTICE EARL SANDERS
BENNETT COHEN

ARCADE PUBLISHING
NEW YORK

FIRST EDITION

Library of Congress Cataloging-in-Publication Data

Sanders, Prentice Earl.
The zebra murders : a season of killing, racial madness, and civil rights / by Prentice Earl Sanders and Bennett Cohen. —1st ed.
p. cm.
ISBN-13: 978-1-55970-806-7 (alk. paper)
ISBN-10: 1-55970-806-9 (alk. paper)
1. Sanders, Prentice Earl. 2. San Francisco (Calif.). Police Dept.—Biography.
3. Serial murder investigation—California—San Francisco—Case studies.
4. Serial murders—California—San Francisco. 5. Hate crimes—California—San Francisco. 6. Whites—Violence against—California—San Francisco.
7. African American detectives—California—San Francisco—Biography.
8. Discrimination in law enforcement-California—San Francisco. 9. Racism—California—San Francisco. 10. San Francisco (Calif.)—Race relations.
I. Cohen, Bennett. II. Title.

HV8079.H6S36 2006
364.152'30979461—dc22   2005029601

Published in the United States by Arcade Publishing, Inc., New York
Distributed by Hachette Book Group USA

Visit our Web site at www.arcadepub.com

10 9 8 7 6 5 4 3 2 1

Designed API

EB

PRINTED IN THE UNITED STATES OF AMERICA

To my wife, Espanola, my daughter, Marguerite, and my son, Marcus: You have given me the strength, courage, and inspiration to meet the challenges of life every day. Thank you for your unconditional love.

And to the memory of Rotea Gilford

Contents

Prologue

IN 1969 PETE TOWNSHEND of the Who produced the only album by a little-known band called Thunderclap Newman, with a song that became the group's sole hit: "Something in the Air." The song reached number one on the British charts and thirty-seven in America. While it may not have topped the charts in the States, the lyrics, which declared that the revolution had arrived and spoke of calling out the fomenters and handing out guns and ammo, perfectly captured the hunger for change that had become like a religion for American youth, and the growing romanticization of violence as a means to that change. The song became a fixture in popular culture and was subsequently included in the sound tracks of numerous films that wanted to capture the spirit of the era, from *Easy Rider* to *The Strawberry Statement* and *The Magic Christian.*

The rhythms on the ghetto streets of the Fillmore and Hunters Point in San Francisco and of West Oakland across the bay during the fall, winter, and spring of 1973 to 1974 were more akin to the funky pulse of Sly Stone, Tower of Power, and the Pointer Sisters than the feathery strains of Thunderclap Newman and "Something in the Air." Yet the sentiment was the same, driven by the passing of the promise felt during the 1960s and the desire, as Malcolm X put it, to change the system "by any means necessary."

This was a time when the entire world seemed caught up in a confusing maelstrom of political chaos, bloodshed, and violence. Native Americans clashed with the FBI at Wounded Knee. Chile fell to Pinochet's fascist junta. The Yom Kippur War raged in the Middle East. Arab terrorists fired on the Athens airport, hijacked planes, took over a train in Austria, and killed schoolchildren in the Israeli town of

Ma'alot. The IRA, Basque separatists, and the Red Army Faction took on the institutions of Europe while the Weather Underground, SLA, and Black Liberation Army did the same in the States. It was a time when even the president, to paraphrase Bob Dylan, had to stand naked as the scandal of Watergate swirled around him and his administration crumbled at his feet. Yet for all the mayhem plaguing the globe, nowhere seemed to be more at the center of the storm than the seven miles square that form the city of San Francisco.

For six months from October 1973 to April 1974, a string of killings that came to be known by the code name Zebra afflicted San Francisco like a curse. Though little remembered or talked about today, the Zebra murders were among the most violent and prolonged cases of domestic terrorism in the history of the United States. This was not a single catastrophic event. Rather, it was an ongoing wave of random terrorist attacks that ultimately numbered nearly two dozen in total and left fifteen dead, eight injured, a population shaken, and a major U.S. city on the brink. It was a time, sad to say, that in many ways presaged our own.

In the wake of 9/11, people in their effort to come to terms with the catastrophe reached for various parallels: Pearl Harbor, the Cuban missile crisis, the assassination of JFK. What sprang to my mind was the flood of terror that washed over San Francisco nearly thirty years earlier.

I was in the Bay Area during the Zebra murders, so I thought I knew a bit about them. By my recollection, a small, radical fringe group inside the San Francisco temple of the Nation of Islam, an organization far removed from the Nation of Islam that exists today, committed a series of attacks in what I understood to be an attempt to alienate whites from blacks and instigate a race war. As I looked further into the Zebra murders, however, I realized that all I really knew was the surface of the story, and that a deeper truth lay beyond the public face. Besides terrorism, the issue at the center of this story was racism, and two very different ways of reacting to it: you can lash out and become part of the madness, or you can struggle to keep your balance and find a purposeful, nonviolent way to fight for change.

I knew the killers chose to do the former. What I didn't know was the story of two other men who were black and similarly outraged by racism, who chose to do the latter. And who chose the course of justice over vengeance while pursuing the very culprits behind the Zebra murders. I didn't know about these men, Earl Sanders and Rotea Gilford, who were the first African American inspectors of Homicide in the history of the San Francisco Police Department, because their story had gone untold for thirty years.

What led me to them was a simple sense of disbelief. I had assumed that the San Francisco of 1973 must have had numerous black officers, and I couldn't imagine that murders committed by an insular group of African Americans such as the then Nation of Islam could be solved without black policemen being deeply involved. Yet that's exactly what the reports I read implied, with every black officer mentioned always relegated to the periphery of the action rather than positioned at the heart of it.

I decided to dig deeper. An Internet search brought up a *San Francisco Chronicle* article from 1995 about an African-American SFPD Homicide inspector named Earl Sanders being promoted to lieutenant, who listed the Zebra murders as one of his more famous cases. More searching revealed that Sanders had since been made an assistant chief, second-in-command of the department, and the highest-ranking black officer in the department ever. So, with little expectation of an answer any time soon, I called his office and left a message, saying I was a writer in Los Angeles and wanted to talk to him about a case called Zebra.

He returned my call that night.

What I learned was a revelation. I was right in my assumption that black officers had been involved in solving the case and bringing the killers to justice. In fact, Earl Sanders said, he and his partner, Rotea Gilford, were among the men who headed up the investigation, working as a team with Gus Coreris and John Fotinos, the two white officers who had been designated the Zebra task force's official leaders. I was wrong, however, in my assumption that a substantial number of black officers were in the SFPD in 1973. The truth, Sanders told me, was that there were only a woeful few back then—no more than seventy-six. Not only that, but at the same time as they investigated the Zebra attacks, which clearly seemed to be racially motivated, Sanders and Gilford were fighting their own war against racism, as they took on their employers, the San Francisco Police Department, in a civil rights action designed not only to end its discriminatory policies but to forever change the face of policing in America.

That first phone call opened a door onto a story, a friendship, and a collaboration that I never expected but which have come to shape and define my life. It also opened a door onto events that, if they are examined properly, might help us to understand not only the past but also the present and perhaps the future as well.

A well-worn adage claims that history belongs to the victors. Someone close to me, however, once observed that like many aphorisms, that old saying is wrong. History belongs to those who have the opportunity to tell it — usually the victors, but sometimes others as well.

Given America's past, it is no surprise that what goes untold about our nation's history often has to do with the lives, accomplishments, and travails of African Americans or other minorities. Telling those stories is not just a matter of honoring the men and women who experienced them but of realizing the full complement of forces that have shaped us as individuals and as a nation, and which continue to do so to this day. To me, there can be few stories as heroic or as inspirational when it comes to the conflicts we face today as that of Earl Sanders and Rotea Gilford, who found themselves caught between racism and injustice on one side and murder and terrorism on the other, and yet who remained determined to stay true to themselves throughout it all both as African Americans and as cops.

This is their story as much as it is that of all San Franciscans who found themselves standing in the eye of a social and political maelstrom during that season at the end of 1973 and the early part of 1974 when the whole world seemed to be going insane.

Bennett Cohen
Los Angeles

THE
ZEBRA
MURDERS

1

A Motiveless Murder

"PEOPLE SAY THE DEAD DON'T SPEAK," Earl Sanders is fond of saying with a wry, knowing smile. "But they do. If you have a body, you have a witness. And if you know how to look at that body, you know how to hear what that witness is telling you." Standing in the autopsy room of the San Francisco Medical Examiner's office on the cool, drizzly Monday morning of October 22, 1973, Sanders, then the most junior inspector in the San Francisco Police Department's Division of Homicide, stared at the body of a young woman and not only heard her speak, he heard her scream.

Her name was Quita Hague. She was twenty-eight years old, with long brown hair and freckles, and even on the autopsy table you could see the pretty, girlish features that made people think she was younger than her years. But that girlishness had been mutilated by the sharp edge of what seemed to be a machete. Hack marks covered her body, neck, and face. There was no pattern to the blows. She had been struck wildly, senselessly, as if her attackers had been fueled by madness. As if they were trying to butcher her like an animal. Or worse. Animals are butchered with a purpose. Here there was none.

"That girl's wounds screamed out hate," Sanders recalls now, thirty years later. "Whoever cut her didn't just cut through flesh, they cut through bone. They cut *deep*."

Two days earlier, on the night of October 20, Quita and her husband of seven years, thirty-year-old Richard Hague, took a stroll down San Francisco's Telegraph Hill, heading down toward the North Beach area that it overlooks. Richard and Quita lived at 399 Chestnut Street, just a block below where Chestnut ends, near the top of the hill. Telegraph Hill has always been San Francisco's promontory point, a place from where the whole bay can be viewed. Today it's known for Coit Tower, a monument built to honor the firefighters who battled the blazes that followed the 1906 earthquake. In the nineteenth century it was a semaphore station, with a huge wooden armature atop it that used flags to relay messages to ships as they came into port. Exposed to the elements, Telegraph Hill is like the city's raised index finger, the spot of land that's first to feel the chilling winds as they cut across the water or the damp mist of fog as it rolls onto shore.

Richard and Quita left their apartment building in the cool of the evening and headed down Chestnut toward Columbus. He was a mining engineer who worked out of the San Francisco office of a Utah oil company. She was a reporter with a small newspaper in South San Francisco. They met in Boulder, at the University of Colorado, and married while still young. Even so, there was a buoyancy about Richard and Quita that made them still seem like newlyweds. They always seemed cheerful, engaging the world with an optimism that impressed everyone who knew them, at a time when both cheerfulness and optimism were hard to come by.

The world seemed to be going mad in the fall of 1973. Chilean president Salvador Allende had just been overthrown and killed in a coup orchestrated by our own CIA. There were airplane hijackings and terror bombings in the Middle East, Africa, and Japan. The Yom Kippur War had broken out in Israel. Here in America, the old radical groups were splintering apart and turning into violent offshoots like the Weathermen and the Black Liberation Army. Just that week, the local papers had been filled with news of BLA members who had been convicted in the murder of a cop out at San Francisco's Ingleside Station. Vice President Spiro Agnew resigned from office because of crimes committed while he served as governor of Maryland. Watergate, which first splashed across the nation's newspapers in spring, was approaching critical mass. And on the very night that Richard and Quita Hague strolled down Telegraph Hill, Richard Nixon, in a blatant attempt to cover his backside that would become known as the Saturday Night Massacre, simultaneously fired special Watergate prosecutor Archibald

Cox, Attorney General Elliot Richardson, and Deputy Attorney General William Ruckelshaus.

Like most of their friends in the hip, youthful neighborhoods of North Beach and Telegraph Hill, Quita and Richard felt shocked by what was going on in Washington. The events of that night would turn shock into outrage, setting off a chain of events that would topple Nixon's presidency. But Quita Hague would never learn of them: another perilous chain of events was about to cut her young life short.

"I'd been in the department almost ten years by the time the Hagues were attacked. I worked in radio cars and on vice, with robbery and homicide. In nine years, you see a lot. Knifings, shootings, beatings, strangulations — pretty much any way you can kill a person, I'd seen it done. But I'd never seen anything like the wounds that cut through that young woman. They took your breath away. It was like looking at a painting that had been hacked at by some madman, the beauty torn and shredded right there in its frame."

Sanders had applied for the SFPD in 1964 almost as an afterthought. At one time he had considered pursuing a career as an officer in the U.S. Army. Getting stationed in Georgia put him off that dream.

"I didn't mind the idea that I might die for my country. But I minded like hell that I had to live someplace where I couldn't buy a hamburger outside the fort, or drink from a water fountain that wasn't marked 'Colored.' I figured if I was good enough to die, I was good enough to drink water or buy a hamburger, so I took a commission in the reserves instead of the regular army, headed back to San Francisco, and worked my way through college."

By 1964 Sanders was working as a data processor with the Social Security Administration. It was his brother-in-law, Calvin Wiley, who wanted to be a cop, not Sanders. But Sanders agreed to help Calvin prepare for the entrance exam he had to take, and after doing so much studying, decided to take the test himself. Calvin didn't do so well. The assertion by Calvin that the tests given to African Americans, both at his exam and others, were unfairly administered would become one of the lead complaints in a civil rights lawsuit that Sanders, along with other black officers, became instrumental in bringing nearly a decade later in federal court as part of their effort to end racism inside the

SFPD. Yet despite that unfairness, which would ultimately be proven in court, Sanders's score placed him third out of eight hundred applicants, including the white ones.

Sanders still wasn't sure he wanted to be a cop.

"The Watts riots had just happened. I lived in that neighborhood for a while, before I came to San Francisco, and the fires down there tore that place up. I mean, they sent in the National Guard. And this wasn't Mississippi or Georgia. This was California. Things were changing. The civil rights movement wasn't just about turning the other cheek anymore. It was about striking back. I didn't relish the notion of having to pick up a baton and face down my own people. But I'd just gotten married, and we were thinking about a family, and I'll tell you this: the hundred and fifty dollars a month a rookie cop got back then was a hell of a raise over what I made as a data processor."

Sanders decided to go ahead and take the required physical. Then he could decide whether or not he wanted to be a cop.

With such a high score on the written exam, Sanders's acceptance into the SFPD should have been a given. The medical exam, however, proved far different from the written one. Up until World War II, the SFPD had been Jim Crow white. In the years that followed, that started to change. But not as much as Sanders thought.

Sanders had just been given a routine medical exam as part of being in the army reserves, so he knew he was in excellent shape. However, according to the doctor conducting the physical for the SFPD, Sanders was a washout, with a vague, unexplained medical condition that made him unacceptable. The doctor, who was not an officer himself, couldn't resist adding a personal comment to his decree, telling Sanders that the SFPD already had enough of "your kind."

"Until then, I wasn't sure if I wanted to be a cop or not. But after that, what I wanted didn't matter. I had to be in the SFPD. I might have never been a cop if that doctor had signed off on my exam. But when he tried to Jim Crow me, I had to stand up to the son of a bitch. Whether I wanted to or not."

It was a question of justice. And his desire for justice was what drove Earl Sanders more than anything else. Sanders threatened to sue the department over the unfair medical exam, demanding to be given the place in the academy that was rightfully his. What began as act of defiance led to one of the greatest loves of his life. As he puts it now, police work became "his mistress": "Other men may spend their days chasing women, or drinking, or gambling. But for me, it's work."

It was his passion for police work that drew Sanders to the autopsy room on the drizzly Monday morning of October 22. Quita Hague wasn't his case. The Homicide inspectors on call when she was killed were Dave Toschi and Bill Armstrong. Sanders and his partner, Rotea Gilford, were working the part of their rotation that called on them to investigate old cases, not take on new ones.

There were eight two-man teams in the SFPD's Division of Homicide in 1973. Each team spent one full week on call, twenty-four hours a day. Every murder that occurred inside the city during that time was theirs. The next seven weeks were spent investigating those new cases, along with the cases they had that were still unsolved. Any involvement in cases outside your own was voluntary. But Sanders was the sort of cop who could never resist an opportunity to learn. In fact, he so diligently studied the latest developments in police work that the older, more experienced Gilford took to calling him School. Or, as Sanders puts it today, Po' School.

"That's what he called me. Gil was never one to study. Never took the test for sergeant or lieutenant. Working cases was enough for him. So he'd look at me bent over my books, laugh, and call me Po' School. But that was the only way I knew to get better. Learn everything I could. Everything."

When it came to involving himself in cases other than his own, Sanders only asked himself two questions: Could he learn something, and could he help? If the answer was yes to either, he'd be there. Without a second thought.

The impetus to be present at Quita Hague's autopsy stemmed from a gathering Sanders had attended in Oakland on October 16. The speaker at the meeting of the recently formed California Homicide Investigators Association, where investigators from over twenty-five law enforcement agencies across the state were in attendance, was an officer from southern California who talked about what he called a new surge of "motiveless killings" that had been plaguing the West Coast. It wasn't clear whether these killings were actually connected, but all were marked by surprising brutality, with victims often butchered by ax- or machete-like blades, and by an apparent lack of motive.

When Sanders heard about the Hague killing, he immediately thought of that speech. So a little after dawn the following Monday, he got up even earlier than usual so he could attend the autopsy, showering and starting to dress while it was still dark. Dressing was a ritual for Sanders, an act of preparation he took quite seriously. To Sanders, dressing well was part of the job. With his background in the military, he looked at a suit as a uniform — the better the suit, the higher the rank. The least he could do, Sanders figured, was look better than the crooks. So whenever he and Gilford got overtime checks, instead of banking them, they'd head straight to the Roos Brothers clothing store on Market Street, hand them over to an old saleswoman there they trusted, and pick out clothes until the checks were gone. It was, as Sanders says, "the price of doing business."

Even though Sanders was hurrying on the morning of the twenty-second, he still took the time to get his attire right, fastening cuff links onto a clean, pressed shirt and fitting a neatly creased silk handkerchief into his coat's front pocket. His costume complete, Sanders headed out of the new home he and his family had moved into that summer. The house was in Daly City, a working-class neighborhood just south of San Francisco, and buying it had proved to be nearly as tempestuous a process as trying to get into the SFPD.

"The first house I bought was in Westlake. But my children were growing, and I wanted what everybody wants for their families: more room, a safer neighborhood, better schools. But there'd never been a black family in the neighborhood I was moving to, and the realtor made it clear that if it was up to the people who lived there, there never would be. I told him I didn't care what the hell people thought. I was buying that house."

Once again, it was a matter of justice. In 1964 California passed the Rumford Fair Housing Act, which said that if Sanders had the money and made the best bid, it was his right to live there.

"I had a rule about racism. Don't knuckle under. But pick your fights. This was one that I knew I'd win."

And he did.

It was already drizzling as Sanders drove north on Highway 101, past Candlestick Park and Hunters Point, heading to the Hall of Justice. The *San Francisco Chronicle* set the chance of rain at 60 percent that morning. This time, at least, the *Chronicle* was right.

The medical examiner's office was tucked away in a corner of the Hall of Justice's first floor. Sanders's office was up on the fourth floor, along with the other downtown divisions of the SFPD. As the examination was scheduled for early that morning, he went straight to the autopsy room, walking in just as Boyd Stephens, San Francisco's chief medical examiner, retrieved Quita Hague's body from the cooler.

Boyd Stephens was a reedy man of thirty-three, thin and bookish, with glasses so fixed partway down his aquiline nose that they seemed congenital. Despite his academic manner, Boyd Stephens treated his subjects with empathy. His job forced him to deal with each victim as a body, evidence to be opened and probed. But he saw them as people. And as he prepared Quita for the grim task ahead, the sadness that he felt for her was evident.

Dr. Louis E. Daugherty, who worked with Stephens, had already performed a preliminary autopsy the day before. Now Stephens was doing another. The others in attendance with Sanders and Stephens were Dave Toschi and Bill Armstrong, the Homicide team that had caught the case. Like most inspectors, they were excellent cops, but they were as different from each other as a madras sport coat and a gray flannel suit.

Toschi was the madras of the two, with a taste for bow ties, flashy jackets, and an equally flashy lifestyle. Dark and with brooding Italian looks that might not be classically handsome but that women seemed to like, Toschi loved the finger-snap of being a cop, the style and pizzazz of it, as much as the actual work. Part of that style was being in the public eye, and Toschi cultivated publicity in ways that often grated on the other inspectors, including his partner.

Armstrong was the gray flannel, tending toward a more conservative, steadfast, and deliberate style, in his life and in police work. He tried to get Toschi to keep their cases under wraps when he could. But this murder was just too good. Nothing was going to stop Toschi from calling his pals at the *Chronicle* about this one. The irony was that although Toschi talked to the press, it was Armstrong, who never trumpeted his cases yet was as hardworking and as diligent as any cop in the bureau, who really handled the case. Toschi had been out of the office on personal business the night of the attack, taking the unmarked car he was supposed to share with Armstrong and forcing Armstrong to get a ride from his wife to make it to the scene of the crime. And while it was Toschi's quotes that were printed in the *Chronicle*, it was Armstrong who went to see the survivor, Richard Hague, in the hospital, talking with him and, over time, bonding with the devastated young man.

Although severely injured, Richard Hague managed to give a remarkably vivid statement to Armstrong from his hospital bed. By Monday, it was front-page news. So Sanders knew the gist of Hague's statement without anyone having to say a word.

Watching Boyd Stephens turn on his tape recorder and begin to catalog the list of wounds visible on the naked body of Quita Hague, Sanders went over in his mind what he knew about the events that led up to her senseless murder, wondering where, if anywhere, a kind of sense could be found.

The air was damp the Saturday that Quita and Richard went for a walk after dinner. They stepped out around nine P.M. It was a typical San Francisco night, just enough fog to put a chill in the air without obscuring the beauty of the city.

Since the early days, North Beach had been the part of San Francisco that most readily welcomed newcomers. Situated by the city's original port of entry, nestled in the coastal hollow just below Telegraph Hill before landfills extended the coast northward toward Fisherman's Wharf and the Embarcadero, North Beach was where the forty-niners came in by boat during the gold rush. It was where the Chinese arrived to work on the railroads. Where the Italians came during their waves of immigration. And where the Beats set down their rootless roots, calling its bars, cafés, and bookstores their home.

It was only fitting, then, that Richard and Quita had settled in this vicinity after coming to San Francisco. Quita had been raised in northern California and always wanted to return. Even though they had made a life for themselves in Utah, Richard got himself transferred to his company's San Francisco office, and they made the move to California. Eighteen months later, both were glad they had. San Francisco was as alive and vibrant as they were. Living there seemed the most natural thing in the world.

Richard and Quita set off down Telegraph Hill toward Columbus Avenue, North Beach's main artery, which is always filled with street life, especially on weekends. They didn't get far. Within a block or so from where they lived, a white van pulled up alongside them. Inside were three African-American men, one of whom jumped out and trained a gun on the young couple, telling them to get in the van.

Reacting quickly, Quita ran off out of range. But Richard had been grabbed by the men and was in their grasp. Thinking that the men only wanted to rob them, and that if she didn't resist, they would let her and Richard go, Quita went back, allowing herself to be captured.

It was the last choice she would ever make.

Sanders got out the pad and pen he kept in the inside pocket of his jacket and started taking notes as Boyd Stephens tried to determine which of Quita Hague's countless wounds might have been fatal. The ones around her head and neck were the best bets. The cuts there ran so deep they had nearly decapitated her, ripping through her carotid arteries, jugular veins, epiglottis, and hypopharynx. Other wounds nearly cut through her cervical spine, hacking away chunks of C3 and C2 along with parts of her scapula and shoulder blades and portions of her jaw and cheekbone.

"Looking at those wounds, and the horror of them, you couldn't help but wonder why. There was no sexual assault. Her husband's wallet was stolen, but there was almost no money in it. Even if robbery was the motive and the killers were just trying to silence them, they could have used their gun. But they didn't. Which meant they didn't just want to kill them. They wanted to mutilate them, to attack them with a violence that spoke of a hate I couldn't even imagine. A hate that went beyond reason."

Richard Hague said he remembered little of the attack. Apart from his fractured memories, the only real clues to a motive were the wounds themselves, which appeared so utterly without purpose that brutality itself seemed to be part of the intent. Which led Sanders to another thought: The victims were white. The assailants were black. Could race have been a motive?

If it had only been Toschi, Armstrong, and Stephens eyeing the wounds of a white woman who'd been brutalized by three black men, the racial angle would have probably been the main topic of discussion. But they weren't the only ones there. Sanders was with them. Which made the racial geometry inside the room decidedly complex.

"The whole racial thing hung in the air during the autopsy," Sanders recalls. "But no one said a word. Probably because of me."

Adding to that complexity was the fact that Sanders and his partner, Rotea Gilford, had reputations in the department as being "militants" who wanted to take down the white power structure that ran the SFPD. The reputation wasn't without cause. At the very moment Sanders stood in that autopsy room, he and Gilford were in the middle of a lawsuit against their own department, claiming a pattern of discrimination by the SFPD that limited minorities in every aspect of employment, from hiring to promotion.

San Francisco was renowned as a liberal mecca in the 1970s, but it was far from that when it came to issues of race. Before World War II, the African-American population of San Francisco numbered no more than a few thousand. That changed during and after the war, as thousands of blacks migrated to the city, settling into neighborhoods like the Fillmore, Potrero Hill, and Hunters Point. Yet while the faces of San Francisco took on new looks, the old attitudes remained unchanged.

Those lingering racial tensions were heightened in October 1973 by the closing of the old navy shipyards out at Hunters Point, which was the very reason many African Americans had come to San Francisco in the first place.

It was work in the shipyards that drew blacks west and caused them to settle among the winds that whipped across San Francisco's southeastern shore, blowing a chill breeze from Potrero Hill to Candlestick Park. That breeze got even icier when the shipyards closed, causing hundreds to lose their jobs and rail bitterly against a government they felt had abandoned them. The situation underlies Otis Redding's hit from the late 1960s, "(Sittin' on) The Dock of the Bay," which had been inspired by San Francisco's African-American population, many of whom felt disenfranchised even then. Redding, along with his cowriter and guitarist, Steve Cropper, wrote of the hopelessness that drove blacks out of the South and led them to San Francisco, where they reached, quite literally, the end of the road, finding only more hopelessness, with no more horizons to head for and little to do except watch "the tide roll away."

Nowhere was that disenfranchisement greater than in the corridors of power that housed San Francisco's civil servants, politicians, and ruling elite. For years it was the Irish who ran San Francisco. By the 1970s, with the election of Joseph Alioto as mayor, the Italian community had begun to gain a foothold as well, but not in the Police Department. In 1973, only one man who wasn't Irish had a rank of captain or higher in the SFPD: Charlie Barca. Barca was Italian, and as captain of inspectors he oversaw all the inspector bureaus, including Homicide. But that was it. Barca was the only member of the department's top brass who wasn't Irish American.

The situation among the rank-and-file officers was no better. There were fewer than a hundred fifty minority officers on the SFPD in 1973. That included *all* minorities — black, Hispanic, Asian, and Native American — out of a force of just under two thousand, for a total of less than 9 percent. Only six minorities had a rank of inspector; only eight were sergeants; and only one, a latino, had reached lieutenant.

Frustrated by what they saw as blatant discrimination, and by a lack of representation in the white-controlled Police Officers Association, the minority officers on the SFPD formed their own union, the Officers for Justice. Officers of any ethnicity or race were allowed to join, but only one non-minority actually did: Richard Hongisto, a progressive, white SFPD officer who was shunned by many of the other white officers on the force but much later was elected sheriff of San Francisco and, for a short while, was appointed chief of the SFPD. In 1973, the number of minority officers in the department was small to begin with, and those who decided to brave the risk of reprisal and join the Officers for Justice numbered even fewer. The estimated membership at the time was no more than fifty or so officers. Unlike the far larger Police Officers Association — led by the conservative sergeant Gerald Crowley, who not only lobbied politicians but also raised money in support of the causes he backed and created ties with other similar-minded police unions across the nation — the Officers for Justice could only defend individual officers with specific grievances. Beyond that, they were powerless.

Then came the lawsuit. It was Sanders's idea. And he hit upon it over a game of dominoes.

Rotea Gilford was going through a difficult divorce in 1973 and had left his house in Ingleside Heights, moving into an apartment in one of the old Victorians built just after the 1906 earthquake in San Francisco's Upper Haight, along the slope of Mount Parnassus that runs above Haight-Ashbury.

Gilford was older than Sanders by ten years, and had been a mentor to him as he came up through the ranks. Sanders was familiar with Gilford from when Rotea was still a uniformed officer walking the streets of the Fillmore and Sanders was a young man hanging out in the neighborhood. Gilford was known to everyone then as Officer Smiley, so named because of the grin he never seemed to lose. Sanders still called him Smiley, but in the days of Gilford's divorce the name often seemed less than accurate.

"Gil wasn't used to living alone, so whenever we had time off he wanted me to drink and play dominoes up in that apartment of his. It got to the point where I thought he was going to get me divorced, too. But he was down. And he'd been there for me when I had needed him. So it was hard to say no."

Playing dominoes and drinking is exactly what Sanders and Gilford were doing one evening in the late fall of 1972, nearly a year before the killing of Quita Hague, when Jesse Byrd, the president of Officers for Justice and the only black motorcycle cop on the force, came to Gilford's apartment along with others from the group, including Troy Dangerfield and Rodney Williams, one of the earliest fully sworn African-American officers hired by the SFPD. They had grown frustrated by the fact that while numerous complaints over racist policies had been filed by the Officers for Justice, nothing had changed, and many were starting to feel that the whole process was a pointless exercise. No one wanted to give up the fight. But no one was sure how to continue, either. As the only African-American inspectors of Homicide, Sanders and Gilford were considered the highest-ranking blacks on the force. And as the first black to be promoted to the rank of inspector, Gilford was uniquely influential. Jesse Byrd and the others wanted his advice.

Listening to their complaints, Gilford shook his head. He, too, had grown tired of the obstacles placed before them by both the police union and the Irish-controlled department hierarchy. However, like the others, he was stumped as to how to make progress. Then Sanders hit on an idea.

"Even though I was an inspector, I was the youngest one there. So no one really looked to me for advice. But as everybody kept going on about how unfair it all was, I thought of a plaque that a lawyer I knew kept on his desk. 'When in doubt,' it said, 'sue the bastards!'

"I thought, Why the hell not? So that's what I said. 'Let's sue the bastards!' Simple as that. At first they all looked at me like I was crazy. But then, one by one, everybody agreed. *Why the hell not?*"

That was the beginning of a civil rights lawsuit in the U.S. Federal Court designed to end the discrimination inside the SFPD, initiated by the Officers for Justice and filed in April of 1973 by the legal firm Public Advocates, led by Robert Gnaizda and William Hastie Jr. Gilford played a leading role in the case early on, with Sanders succeeding him as it dragged on over the years, eventually being elected president of Officers for Justice and becoming, in Gnaizda's words, the public face of the lawsuit, whose unquestionable excellence proved the lawsuit's point. It was Calvin Wiley's claims from nearly a decade earlier that served as the suit's lead complaint, but the abuses it intended to redress went far beyond that, giving the lawsuit the potential to be a precedent-setting case. If successful, the suit's scope would alter the makeup of departments throughout America, bringing in not only more minorities but more women as well.

From the moment the suit was filed, it caused a huge backlash among the largely Irish and entirely white old-boy network that controlled the SFPD. The Police Officers Association began lobbying and raising money to fight it, with the union's leader, Sergeant Crowley, declaring, "We're entering an era where politics will become part of being a policeman." At the same time, the department initiated a series of measures to make it look as though the suit was unnecessary or even counterproductive, claiming they were about to make a new recruitment drive among minorities and that the lawsuit was impeding progress. But the reaction that unnerved Sanders and Gilford the most was the personal backlash from fellow officers, whose rancor and bigotry turned to hate and threatened to transform the SFPD into a police force that was more than ever divided against itself along racial lines.

The hearings, which began in May, continued through summer and early fall and would pick up again later in the year. By the time Richard and Quita Hague took that walk down Chestnut Street, the racial tensions on the force had reached a level of bitterness and anger that went beyond anything that Sanders could recall. Speaking about the lawsuit and the reaction it caused, he cited two incidents that occurred around that time, which epitomized the kind of hate he and Gilford faced inside the SFPD. The first incident came before the assault on the Hagues. The second came afterward.

"The trial was getting started, and Gil gave one of the first depositions about racism inside the department," Sanders said. "The deposition was in the Federal Building on Golden Gate. When Gil and I walked out after his testimony, there were some two hundred of our 'fellow officers' — all white — waiting to give us hell. They called us everything in the book, from the 'N' word on down. Gil was the cool one back then. He was ten years older and knew how to let that shit roll off his back better than me. So he kept pushing through the crowd, just trying to get us out, while I kept getting hotter and hotter. Then I heard one son of a bitch call out, 'Somebody ought to take a contract out on those two niggers!' That was it. I lost it. I stopped in my tracks, looked to where I heard the voice, and yelled, 'Why doesn't the asshole who said that come over here and try to make good on that contract himself!' I was ready to take on that cracker right there. But before anyone could say another word, Gil grabbed my arm and pulled me away, whispering, 'C'mon, man, c'mon, let's go.'"

The other incident occurred in the late fall of 1973, when Sanders and Gilford were working on a homicide in San Francisco's financial district. They were in their car when they heard on the radio that a robbery had occurred near where they were. Then they saw someone running on the street who fit the description of the robber.

Sanders and Gilford took off after the suspect, chasing him down in an empty lot. Sanders picks up the story from there.

"The radio said the suspect was unarmed, so we decided to try to capture him without using our guns. Gil had been a defensive back at the University of San Francisco and spent a little time with the old Chicago Cardinals of the NFL. So he was fast. And tough. He reached the guy first and tackled him. But that guy was strong, and high on something, because he was crazy. Gil couldn't hold him. So I piled on too. Then I tried to keep him down while Gil got out his walkie-talkie to call for help. We were so winded from the run and the struggle that the two of us couldn't hold him much longer. That's how strong he was.

"Gil got on the radio, gave our location, and said we needed some buddies as backup. For a moment there was silence. I'll never forget what I heard next. A man — we never found out who — came on and said, 'You two ain't got no buddies out here.'

"That's when I saw that the report we'd heard about the suspect was wrong. He did have a gun, tucked in his pants. And he was trying to grab it. You won't believe how fast I got my energy back when I saw that. I grabbed my own gun before he could reach his, shoved it in his face, and told him I'd blow his head off if he made another move. Then we cuffed him and took him in. From that point on, we knew what the score was. If we wanted to take on the department, we weren't going to have any 'buddies' out there. We were on our own."

The one exception was Homicide. It wasn't that the cops there were free of racism. It was just that, in their minds, they had bigger things to think about.

Sanders knew that Toschi and Armstrong had not been part of the group waiting for him and Gilford outside the federal court, shouting out insults. Yet he also knew that the lawsuit had made him and Gilford synonymous with issues of race inside the department. And as he and the others stood in the autopsy room, Sanders knew that the pretty young white woman lying on the table in front of them, butchered by a group of black men, crystallized those issues in a way few things could. The Officers for Justice trial wasn't enough to put a wedge between Sanders, Gilford, and the others on Homicide. However, as he sensed the tension in the room and the racial geometry his presence caused, Sanders realized that a crime this brutal, this senseless, and this filled with hate could become that wedge.

As soon as Richard and Quita Hague entered the van, they were grabbed and thrown to the floor, their hands tied behind their backs with rope. From that point on, Richard could see only glimpses of what was going on. But he could hear it all as the van's engine started up and they took off. As they drove, he heard one of the assailants begin to mess with Quita somehow. Fearing that he might sexually assault her, Richard tried to look up and ask him what he was doing. As he did, another man hit Richard and told him to keep his head down. When the first man continued to mess with Quita, Richard tried to look up again. This time the response was even more violent, as out of the corner of his eye Richard saw the assailant who had struck him pick up a wrench and smash him in the jaw and skull, shattering bone and beating him into unconsciousness.

The killers drove out of North Beach and wound their way south through the city toward the more desolate industrial region that surrounded Potrero Hill, some four and a half miles away.

The van stopped near the Southern Pacific tracks at Twenty-fourth Street and Minnesota. The killers dragged out Richard and Quita and threw them onto the rails. Richard was already bloody and unconscious, so they slashed at his face and neck a few times with the long machete-like blade they had, then left him for dead.

The next thing Richard knew, he was walking among train tracks, his hands still tied behind his back. His thoughts were a fog. He didn't have a clue where he was or how he got there. He knew he was in pain, but he wasn't aware yet that his head had been hacked at with a long blade, slicing open his face and cutting into his facial bones. Nor did he realize that he was covered in blood, which had already started to clot in his wounds and dry on his skin, matting his hair and clothes. The one thing he was aware of, however, and painfully so, was that Quita was not with him.

Richard roamed the train tracks, uncertain where Quita was or what had happened to her, until a college professor driving through the area with his wife found him. The couple took him to the Potrero police station, from which Richard was taken to San Francisco's General Hospital, where he was admitted in serious but not critical condition. His wounds would scar. But he would recover. Quita would not.

Sanders, Toschi, and Armstrong looked on as Stephens compared the evidence offered by Quita's body with some of the evidence found at the crime scene. But as Sanders relates, the terrifying story of what happened was best told by the wounds themselves.

"There were no broken bones or signs that she'd been clubbed, so the odds were she was awake right up until she was killed, aware of everything. From the blood on the tracks we knew that the attack occurred there. But death didn't come quick. She'd been bound, so there were no defensive wounds. But there was tearing in most of the cuts, which meant she was struggling, trying to twist away from the blade as it came down toward her.

"The wounds were across the front of her face, shoulders, chest, and torso. That meant that the killers attacked her while she was on her back, facing up. So she could see it. So she could witness her own murder."

Autopsies are curious things. As serious as they are, there are times when a kind of gallows humor can take over as a way to let off steam. People laugh, relax, talk about sports, women, anything but the case at hand. Not here. Nothing said was off point. According to Sanders, little was said at all. The brutality of the murder knocked the wind out of everyone. And they all felt relieved as the autopsy started to wind down, with Stephens putting the last of his observations and commentary on tape.

Between the statement of Richard Hague and the physical evidence offered by both the crime scene and the body, Sanders and the others had been able to piece together much of what happened. However, the two most crucial questions remained a mystery.

Who did it? And why?

The "who" part of the equation is something cops are used to not knowing. But it's rare that they are so wholly in the dark about the "why."

"We knew it was possible that there was simply no motive," Sanders said as he recalled the autopsy, looking back some thirty years. "That it could've been a 'thrill kill,' a murder done at random, for no other reason than to get high off the bloodshed."

Sanders paused in the midst of his recollection and shook his head, as if reliving the dissatisfaction he felt at the time with that explanation.

"Thing is, there'd usually be evidence of some kind of sexual assault in cases like that. Maybe not penetration, but something. Here there was nothing. Which would've made it the rarest of all murders, one that was random in every way, without any reason or purpose. Unless . . ."

The randomness, Sanders muses, was not absolute.

"The killers might not have been after the Hagues. But they may have been after a couple 'like' the Hagues. A couple their race. A couple who were white."

The black-versus-white theory remained unspoken in the room, but Sanders knew it was on everyone's mind. If it was true, it would answer two things that otherwise didn't make sense: the lack of any other seemingly meaningful motive, and the insane rage with which the couple was attacked.

Yet if it answered some questions, it created others. What would a case like this do to race relations in the city? Or the SFPD? Or Homicide? Would people become more polarized, the battle lines even more sharply drawn?

Those thoughts were in Sanders's mind when, as Boyd Stephens prepared to put Quita Hague back on ice, Dave Toschi turned to Sanders and asked him what he thought of the crime.

Sanders paused a moment. He knew that implicit in the question was the concern that he might feel some sort of allegiance to something other than the SFPD. The truth was, he did. It was the same allegiance that had caused him to fight his way onto the force in the first place. And to buy a house in Daly City. And to bring a civil rights lawsuit against his own department.

Finally Sanders answered.

"I'll tell you what I think. I think anybody who could kill like that, without reason, is crazy. And if they had a reason, then that reason is crazy. And we better get the goddamn motherfuckers before they can do it to anybody else."

It was a matter of justice.

And that, more than anything else, was where Earl Sanders put his allegiance.

No matter where the pursuit of it would take him.

2

A Deathbed Promise

JUSTICE WAS ANYTHING BUT A BIRTHRIGHT for Prentice Earl Sanders. Born in the rural East Texas town of Nacogdoches on October 12, 1937, Earl uses a little-known statistic to encapsulate what it was like to grow up in Texas as an African American during the era of Jim Crow. The two states in which lynchings were most common during the hundred years between Emancipation and the civil rights movement were Mississippi and Georgia. But the state that comes in third on that shameful list is not South Carolina, Louisiana, or even the Deep South state of Alabama. It is the Lone Star State, Texas. That fact may be a surprise to some, but not to Earl Sanders.

"People talk about Texas in mythic, all-American terms, going on about the Alamo and Davy Crockett and longhorns and oil wells. But the reality in East Texas was more about Jim Crow cotton culture than any of that, and the kind of racial tensions that often seemed little more than a breath away from slavery."

It is taken for granted that the history of Texas is closely linked to the history of relations between the United States and Mexico. Less appreciated is how bound up the history of Texas is with the story of race relations between blacks and whites in America. Nicholas Trest, whom President Polk called upon to draft the Treaty of Guadalupe Hidalgo, which paved the way for Texas to become part of the United States, was also the author of a series of racist tracts and, while U.S. consul to Havana, made it possible for Cuban slavers to import their inventory into the United States. When Texas entered the Union in 1848, its admission as a slave state triggered a string of maneuvers that ended in 1850 with the passage of the Fugitive Slave Act, a draconian set of provisions that, according to Sanders, resound to this very day in the attitude of blacks to law enforcement.

"The Fugitive Slave Act gave police carte blanche when it came to crossing state lines and chasing down runaway slaves, and it forced federal marshals to help them under penalty of law. Even before that there had been 'slave patrols' down South, which had the right to stop and search, or what the streets call 'jack up,' any black they saw on the street and make them prove they weren't runaways. But the fugitive slave laws went even further, denying every black in America who was tagged as a 'fugitive' the right to testify or have a trial by jury, making them subject to the whim of any racist policeman, prosecutor, or judge who wanted to jack them up and send them off in chains, even if they'd been free all their lives and had never set foot south of the Mason-Dixon line.

"The mistrust that caused didn't end with slavery. It didn't even end with Jim Crow. It's alive every time an African-American kid gets jacked up by a cop today, or stopped for 'driving while black,' or sentenced to more time than a white would be. People may not know where the anger comes from, but it gets handed down from generation to generation, and they feel it whether they know the history or not."

Sanders's own history can be traced to a legacy that, as for many African Americans, is a mixture of black, white, and Native American. His father, George Sanders, had a grandmother who was a full-blooded Cherokee. His maternal grandfather, Henry Baxter, was — as Sanders calls him — mulatto, born in Macon, Georgia, in the years just after the end of slavery to a white father and a black mother. It was a situation that was far from uncommon.

"My grandfather never discussed the relationship between his parents, but the fact was that even after Emancipation, many former masters of slaves kept treating their workers as if they still owned them. They might have changed the semantics, using words like 'tenant farming' instead of slavery, but the reality was the same. And if a white man wanted a black woman, he did what he wanted and that was that. Especially if he had money or land or any kind of power over her."

Though Texas may not have offered the equality blacks hoped for after Emancipation, it did allow for a kind of frontier independence. The men on both sides of Sanders's family had been wranglers, working the horses on their masters' plantations, and it was the children of those slaves that headed west, where the cowboy culture of Texas gave them a chance to put their skills to use. Cowboy culture offered blacks something else, as well: guns. Firearms were necessary tools on a ranch, and as Sanders points out, "While having a gun didn't give a black man the right to vote, or enter someone's house by the front door, or eat inside a restaurant, it did give him a way to defend himself. Guns didn't stop whites from lynching blacks. But it let them know that they had better bring a lunch with them if they had lynching on their mind, because they were going to have to work all day to do it."

Sanders can recall no single story in Texas where blacks took up arms against whites who had "lynching on their mind." However, he does remember what he refers to as "stories of stories."

"We didn't have much in the way of a written history. So we developed oral history instead, stories handed down from mama to daughter and daddy to son, telling what went on over generations. Some stories talked about blacks in Texas defending themselves, but some talked about men who, after a rape or lynching, took revenge by going out and randomly killing a white. It wasn't that the person they went after had anything to do with the crime. It was just that they had no other recourse except to spill blood for blood."

Leon Litwack, in *Trouble in Mind,* his eloquent history of the Jim Crow South, documents similar incidents throughout the South, including one written about by the novelist Richard Wright that tells of a woman who, after her husband had been shot by whites, blew away four of those responsible with a shotgun she had hidden beneath her skirt. Litwack also quotes a black news editor in Montgomery, Alabama, who told his readers that, if faced with racial violence, they should kill two or three "white devils" rather than die alone.

Decades later, as Sanders tried to keep the peace on the streets of San Francisco, seemingly far away in both time and place from the Montgomery, Alabama, of the Jim Crow South, that statement would sound prophetic.

*   *   *

Earl Sanders was born not as Prentice Earl Sanders but "Prettiest" Earl Sanders. The spelling was a mistake on the part of the midwife who guided his entry into the world. The birth took place in the little shack into which his father, George, and his mother, Kissie, had just moved. George was nowhere to be found during the event, setting a precedent that would sadly hold for the rest of his life. Kissie, who had intended to name her son Prentice, was still recovering from the throes of birthing when she told the midwife the child's name. The midwife either misheard Kissie or else just wrote it down incorrectly. Sanders put an end to the mistake as soon as he entered school. In the rough-and-tumble, red-dirt, six-gun world of rural East Texas, Prettiest just wouldn't play.

In 1937 George Sanders was a handsome young man in his twenties, renowned in Nacogdoches and the surrounding area as both a horseman and a street fighter. One story Earl Sanders tells points to how both qualities came together to define him.

"My mother was walking with my father soon after they got married, and the deputy sheriff of Nacogdoches, who was white, pulled a gun on my father to arrest him on some charge or other. Well, my father knocked that gun from the deputy's hand, grabbed his billy club, and beat him with it until he was lying on the ground. My mother was terrified. Blacks got lynched in Texas for less than that. She was sure she'd be a widow. But my father broke horses for the richest man in Nacogdoches, and that rich white man cared more about his horses than any deputy sheriff, so he made damn sure that my father stayed alive and out of jail."

What no one could do, however, was make sure that George Sanders stayed true to his responsibilities as a husband and father. Even before Sanders was born, his father was treating his young wife with disdain, taking off for days at a time and carrying on as if he were single. Nor did he change when Sanders arrived, two months premature and in need of constant care. That winter was one of the coldest that Texas had endured in years, and eighteen-year-old Kissie was left alone to care for both herself and her infant son, with little to warm them in their clapboard shack except the heat of their own bodies and what firewood she could afford. Finally George Sanders's sister Mamie came to visit with a gift of twenty dollars and some advice for the young mother: go home. Kissie's father, Henry Baxter, who had opposed the marriage, broke from his daughter when she stubbornly followed her own mind. Now, with a sickly child and almost no way to support herself, Kissie had little choice but to suck up her pride, ask for forgiveness, and move back in with her family. She never looked again to George Sanders for help, and it would be over twenty years before Prentice Earl Sanders set eyes on his father once more.

The Texas Sanders remembers from his youth was, despite the hardship, an idyllic place to grow up, with many a joy. Not long after moving back home, Kissie went to Houston to work as a domestic and cook, leaving her young son to be raised by the aging patriarch Henry Baxter, a man Sanders remembers as both stern and fair, and often gentler than expected.

"My grandfather was the kind who believed in 'spare the rod and spoil the child,' and any time I did something wrong, he'd go to a tree by the house, tear off a branch, and use it as a switch on me. Those things never broke, no matter how hard he whupped. Well, it wasn't long before I had my fill of that tree, and I decided to do something about it. My granddaddy raised Clydesdale horses, huge draught animals. So I went to the barn, got one of those horses, hitched it to that tree, and pulled the damn thing right out of the ground, roots and all. My grandmother was furious. She told old Henry to get a switch from another tree and give me a lickin'. But he said no. That kind of industry deserved to be encouraged, not punished."

The extended family that Sanders grew up in during his first few years was a complicated skein of cousins, uncles, and aunts, one of whom was actually younger than he was. At the core of the convolutions was the fact that his grandfather had two families, one in Nacogdoches with Earl Sanders's grandmother and Henry Baxter's second wife, Equilla, and one in nearby Tyler, with the wife Baxter had married years earlier. Henry Baxter never divorced his first wife. What he did, after a long marriage, was marry a younger woman and start another family, balancing his time between the two. It was an arrangement everyone knew about, and, despite the tensions it created, everyone accepted. It seemed evident that Henry's love for Equilla was the greater passion, but he never failed in his responsibilities to either family, or either wife.

Sanders's idyll in rural Texas ended when his mother married Lewis Lacy, a laborer and musician she had met in Houston. Sanders left his grandfather's ranch and moved in with his mother and stepfather in the city, where she soon gave birth to another son, William. Sanders and his younger brother accompanied Kissie and Lacy as they went from job to job, often living in the servants' quarters of the white homes where Kissie would work as a cook.

Houston gave Sanders his first bitter taste of racism. He always knew there was a dividing line between whites and blacks. However, the sparsely populated countryside offered a cushion of detachment, allowing him to remain at least somewhat ignorant of racism's painful reality. Houston, by contrast, was like a slap in the face. Living with white families, Sanders received a rude indoctrination about the separation between whites and blacks in the Jim Crow South.

"I always knew there was a line you didn't cross if you were black. But that line became a brick wall in Houston. Since we lived in the homes of the white folks, I naturally fell into playing with their children. It didn't matter to me that they were white. And it didn't matter to them that I was black. But the adults let us know that we could only play in the backyard, out of sight of the white neighbors. Once we stepped into the front yards, they were on another level. And there wasn't to be any mixing."

One memory that stands out for Sanders is of being on a bus heading from the white neighborhood where he lived with his mother and her employers to the black neighborhood across town, where he was permitted to attend school. There were signs on the buses in Texas during Jim Crow, labeling the "Colored" and "White" sections. The white sections were always to the front, the colored sections always to the back. One day the seven-year-old Sanders sat under the sign that separated the two, at the very front of the colored section, even though there were empty seats further back. Officially, he was in the colored section. However, a white man who got on the bus after Sanders thought he was cutting it too close.

"He stopped short as he got on," Sanders recalls, "looked at me like I was dirt, pointed to the rear of the bus, and said, 'Get back where you belong, nigger.' I couldn't believe it. The bus was almost empty. If I'd been a grown man, I'd have challenged him. But I was a child. So all I could do was stand up, walk to the last row, and sit back down. It was the kind of humiliation that you never forget. And you never forgive."

The story that best illustrates how devastating the Jim Crow era was for blacks in Texas comes not from Sanders but from his wife, Espanola. This is not a fable from some distant past, but a true occurrence from the mid-1950s, the era of Eisenhower and the early cold war, a time when history tells us that America had begun to take steps along the long road toward civil rights. Perhaps it had, but those steps had not changed Texas.

Espanola Wiley was born during World War II to a family rich in tradition and history. On one side were the Wileys, descended from both slaves and slave owners and the founders of Wiley College, one of Texas's first black colleges. On the other side were the Terrys, descended from an African patriarch who had entered the United States as a freeman and traced his heritage as a member of the Ebo tribe back for generations. Both the Wileys and Terrys were leaders in the black community, with a long record of accomplishment, and counted among their numbers doctors, preachers, and teachers. Espanola's father, Henry Wiley, was a rancher and businessman who, by the time she was born, already had a lifetime of success behind him. Henry Wiley may not have been rich by any urban accounting, but in the rural African-American world of East Texas he was a man of means, with hundreds of acres, a mansion for a house, and a number of servants. Yet none of those things could protect him or his family from the bitter taste of Jim Crow.

Espanola was only thirteen when she began to notice that the twenty-something son of one of the most powerful white families in Crockett was paying her what seemed to be an inordinate amount of attention. The year was 1956. Elvis was topping the charts, Jackson

Pollock was thrilling the art world, GE was creating the "all-electric kitchen," and everything seemed to be shifting to the new and modern. But the menace that was about to overtake Espanola's young life was as old as the Middle Passage and, for a young girl, served as a heartbreaking reminder of an injustice etched so deeply into the landscape around her that it seemed like it would never be erased.

"Espanola's father, Henry Wiley, and her mother, Odessa Terry Wiley, were leaving church one Sunday," as Sanders tells it, "when the young man approached her father and said, 'Henry, I'd like to come by and see Espanola.' First off, it wasn't lost on Henry Wiley that if he were a white man instead of black, that green young kid would never even dream of addressing him as 'Henry.' Second, he knew that kid didn't just want to play Parcheesi. Espanola was thirteen, and to someone like Henry Wiley that was too young for any man to come calling on her, white or black.

"But that kid wasn't asking for permission. He was merely stating what he was about to do. Henry Wiley couldn't say no. It didn't matter that he had land, or a big house, or servants. He was black, and that kid was white. And in East Texas, that meant he could do whatever he wanted to Henry Wiley's daughter. Period. There was nothing Henry could do about it. No police would help him. No court. No judge. The whole concept of justice simply didn't exist for blacks.

"But what might happen to Espanola was only the start of the kind of tragedy that Henry Wiley knew was possible. Espanola came from a big family, with a whole bunch of brothers, and none of them were shy or retiring. If any man touched their sister, there'd be hell to pay. Which meant that there was no telling where the sorrow might end. Nineteen fifty-six was the same year Emmett Till was killed for doing little more than breathing. So God knows what would happen if they got into it with some white kid who went after their sister.

"From Henry Wiley's point of view, there was only one thing to do: get Espanola out of Texas. So she went off to live with relatives in Detroit. Espanola was only thirteen, but she could never again live at home, never again be raised by her father and mother, never again set foot in Texas except for short little visits during summer. Her whole life was turned upside down, and it was months before she stopped crying herself to sleep at night, wondering why she had been sent so far away. And when you boil it down, there was only one reason for it all. She was black.

"But as sad as it was, what's probably most chilling is that it wasn't that unusual. Every black who grew up in Texas back then knew stories like hers. And worse. And most black parents in Texas had the same advice for their kids: get the hell out."

There were two great migrations of African Americans during the twentieth century. The first began during World War I, with blacks pouring out of the South and heading north on the railroads that had recently been built, in search of the jobs that were said to be opening up because of all the young men leaving to fight. The second, and far less documented, migration began during World War II. This exodus came more from Texas and Louisiana than from elsewhere in the Deep South, with blacks heading west this time instead of north, traveling along the newly built highways instead of rails, once again chasing the jobs that were said to be opening up as the young men of America headed to war. Like many blacks now on the West Coast, Sanders was part of this later migration. But it wasn't work that caused his mother to head to California. It was the promise of something she thought would be a key to her young son's life: school.

"My mother never went to college, but she saw it as the only means blacks had to raise themselves up out of the mire of racism. She made the notion so much a part of me that, even years later, when Gilford got fed up with me studying and started calling me School as a nickname, I never minded. Because every time I heard it, I knew it was a testament to my mother."

In Kissie's mind, the specter of Jim Crow was too steep a barrier for a young black man to surmount to get the education he needed to succeed. The only way around it was to get out of Texas, and travel as far north of the Mason-Dixon line as possible.

"Lacy was happy in Texas. But my mother wouldn't stay put. So he went to California in the summer of '47 and found work in Los Angeles. And that August my mother, me, and my little brother Bill followed, riding the Greyhound bus from Houston to Los Angeles."

The summer of 1947 simmered with uncommon heat. By August

the Southwest was sweltering, turning the bus that Sanders was on into
a rolling oven, and the only way to cool things down was to lower the
window by his seat the few inches that its mechanism allowed. Yet, as
stifling as the ride might have been, to Sanders it was a liberation.

"Even though Greyhound was a national company, as long as we
were in Texas, we were bound by the laws of Jim Crow. From Houston
to El Paso, my mother, my brother Bill, and I had to stay in the back
of the bus, where the 'colored' were allowed. But the moment we left
El Paso and crossed into New Mexico, everything changed. For the first
time in my life I could sit wherever the hell I wanted on a bus, and no
one could say a goddamn word."

When Earl Sanders speaks today about arriving in Los Angeles in
the late summer of 1947, two things spring to mind. Cars. An endless
stream of them, heading in every direction on what seemed impossibly
wide and grand avenues. And grapefruit. Huge, luscious, costing only
two cents a pound, and seemingly so plentiful that there was no way even
the vast numbers who filled the city of Los Angeles could ever manage
to eat them all. Like a southern California variation on milk and honey,
cars and fruit came to embody a land that felt like a modern-day Eden
to Sanders, where the skies were always sunny and any bus, restaurant,
or bathroom was available for anyone to use, black or white.

Sanders settled with his family in the downtown area of Los Angeles, just south of Exposition Boulevard. With time, though, they fell
into the same peripatetic pattern of living they had had in Texas, moving into the homes of a succession of wealthy white families for whom
his mother worked as a cook. Sanders even had a brush with the glit-
tering fame of Hollywood, living in the servants' quarters at the home
of Loretta Young while his mother worked for her as a cook. Eventually
the family settled in Santa Monica, which, with its wide beaches, laid-
back atmosphere, and temperate weather, became Sanders's favorite part
of the city. But as sweet as this newfound paradise seemed, it would soon
become a paradise lost.

Sanders's stepfather was a talented musician who never realized his
ambitions in life and was prone to the kind of anger that can tear families apart. Sanders tried to give Lacy the respect he thought a father de-

served, but Lacy's fits of rage and violence eventually caused him to shut down all feeling for the man.

"It got so bad when we were in Santa Monica that I finally decided I couldn't take it anymore. I was thirteen, and he was a grown man, but it didn't matter. I didn't give a damn what he did to me. I couldn't let him hurt my mother anymore. So one night I broke up a fight he had started in the kitchen and swore to him that if he ever hit her again, I'd kill him."

Though able to protect his mother from Lewis Lacy, Sanders was powerless against the heart disease that had begun to sap her health, affecting her more than any of Lacy's blows. The vulnerability of African Americans to heart disease is common knowledge today, but in the early 1950s few had a clue. Kissie Lacy, formerly Sanders, née Baxter, was only thirty-two years old when heart disease forced her into Los Angeles County General Hospital. When she was thirty-three, she would die there. Heart disease can be a cruel killer. For Kissie it was especially so, disabling her still young body bit by bit with an illness that was mystifying, but which in retrospect seems to have been a series of strokes, affecting her ability to see, walk, even breathe. The hospital stays grew longer and longer, until finally it became clear that she would never get out.

County General is far from Santa Monica, set in Lincoln Heights, on a small hill that rises up above East Los Angeles. Each day Sanders would go there by bus or on his bike. Children under sixteen weren't allowed in the wards unless accompanied by adults, but the nurses ignored the rules for him, letting Sanders in by himself and allowing him to stay long after visiting hours were over, even turning a blind eye when he curled up in a chair to spend a night by his mother's bedside.

"It reached a point where she could barely catch her breath, her eyes were half blind, and it was only a matter of time before her heart just flat gave out. We knew it. She knew it, too. That's why she grabbed my hands one day when I came to see her, squeezed them hard, and wouldn't let go. She knew she was going. So she pulled me close and made me promise two things right there on her deathbed: that I would finish school and get a college degree, and that I would never go to jail.

"I had to choke back tears, but I promised her that I'd do both. Then I kissed her good-bye and made the long trip back to Santa Monica.

"It was the last time I ever saw her alive."

With his mother gone, Sanders decided that he couldn't continue living with Lacy. It pained him to leave his little brother Bill. However, he had an uncle in San Francisco who said he would give him a room, and, fearing the tension between him and his stepfather would ultimately lead to violence, he decided that was the only option. He left without even bothering to say good-bye to Lacy.

The first thing Sanders felt as he stepped off the bus in San Francisco was fear. The old Greyhound depot was situated in San Francisco's downtown area south of Market, which, though becoming fashionable today, was then the city's skid row, filled with flophouses and the sort of "bucket of blood" bars that attracted the lowest class of crooks.

"It was a place where they'd cut your throat for a nickel if you didn't watch your back. But it wasn't the area that scared me. Bums and junkies were something I could see. What frightened me was the future. Because that was a mystery, and I didn't have a goddamn clue what was coming."

The rarely discussed truth about blacks in San Francisco is that prior to World War II, they were so few in number that they were barely even a factor in the city's racial calculations. The census of 1900 shows that out of the approximately 350,000 people listed as residents of San Francisco, just a little over 1,500 were African American. By 1940 there was only a slight increase in that ratio, with the city's population nearing 650,000 and blacks numbering just a little over 4,500, still well under 1 percent. Ralph Ellison dubbed the pre–World War II black as "the invisible man." In San Francisco, that seemed an understatement.

The laws of the city reflected the utter lack of power that blacks had, allowing for a kind of backdoor Jim Crowism. One old city statute that lingered on the books until early in the twentieth century stated that blacks were not allowed on the sidewalk, forcing them to walk in the street instead. Even into the 1930s, the police had a policy of stopping mixed couples seen in public, often citing them on trumped-up charges.

With the start of World War II, the number of blacks in San Francisco and around the Bay Area began to increase exponentially. Yet the racism remained largely unchanged. Redlining was standard practice when it came to housing, limiting blacks largely to the Fillmore, Bayview, and Hunters Point districts. Hotels and rooming houses were similarly restrictive, with only a few allowing African Americans as guests.

The not-so-subtle message to blacks in the Bay Area was simple: stay out of white neighborhoods. Troy Dangerfield, who along with Sanders became one of the earliest members of Officers for Justice, tells of visiting Richmond, just across the bay from San Francisco, as a teenager in the late 1940s and being stopped by a local cop, driven out to a garbage dump, and told by the officer that if he wanted he could put a bullet in Troy's head and dump his body and no one would know the difference. Then he took Troy to the city limits and ordered him to keep walking and not come back. Needless to say, Troy did as he was told. The fear he felt, and the anger that fear inspired, would affect him for years afterward.

The uncle who took Sanders in was Raymond, the wildest of his mother's many brothers. Ray lived in Laurel Heights, one of San Francisco's few mixed neighborhoods, and treated Sanders as if he were already a man, including him in the parties he held in his home and introducing him to such adult attractions as whiskey and women. The flip side of treating Sanders like a man was that when Ray wanted his house to himself again, he sent the fourteen-year-old packing. Sanders could use Ray's address when it came time to enroll in high school, but that was all Ray would do to help. So Sanders took what little money he had, rented a room in a Fillmore boarding house, and got a job washing dishes at the Fairmont Hotel, supporting himself from that day on.

That fall, Sanders registered at Washington High, which was close to where his uncle lived and was considered one of San Francisco's best. In order to attend, Sanders created a fictional family life for himself. Any correspondence from school was mailed to his uncle's house, where Sanders would collect it during periodic visits, forging his uncle's signature to any paperwork that needed to be returned. The ruse worked well, allowing him to go to school during the day while working nights. Sanders even tried out for the football team, getting selected for varsity and becoming one of the team's starting linemen.

Eventually his counselor at school, Eleanor Parsons, realized that the handwriting of the signatures she kept seeing on his notes was his own. Instead of exposing him, Miss Parsons decided to help Sanders keep his secret, telling the truth only to the football coach, Mr. Madfus, so that Sanders could better juggle the demands of practice with those he faced in school and at work. Over time, Miss Parsons and Mr. Madfus became like surrogate parents to Sanders, making sure he never took on more than he could handle.

Some teenagers might have been worn down by the kind of hardships Sanders faced, allowing adversity to dim their spirit. For Sanders it was the opposite. Instead of seeing the misfortune in his life, he saw the selfless grace with which others stepped in to help him. Sanders knew there were bad people out there. As a young man who had to defend himself in the world, he had met, and fought with, more than his share. But he knew, too, that there were good people, both black and white, and that if you opened yourself up to them, more often than not they would do the same for you.

When he was seventeen, Sanders moved in with his best friend, Kelly Waterfield, another African American attending Washington High School. Kelly was one of the few who knew the truth about how Sanders really lived, and he was so concerned that he finally told his parents, who decided to take Sanders in. At first Sanders continued to work, and even paid rent. However, in his senior year he got laid off from his job, and instead of demanding that he find another, the Waterfields embraced him as if he were equal to Kelly and his younger brother James, telling him to forget about work and rent and simply be a teenager for what little time left he had to do so.

After his senior-year idyll, Sanders was back at work and living alone, as he supported himself while starting college at Golden Gate University, a small liberal arts school in downtown San Francisco. By then he had also joined the army reserves, attending their Officer Candidate School and considering a career in the military.

"There were a lot of things I liked about the army. In a way it was like football. There was an order to it, a sense of organization, and a spit and a polish that made you feel like you were part of a team. There was something else it offered that was also like sports. It seemed to truly be a meritocracy. If you achieved, you rose up the ranks, whether you were white or black. I'm sure at higher levels all sorts of other issues entered in, like connections and privilege and race. But from where I stood, it seemed as fair a world as I'd ever seen. There was only one problem. Most of the bases were in the South. So the moment you stepped outside your fort, you left any semblance of fairness or equality far, far behind."

Sanders was at Fort Benning, Georgia, when he realized the incongruity, at least for him, of a black man trying to find a career in the U.S. military. The Suez crisis had just ended. Sanders and his unit had come within twenty-four hours of being called up on active duty. Yet even though he was about to risk dying for his country, he still faced the blatant racism of Jim Crow every time he stepped outside the fort. "That was it. From then on, I didn't want any part of a career in the army. Not if it meant being stuck on some southern military base. My mother fought too hard to get me out of the Jim Crow South for me to want to put myself back in it."

By the time he was in college, Sanders had fallen in love with his adopted hometown of San Francisco. He knew, as all blacks in the city did, that its image of being a wide-open society, free of the kind of bigotry or prejudice that plagued less enlightened places, was more facade than reality. But there was something about San Francisco that caused him to love it despite its flaws.

"Racism in San Francisco wasn't like down South. There wasn't some scowling cracker on the other end of the whip. In San Francisco, racism came at you with a smile. Like they were doing you a favor when they told you that they didn't have any jobs open after you'd seen a half dozen white guys fill out applications, or that you couldn't buy a house when they'd just sold one to a white who made less money.

"Despite all that, something about San Francisco seemed to hold the promise of opportunity. Maybe it went back to the gold rush. San Francisco was a boomtown that never went bust. It still had the smell of the frontier to it, an 'anything goes' quality that kept things exciting. It was a city where you could imagine being free, even if it hadn't yet made it a reality. And on top of that, it was beautiful, with a mix of fog and sunshine and views that took your breath away."

It was at Golden Gate University that Sanders met Espanola Wiley, a beautiful young woman who was also a student there, and whose keen intelligence was immediately apparent to all who met her. Espanola had little reaction to their first encounter, a chance meeting on campus among mutual friends. Sanders's reaction was stronger. He knew he wanted to go out with Espanola the moment he laid eyes on her, and soon he began to pursue her with the same vigor with which he went after everything else he wanted in his life.

Now in his early twenties, Sanders was young and athletic, with a charm and charisma that made him a natural leader among his friends. What drew Espanola to him more than anything was his seriousness. Other young men she knew spent most of their time worrying about how to have fun. But Sanders, who by then had already supported himself for nearly a decade, worried about the job he had to get to, the studies he had to finish, the feeling he always had within him that he must succeed. His determination would lead him to graduate Golden Gate with honors and then go on to do the same when he earned his master's there.

"I think some kids grow up with a sense that they always have something to fall back on if they don't make it, parents or family to take them in and give them a hand. I knew I didn't. And that if I didn't make it on my own, I'd have nothing. Absolutely nothing."

Sanders was majoring in the new field of computer engineering when he and Espanola married in 1960. While attending classes, he worked full-time as a programmer for the city, handling the punch cards that formed the primitive media of early computing. The last thing he ever imagined he would be was a cop. The idea makes him laugh to this day.

"I don't think I knew any black kids back then who grew up wanting to be a cop. For one thing, cops were pretty much all white. And in my world, they were people you did your best to stay away from, not to emulate. But from the first moment I touched police work, I took to it like a fish takes to water. At least, I took to the work of being a cop. The bullshit that surrounded it, however, was another story."

Although San Francisco made a show of bringing a handful of African Americans into the police force in the early 1960s, the SFPD was far from ready to embrace the notion. Once Sanders began his training as an officer, it became clear to him that racism was rampant in the SFPD, embedded not only in the minds of individuals but deep within the warp and weave of the police department itself, in its very culture and practices.

"The department was a creature of the city, cut from the same cloth. Blacks never came close to serving until World War II, when the department was strapped for manpower. Even then, it was in a temporary capacity. The first black to be a 'permanent hire,' with a bona fide patrolman's shield, was Richard Finis, in '48. But by the time I came on the force in '64 he'd already quit, fed up with the racism that made the job a constant struggle."

A handful of other black recruits followed Finis during the late 1940s and '50s, drawn by the security and benefits that blacks then could find almost nowhere except in government jobs. All faced the same obstacles as Finis, and like him, some would decide the job was not worth the humiliations the department heaped upon them. Others who joined the SFPD during those years, trailblazers like Rodney Williams and Rotea Gilford, who would become Sanders's first partner in Homicide, refused to walk away and were determined to change the department and open it up to minorities rather than let it remain "Whites only." Even so, when Sanders entered the academy, little progress had been made.

"When most white officers talked about blacks in the third person, they still called them niggers without so much as a second thought. Many addressed blacks that way on the street. And if it wasn't 'nigger,' it was 'boy.' But it wasn't just attitudes that were racist. Even the policies of the department were filled with bias. Blacks were still being called 'colored' in reports, and when cops described the color of a black man's eyes it was 'maroon,' an eye color that doesn't exist in nature. Human eyes are either brown or variations of blue, mixed with gray, green, or whatever. Blacks were listed as having maroon eyes, as if they were something other than normal."

Not only the nomenclature was unjust. As Sanders soon discovered, performing police work in a biased manner was actually part of the training at the academy.

"There was no legal basis for stopping two people on the street just because one was black and one was white. None. But that's what we were told to do. The assumption was that if a black was mixing with a white, they were up to no good. We were supposed to jack them up and check them out, whether they were driving, walking, or feeding pigeons in a park.

"My best friend in the world back then was John Pryor, who I met in the reserves and who was as white as white could be. But as far as the SFPD was concerned, he and I together was bad news. I couldn't believe it when I heard it, so I did what you're never supposed to do as a recruit: I questioned the training. Stood up in class and asked why. The instructor just said that's the way it is. I told him that wasn't good enough. And unless I was given a direct order, I wouldn't do it."

Sanders's confrontational attitude in the academy may have alienated some, but his excellence was impossible to ignore. Sanders's test and performance scores in the academy were so good, he placed higher than anyone in his year. Two other cadets used the extra points they got as veterans to pass him in the official rankings, but on grades alone, Sanders was first in his class.

At Sanders's graduation, Rotea Gilford was also honored. Having joined the force in 1960, Gilford was the first African American in the history of the SFPD to drive a patrol car, what was then called a radio car. Prior to that, the SFPD had claimed that insurance for black drivers was prohibitively expensive. The problem with that excuse was that the SFPD was self-insured: they could let anyone they wanted drive a car. Gilford broke through that wall in the early 1960s, taking the wheel of the Number 4 car in the Fillmore and becoming a fixture there, known by all as Officer Smiley.

The day that diplomas were handed out to Sanders's class, Gilford was given a First Grade Meritorious Service accommodation, the highest such honor an officer can get, so rare that it is usually awarded posthumously. He had earned it by taking on an armed burglar with his bare hands, not having had time to draw his gun but still able to make the arrest. That honor brought him something else, as well: a promotion from patrolman to inspector, with an assignment to the Burglary Bureau. For the first time in the history of the SFPD, an

African American wore a gold shield instead of a silver one, marking him as one of the exclusive few who could call themselves inspectors.

Seeing Gilford become the first black inspector in the history of the department deeply impressed Sanders, who recalled Officer Smiley from when he was a young man hanging out on the streets of the Fillmore.

"He used to come up to us when we loitered on the street, wave his billy club, and say, 'Give me my corner,' meaning it was time to move on. Now here he was being honored as a hero. I wanted to be like him, to rise to that kind of excellence. And it made me think that maybe, just maybe, some sense of fairness might seep into the walls of the Hall of Justice."

Unfortunately, any fairness seeping through the cracks in the Hall of Justice was doing so at a very slow drip. Most rookie cops who graduated as high as Sanders were given a plum assignment downtown. Not Sanders. Like all blacks, he was sent straight to the ghetto, going to Potrero Station to ride the Number 3 car and patrol the area of the city that was known as its roughest: the project-filled hill at the top of Hunters Point.

3

The Real Cops

IN THE STRUGGLE FOR CIVIL RIGHTS, 1964 is known for four historic milestones: the adoption of the Twenty-fourth Amendment to the Constitution, ending the use of poll taxes to prevent blacks from voting; the campaign of the Freedom Riders, who traveled to Mississippi to militate for the voting rights of blacks; the murders of three civil rights workers who were part of that effort; and passage of the Federal Civil Rights Act, which expressly prohibited discrimination and was voted into law by Congress at the urging of President Lyndon Johnson. That year San Francisco had its own milestones as well, events that would likewise prove transformative in a city most would have never thought so lily-white.

It was in 1964 that Mayor John Shelley, part of the Irish old-boys' network that had run the city for generations, showed himself above such petty allegiances by appointing Terry Francoise, an African-American lawyer from Louisiana who had migrated to San Francisco after World War II and became one of the local leaders of the NAACP, to be the first black supervisor in city history. That same year, Willie Brown, a lawyer who had come from Texas around the same time that Terry Francoise journeyed from Louisiana, became the city's first black assemblyman, representing the Fillmore district. And, with less fanfare, Prentice Earl Sanders, who nearly forty years later would become San Francisco's first African-American chief of police, entered the SFPD as a patrolman, one of still only a handful of black officers on the force. Odd as it may sound, in 1964 San Francisco was probably more prepared to welcome a black supervisor and assemblyman than black cops. And in some instances, it wasn't just whites who felt that way.

"There'd been so few black cops for so long that no one knew what to make of us. It was like the moment we put on a uniform, we turned into some strange kind of creature, not quite black to blacks; not nearly cops to cops. I used to say that we were 'Toms' outside the Hall of Justice and 'niggers' in it.

"Soon after I started at Hunters Point, my first partner, who was white, showed me a round of ammunition and asked me if I knew what it was. Colt had just come out with the .357 Magnums back then, and that was what he had, but I hadn't seen them yet. The cartridge looked huge, bigger than any I'd seen. So I told him no. Then he looked at me and smiled and said, 'These're nigger-stoppers.'

"I had to be torn away from the son of a bitch."

The incident made Sanders realize that he needed a different partner. Yet he knew it would be impossible for him to make such a request merely on the basis of racism; his white superiors would dismiss him as being too "sensitive." But a second incident was different.

"We were on Third, the main drag in Hunters Point, and saw this car heading the wrong way in the wrong lane. So we turned on the siren and pulled him over. The guy was drunk as a skunk, a merchant marine who had just gotten paid and was blowing it all on booze. My partner asked the driver for his wallet. When he took it, I saw it was thick with cash. But when he handed it back, it was pancake thin. That cash had made its way into my partner's pocket. And instead of writing the guy up for DWI, he sent him on his way. The driver, as the saying goes, had 'made bail.'

"I decided in the academy that no matter what else, the one thing I'd never be was a dirty cop. One reason was the promise I gave my mother that I'd never go to jail. But another reason was survival. I knew there were different rules for white cops than there were for blacks. Whites could get away with things. They were part of the club. Blacks weren't. And if they were dirty, they'd be the first to go down when the shit started to fly.

"I didn't make any specific charges against my partner. Back then someone like me couldn't, because I couldn't be sure if the people I was reporting to were any cleaner than the guy I was reporting about. But I made it clear that something happened that I didn't want any part of. The lieutenant who ran Potrero Station understood. And I had a new partner by the end of the week."

Harold McCoy was nearly ten years older than Sanders but had been in the SFPD for only two or three years when Sanders was teamed up with him. McCoy was a tall, lean African American, built, as Sanders recalls, like a point guard in basketball.

"He was about six-two and not an ounce over one-eighty. Quiet, but tough. Harold was from Marshall, Texas, and he and his wife, Opal, both went to Wiley College there, which had been started by relatives of my wife, Espanola. So he was well educated. But he had that Texas, take-no-bullshit way about him. We got along well, and we watched each other's back. You had to when you rode the 3 car in Hunters Point, no matter what color you were."

Long considered San Francisco's most crime-infested ghetto, Hunters Point began its history as a respectable working-class enclave. Named for the family that first settled there, the Point, as it is commonly called, is set on a rocky outreach at the end of the city's southern shore and is a naturally beautiful neighborhood, blessed with steeply pitched streets in the classic San Francisco style, warm, fogless weather, and spectacular views. The lifeblood of the Point was shipbuilding, with dry docks that date back to the 1860s. In the 1940s, when the federal government took over the docks as part of the war effort, the navy became the biggest employer in the area, creating a wealth of civilian jobs and prompting thousands of African Americans to journey from Texas and Louisiana in the hope of finding work.

For a short period of time, prosperity seemed as accessible to blacks in Hunters Point as it was to whites. But when the war ended, many of the jobs that had been opened up to blacks were suddenly withdrawn and given to the mostly white returning heroes. A decade later, the building of the public housing projects began, and the area continued to decline. Set high at the top of the Point, the projects became both an infection and an emblem, radiating poverty and despair.

This was the Hunters Point that Earl Sanders and Harold McCoy patrolled in the summer and winter of 1964. Surprisingly, although they were among the first black officers deployed there, they often felt no more welcome than the white officers had been. In fact, among some blacks they seemed even less so.

"It was a strange thing, but some blacks would look at us in uniform and simply not believe it. One response we used to get when we showed up in the ghetto was people looking at us with a kind of haughty disdain, saying that they wanted the 'real cops,' not us. As if we weren't good enough, weren't up to the job."

Sanders traveled a lot growing up, accompanying his mother as she moved from one job to another, and over time he had discovered a way to quickly gain respect in the pecking order of any new neighborhood he entered.

"What I'd do is pick out the toughest kid in school and challenge him to a fight. There'd be one of two outcomes. Either I'd beat him or we'd reach a draw, and I'd be looked on as so tough that no one else would mess with me. Or he'd beat the living hell out of me, and I'd be looked on as so *crazy* that no one else would mess with me. Either way, no one hassled me from that moment on."

Sanders and McCoy chose a similar tactic to establish their authority at Hunters Point.

"We looked around for the toughest gangster we could find, the guy no one would even think of messing with. Then we picked him up and took him for a ride. We didn't beat him up; we just let him know in a way he wouldn't forget that as far as we were concerned, he was in charge. And if anyone pulled any shit, we wouldn't go after them — we'd go after him."

The tactic proved winning. Sanders racked up an outstanding record while patrolling Hunters Point in his rookie year, excelling on the street as much as he had at the academy. Part of his success lay in the talent he had for police work. But part of it came from the comfort he felt being stationed in the black neighborhood.

"White cops who'd patrolled Hunters usually felt out of place. We didn't. So for us, it was like throwing the rabbit in the briar patch. You may think you're doing him in, but the truth is, you're just sending him home."

Sanders shone so much that by the end of his first year he was

given the kind of plum assignment he had been denied when he graduated from the academy. He was sent to Richmond Station, at the
western edge of the city, and assigned the Number 4 car, covering the
majestic stretch of beach known as the Great Highway.

"I loved it out there. The crime was minimal. The coastline was
beautiful. And I had a brand-new radio car to drive in. Probably the
biggest problems I ever faced were the hot-rodders by the beach. As far
as I was concerned, I could have stayed there forever."

Once again, however, the ease with which Sanders adapted to his
work as a cop brought him success that his superiors could not ignore.

"The department was looking for black officers to do undercover
work in narcotics, which was then part of Special Services, located
downtown in the Hall of Justice, and a call came in for me to transfer.
But undercover details were discretionary, so I wrote a note turning the
transfer down. Captain Meehan, who ran Richmond Station, called
me into his office. He wanted to talk to me before sending the note in.
Meehan was one of the good guys, the kind who reach out to young
cops no matter what color they are. He said he understood that I liked it
at Richmond, but when they call you downtown, it's always good to go."

Sanders took his advice, heading downtown to work in plain-
clothes and joining four other black officers as part of Special Services:
Herman Clark, Ron Carson, Richard Gamble, and Willie Johnson.
Sanders never cared for undercover work. He knew too many people in
the city to feel at ease trying to pass himself off as a crook. Instead of
complaining, though, he threw himself into his assignment and soon
was able to switch from narcotics to prostitution, working in a more
traditional detective mode. When Herman Clark decided to go back
on patrol, the remaining four black officers were paired into teams,
with Sanders working alongside Willie Johnson.

"The best way to describe Willie Johnson is with two words:
Sonny Liston. He looked like Liston, moved like Liston, and even had
a little mustache like Liston. Whenever he walked in a bar, word spread
that Liston was there, and people would come up to Willie and ask for
his autograph. He'd always try to tell the truth, but they never believed
him. After a while he'd give up and just start signing Liston's name for
them. There are probably people in the Bay Area today who still have

autographs tucked away somewhere that they think were signed by Sonny Liston but really were signed by Willie Johnson."

By the mid-1960s, the sexual revolution was in full swing, and prostitution was rampant in San Francisco. In the past it had largely been restricted to whorehouses, which generally paid off cops so they could remain open while the streets were kept clean. But in the 1960s all that changed. The whorehouses began to lose their clout, and the pimps took over, flooding the streets with the girls they "turned out" one after the other. It was up to Sanders, Johnson, and the other cops in Special Services to try to stem the tide.

"A whole new class of crook started to emerge back then. People romanticized them, calling them macks and pimps and players, but there was only one name for them in my book: scum. Most cops went after the hookers, because they were the easiest marks. But Willie and I began to target the other two parts of the equation, the johns who fueled the industry with cash and who we called 'tricks,' and the pimps who preyed off the women.

"We found a Superior Court judge who was willing to bring charges against the tricks, which pissed off some of the old-school cops, who thought men seeking sex should be above the law. But pimps were a tougher nut to crack. You had to show they were taking money from the girls to charge them with pandering, and to do that you had to convince the girls to talk, which was hard, because they knew the pimps would beat them up."

While pimps could avoid charges, scofflaws could not. Almost all the pimps drove flashy Cadillacs that were easily recognizable. So Sanders and Johnson made sure that patrolmen knew which cars were theirs and had them ticket the cars as often as possible, costing the pimps thousands in fines and, since they almost always refused to pay up, allowing them to be brought in on charges.

Sanders and Johnson made so many arrests they earned a reputation as the "Soul Brothers," the two cops in San Francisco that crooks did not want to mess with. At about the same time, the fairness with which they approached their work bought them the respect of the prostitutes. And respect brought them something else along with it: information.

"The two best sources of information about the crime world of any city are cabbies and hookers. Cabbies always know who's new in town and who's got money to burn. But the girls know even more. Because when a crook makes a score, they almost always want to spend some of it on women. And the second thing a man does most often in bed, after he's done with the first thing, is brag. So the hookers end up knowing all their business. If you're a cop who treats hookers right, you might, too."

Sex was not the only revolution brewing during the mid-1960s. The civil rights movement, which in the 1950s and early '60s had been led by the peaceful resistance of Martin Luther King Jr., began to drift to the left, fueled by frustration at the slowness of change and the violence with which its actions were met. Leaders like Malcolm X and Stokely Carmichael gained influence, preaching an eye-for-an-eye doctrine that met violence with violence. When the fighting in Vietnam escalated, tensions rose even more, as blacks, less able than whites to avoid the draft, started dying in disproportionate numbers. Beginning with Watts in 1965, those tensions began to explode, combusting in the summer heat in a series of riots that spread from city to city: Cleveland, Chicago, Newark, Detroit. One after another, America's urban ghettos erupted in violent uprisings that, in almost every instance, began with what was perceived as an act of police brutality.

In 1966, the violence spread to San Francisco.

The first flare-up came in July. Herman George, an African-American SFPD officer who was a friend of Sanders and had been in his class at the academy, was off duty in the Fillmore late one Saturday night when he saw a group of young blacks robbing a white couple. While trying to break up the robbery, George shot one of the blacks. The young man survived, but the incident drew a crowd, and soon scores of blacks from the community had surrounded George, deriding him as an Uncle Tom and crying for revenge. George had to call for backup, and in the melee that followed, storefront windows were broken and cars were burned.

As riots went, this was a small one; but it was only a prelude.

September 1966 was unseasonably hot in San Francisco. Like many U.S. cities, it had endured a long, sweltering summer. On the night of the twenty-seventh, its patience came to an end.

At fifty-one, Alvin Johnson was still a patrolman attached to Potrero Station, working in the same Number 3 car that Sanders had once driven in Hunters Point. Johnson, who was white, received a bulletin about a car theft while he was on patrol and caught sight of the stolen vehicle. When he pulled the car over, the two young black men inside immediately jumped out, running off in opposite directions. Johnson pursued sixteen-year-old Matthew Johnson, calling for him to stop. When Matthew kept running, Officer Johnson fired three shots. The third hit the fleeing youth in the back of the head, killing him almost instantly.

"For a white cop, getting detailed to Potrero Station back then was like punishment. And for a cop with as much seniority as Alvin Johnson must have had, it was doubly so. To be honest, I only remember him vaguely. From what I recall, he was like a lot of cops. A guy who showed up and did his job, neither particularly good nor particularly bad. His judgment when it came to firing at the kid was wrong. But the real sin underlying the incident was the fact that in terms of police policy, there was nothing illegal about it. An officer was within his rights to fire at a fleeing suspect, whether that suspect was a danger or not. It was a terrible policy. When I was president of Officers for Justice, we filed an amicus brief in a case that finally brought it to an end, citing the shooting of Matthew Johnson as an example of how it could go wrong. But back then it was seen as appropriate. So when the people rioted, it wasn't without cause. It wasn't just one officer who was wrong. It was the department itself, and how it went about policing the community."

As understanding as Sanders is now of the uprising in Hunters Point, at the time he was focused on mere survival. Bullets, rocks, and Molotov cocktails were flying, and more often than not they were coming his way. Black cops and black radicals may have had common enemies, but when it came to the streets, they were on opposite sides.

"A lot of the guys I grew up with joined the Panthers. We came from the same place and wanted the same results. But we disagreed about how to get it done. I believed the way to change things was from the inside, beginning with the institutions themselves. They believed the only way was to tear it all down. They wanted armed revolution. I told them they were fools. I trained at Aberdeen Proving Grounds, so I know what kind of artillery the military has. They have cannons in San Francisco that could take out the whole Fillmore with just a few rounds. You can't beat an opponent that has superior firepower. That's just a fact of war. And the United States has the most advanced weaponry in the world. So if you want to change the status quo, you've got to find another way to do it."

After four days of rioting, the gunfire, bomb throwing, and bloodshed finally came to an end. The largest black neighborhoods, the Fillmore and Hunters Point, were in shambles. Yet, as was the case with all the rioting in the 1960s, the white neighborhoods remained untouched, a fact that, in many ways, underscored Sanders's point. If those who were outraged by police violence wanted to change things, they had to find another way. The question was, how?

Herman George, who had played an inadvertent role in the rioting in July, found himself at the center of another rebellion he had little control over and little to do with beyond setting it in motion.

Tall and athletic, George was the kind of officer who, if he had been white, would have cut the classic figure of what a cop was meant to be, with a warmth and charisma that appealed to all who knew him. However, Herman George was black. And despite his positive qualities, he was also a man flawed like any other, as imperfect as he was inspiring. Those two qualities, the fact that he was imperfect and the fact that he was African American, came together in a way that helped begin the process that led to the transformation of the SFPD.

"Herman was a good man," Sanders recalls as he talks about his friend, "but he was never very faithful in his marriage. The truth was, Herman had outside women, and one time a merchant marine who was seeing the same woman as Herman pulled a gun on him and shot him in the shoulder. Then Herman made things worse by lying, saying he'd accidentally shot himself on the job. He didn't stop to think that if he'd shot himself while working, there'd be a hole in his uniform.

"Herman's superiors figured out the story was fishy and brought him up on charges. Herman was a dues-paying member of the POA, the Police Officers Association, so the POA was supposed to defend him. But the lawyer they had on retainer told Herman that he'd be caught dead before he'd defend a nigger, and turned him down. When the blacks on the force heard that, we went ballistic. Wrong or right, Herman deserved counsel. That was the impetus that started Officers for Justice. We decided that if the POA wouldn't treat Herman George the same they would a white cop, we wouldn't be part of it. So a group of us resigned and started up an organization of our own."

Herman George never joined Officers for Justice, but he never had much of an opportunity to do so. Less than a year later, on November 13, 1967, he was gunned down in cold blood, the first African-American officer killed in the line of duty in the history of the SFPD. The sad irony was that it was not some crook he was trying to arrest who took Herman down. It was black revolutionaries.

Herman was doing paperwork in an office the police used in the housing project at Hunters Point when the shooting took place. According to Sanders and other officers who investigated Herman's murder, he was killed by members of the Black Panthers, assassinated, at least in part, because of his involvement in the Fillmore and Hunters Point riots of 1966.

The Black Panther Party was formed across the bay in Oakland in October 1966, two weeks after the rioting in Hunters Point. The Panthers embraced the notion of taking up arms, combining traditional antipoverty programs with shotgun-wielding, in-your-face debate.

"The Panthers were started by Bobby Seale and Huey Newton, and while they did some good work in the community, there was a touch of hustle to them, especially Newton. And that criminality ultimately brought them down. It's known that Newton became a crack addict in the late 1970s. But even when they started the Panthers, they were funding much of their operations by acting like a mini-Mafia, demanding a piece of the criminal action that went on around their chapters and telling business owners that if they wanted to stay open, they had to pay protection money."

According to Charlie Walker, the Panthers were not always up to their swagger. Charlie Walker is known today as the unofficial "mayor of Hunters Point," having run a trucking business there for more than a generation. Trucking is only one of the many businesses Charlie has had over the years, and by his own admission not all of those other enterprises have been legal. In the 1970s he bought a nightclub in the Fillmore called the Half Note, and, as Sanders recalls, the purchase brought him a visit from Huey Newton.

"Newton called Charlie and told him he wanted to come over for a meeting. Charlie knew the kind of shit Newton was pulling in Oakland, so he had no doubt what the meeting was about. Sure enough, when Newton entered with another Panther he pulled a gun on Charlie and told him that if he wanted to stay open, he had to cut him in on the take. But Charlie was ready. A friend of his had just got out of San Quentin, and Charlie had tucked him away in the room behind where he knew Newton would be standing. So when Newton pulled a gun on Charlie, Charlie's pal stepped out with a sawed-off shotgun pointed at Newton's head. Then Charlie pulled a gun and told Newton to get the hell out or else there'd be some killing. Newton never bothered him again."

It was one thing for Newton to back down in private to another African American. Backing down to a white cop in Oakland, in full view of his friends, was inconceivable. And on the night of October 27, 1967, that fact led to a tragic outcome when two Oakland cops stopped Newton and another Panther as they were driving along the streets of West Oakland.

Exactly what followed is a matter of debate, but shots were fired, and by the end one cop was wounded, one was dead, and Huey Newton was on the run. The Oakland police, who had always been hard on the Panthers, redoubled their efforts against them after the incident. The Panthers responded in kind, and they did so against all cops, not just in Oakland. Nor did it make any difference if the cops were white or black. In the parlance of the time, "pigs" were "pigs," "swine" was "swine," and color "didn't mean shit."

"They had special names for us," Sanders recalls now, the sting of the memory evident in his face. "Things like Brother Pig or Nappy Fuzz. We weren't just cops to them. We were traitors. Collaborators. And to many, we became targets."

According to Sanders's sources, a meeting was held between Panthers and other radicals in the public housing project at the top of Hunters Point in November 1967, not long after Huey Newton went on the run. It was decided that Herman George should be killed because of his so-called crimes, among them the off-duty shooting in the Fillmore. Volunteering for the job were three members of the budding San Francisco chapter of the Panthers. The place chosen for the hit was in the same complex where the death sentence was being handed down, the housing project at the top of the Point.

Potrero Station is so far from Hunters Point that the officers who patrolled the Point used the Housing Project Police office there to do their paperwork. Herman George was there writing up a report on the night of November 13, 1967, two weeks after Huey Newton was arrested for murder in the Oakland shooting, when the men chosen to take him out approached the office's first-floor window with what Sanders describes as "murder on their minds."

"Herman was working with my adopted brother, Kelly Waterfield, that night. Kelly entered the academy a year after I did, and he and Herman were working the same area I had worked with McCoy. I was with my family in Yosemite that week, but I heard later that it had been a warm night in the city, so the windows were open in the office. One of the housing cops, Wayne Summerlin, was with them. Kelly was by a file cabinet, and Herman and Summerlin were sitting at the desks. Then the three sons of bitches stuck war-surplus M1 carbines in the window and didn't stop firing until their rifles were empty."

Over thirty shots were fired at the officers. Kelly Waterfield took cover behind the metal filing cabinet and managed to avoid getting hit. Summerlin was less fortunate. Three bullets hit him before he fell to the floor. But it was at Herman George that the assassins were aiming, and he took eight shots to his body before the shooting was over. The first bullet stood him up from his chair, the next turned him around to face the window, and the six that followed held him up in the air, keeping him aloft with the force of their impact as they entered his midsection, one after another. Then the deafening staccato ended as the bullets ran out and the assailants ran off into the night, disappearing among the rows of apartments that made up the hilltop project.

"I heard about it the next day in Yosemite and drove all the way back to San Francisco that night, then went to see Herman in the hospital. It was amazing how strong he was. The bullets tore up his insides. There was nothing the doctors could do. But he didn't die. Not right away. He held on for weeks, fighting, until sepsis set in and then, finally, his body gave out.

"Bill Armstrong was the Homicide inspector who drew Herman's case, and I'll never forget how moved he was by what Herman went through. Bill was white, and if you just went by appearance you might think he was like a lot of the old guard, looking on black cops more like threats than colleagues. But Bill was as different from that as night was from day. He had tears in his eyes when Herman died, and later he told me that watching Herman suffer was one of the toughest things he ever dealt with. Bill didn't see color when he looked at Herman. He just saw a man. And a cop."

Some Homicide inspectors seem to owe their success to innate cynicism, something inside them that doubts and questions everything they see. William Armstrong, however, made use of two very different qualities in his work: a dogged attention to detail and a quiet but evident sense of empathy. Compassion shaped every aspect of Armstrong's life, including his attitude toward minorities. One would never call Bill Armstrong overtly political, but one would also never call him anything other than fair. His sense of fair play caused him to reach out to Earl Sanders and Willie Johnson to help him solve the Herman George murder. Neither was in Homicide. Neither was even an inspector yet, but Armstrong knew they would have contacts inside the black community that went beyond his own, and to him getting the job done was all that mattered.

Looking back at the investigation, Armstrong remains impressed with the determination that Sanders and Johnson brought to the task of discovering who had killed their friend. Especially Sanders. Some white cops felt on shaky ground when teaming with black cops against black suspects, wondering whose side the black cops would be on. Armstrong had no such doubts. In fact, what struck him most about Sanders was how relentless he could be with suspects, regardless of color. He recounts how the following incident made Sanders's determination clear.

"Earl and Willie Johnson picked up an informant who was connected to the Panthers and who they believed knew the identity of the killers. But he wouldn't talk. So they took him to the Hall of Justice, Willie driving and Earl sitting in the back with the suspect. Earl was sure the guy had information and was hoping he would open up, but the guy kept acting tough, calling Earl and Willie pigs. Well, Earl lost it. He had a big automatic back then, a .45-caliber, and he jacked out one of those cartridges, held it up so the guy could see how huge it was, and told him 'I'm saving this for you if you don't talk!' Then he slammed it back in the chamber and let the guy get a glimpse down the barrel, so he could imagine what it would be like coming his way. When that informant got downtown he was begging us to keep Earl away from him, calling him crazy and ready to tell us everything he knew."

The murder of Herman George was never officially solved, but Sanders and Armstrong believe they know who the killers were. All three suspects went on the run. Two were brothers who had been raised in the same housing project where George was killed, and later died themselves in a shootout with the Denver police. The third suspect took refuge in Algeria, and has never been brought to justice.

Sanders was left frustrated by his inability to catch the men who killed his friend. However, his efforts earned him the respect of the cops on the Homicide Bureau. No one could question his toughness and resolve, or his devotion to justice.

"The perception the white cops had was that I was coming on so tough because I was after a cop killer. That was part of it. But there was another part they couldn't understand, a battle going on inside the black community. The Panther paper printed pictures of Willie, Kelly, and me because we worked on the case, marking us as traitors. We were on a battle line between two armed camps, and most of the time it felt like the only people who really had our backs were other black cops. White cops talk about being part of a brotherhood. Let me tell you something: they don't have a clue. Black cops back then were like a motherless child. Nobody wanted us.

"But at least we were all motherless together."

Earl Sanders and Willie Johnson worked together in Robbery from 1966 through 1970, racking up arrests and convictions at a rate that solidified the reputation of the Soul Brothers. As the decade came to a close, and 1970 crested into 1971, their celebrated partnership came to an end.

Although Rotea Gilford often worked with Sanders on cases while in Robbery, his official partner was Richard Miller, a white inspector with whom he had been teamed ever since he was first promoted to inspector in 1964. In early 1971 Gilford was informed that he would become the first black ever transferred into Homicide on a permanent basis. Miller, however, would stay in Robbery. Gilford was to have a black inspector as a partner, and, in a rare show of deference, he was allowed to choose him.

Gilford chose Earl Sanders.

Rotea Gilford was born in 1927 in Willis, Texas, a small, rural town set in the middle of nowhere, forty miles north of Houston and ninety miles east of Austin, not far from Lake Conroe, where, if one believes Gilford's stories, endless amounts of largemouth bass could be caught with ease.

"If there was an Olympics for storytelling, Gil would have got the gold." When Sanders speaks today of Gilford, who died in 1998 of complications from the diabetes he had suffered for over forty years, it is with a smile, wistful at some times and sad at others.

Gilford left Texas with his family in the 1930s, moving to San Francisco when it held few African Americans. He lived in the Fillmore, then a mixed neighborhood that served as home to more Japanese than blacks. That changed with the war, as thousands of blacks flooded into the city and thousands of Japanese were forced out by the U.S. government and sent to internment camps.

"Gil used to talk about Soji Horikoshi, who later became the head criminalist for the SFPD, and who lived just a few blocks from him in the Fillmore. Every morning Gil would get up, go to Soji's, and walk with him to school. One morning he went over, and Soji wasn't there. No one was. The government had come in the middle of the night and rounded people up. Every home that had a Japanese family in it was empty."

Gilford went to San Francisco State in the late 1940s, starring on its football team and becoming close friends with crosstown rivals Ollie Matson and Burl Toler, stars of the famous undefeated 1951 team at the University of San Francisco, both of whom helped to break the color line in the NFL. Gilford tried out for the pros himself, earning a cup of coffee with the Chicago Cardinals, but a shoulder injury cut his athletic ambitions short, and he returned to the city. A friend from college, Willie Brown, who later became speaker of the California Assembly and eventually the mayor of San Francisco, was a young lawyer who had already begun to cultivate political ambitions. They began working together to end the pattern of racial injustice that had so long plagued the city, Brown determined to change the face of politics in San Francisco, and Gilford determined to do the same in the city's civil service. Gilford was at the forefront of breaking through the barriers that had been raised against blacks, working as one of the first African-American toll takers on the Bay Bridge, and later becoming a Muni bus driver and working as a conductor on San Francisco's fabled cable cars. All along, Gilford's most cherished goal was to break through the wall that had been built up around the nearly all-white police department, and when he could, he took a first job as an Alameda county sheriff and then, finally, gained admission to the SFPD academy.

Gilford's rise in the department was as swift as Sanders's would be a few years later, and it was generally assumed that when a black was promoted to Homicide, the department's most prestigious inspectors bureau, Gilford would be the one chosen. Officially, that turned out to be true. Unofficially, though, another black was detailed there before him: Herman Clark, who had grown up in a middle-class neighborhood that was nearly all white. Clark was given a temporary assignment to Homicide, which he hoped to make a permanent appointment. Soon those hopes were dashed when he was sent back to Robbery. Sanders recalls Gilford's comment to him that it was the white cops' way of telling Herman he was still black.

"Gilford said they were sending Herman a message. It doesn't matter what neighborhood you're from or how many whites you count as friends. Black is black, and in Gil's mind they didn't want anybody to forget it."

Rotea Gilford and Earl Sanders may have made inspector in the Homicide Bureau, but on their first day they weren't given a desk there. No one would lend a hand in finding one, either. Finally, Gilford turned up an abandoned desk elsewhere in the Hall of Justice, and he and Sanders lugged it to Room 450 on the fourth floor, the home, then as now, of the bureau.

"The first cases we were given were 'roundnecks,' deaths that were either considered unsolvable or which wouldn't lead to an arrest. I remember the very first was in Japantown, on Bush, where a married couple had both died from carbon monoxide while in bed. That was when I found out that Gilford couldn't stomach dead bodies. The couple had been dead for a week by the time we found them. Gil couldn't take it, covering his nose and heading out to 'canvass the neighborhood.'"

The case that followed also failed to yield an arrest. When they returned from their second "roundneck," Eugene Fogarty, a hard-drinking, old-school Irish cop who, as Sanders puts it, was "less than sensitive when it came to issues of race," told the new team that Homicide was like baseball. They now had two strikes against them. One more, and they were out.

"Fogarty would have probably laughed about a new white cop on the bureau getting nothing but roundnecks. But not with black cops. We had to be on our game all the time, and if we slipped at all, the old-school cops would come gunning for us."

Soon the new duo of Gilford and Sanders turned things around and were achieving at a level as high as, or higher than, any other team, solving a string of homicides and cementing their position inside the bureau. Part of what helped them achieve so much so fast was their willingness to work long hours, coupled with their own natural abilities as detectives. They also had an advantage that the white cops never quite realized. The black community tends to be wary about giving information to the police, especially when lives might be at stake. With black cops, however, that wariness breaks down. Since there had never before been any blacks in Homicide, Gilford and Sanders had years of cold cases in the black community to go through. Digging into killing after killing that had never been solved, searching for new sources of information, they may not have succeeded in every case, but they solved enough to clearly be among the rising stars of the bureau.

Although some inspectors in Homicide were reluctant to welcome black cops into the fold, others proved repeatedly that they were oblivious to the whole notion of race. Ken Manley, the old sage of the bureau, who served as the technical adviser for Clint Eastwood's "Dirty Harry" movies, went out of his way to tutor Sanders on the ins and outs of Homicide. Bill Armstrong, who worked with Sanders on the Herman George killing, also welcomed them. But the two homicide cops who were more oblivious than anyone to even the idea of prejudice were Gus Coreris and John Fotinos, then considered to be the most successful team in the bureau.

To Sanders and Gilford, Coreris and Fotinos were "the Greeks," tough, unsentimental San Francisco natives who grew up dirt poor and, being neither Roman Catholic nor Irish, were nearly as much outsiders in the SFPD as the black cops.

"Gus went to the same high school Gil did, and while they didn't run in the same circles, they had the kind of respect tough kids always have for each other. John grew up even rougher than Gus, south of Market. They wouldn't back down from anything. And when you tried to talk to John about the privileges of growing up white, he'd just laugh in your face and tell you, 'I'm not white. I'm Greek.'"

It was Coreris's wife, Katherine, who possibly made the most pointed act of reaching out to the new black officers who had broken the color line in Homicide. She did it with a gesture directed not at either Sanders or Gilford, but at Sanders's wife, Espanola.

"They used to have parties in Homicide, dinners at various restaurants in the city where everyone was invited, including wives. And at the first one we went to, Espanola felt nervous. Gil was still married to Pat, his first wife, then. But they couldn't make it. So it was me and Espy and a sea of white faces. I could b.s. with the guys there, because we had already established a relationship, but Espy felt pretty damn alone. That's when Katherine stepped in.

"Katherine was like Gus, middle-of-the-road when it came to politics, but the salt of the earth when it came down to being a person. She was also someone who all the other wives looked up to. And she went over to Espy, took her by the hand, and said, 'You sit with me.'"

The murder of Herman George in 1967 had made Sanders realize the danger that cops, especially black cops, faced from the growing threat of radical groups. But in early 1973, an incident occurred that brought home to him in a very personal way how great the stakes were at every turn.

It started when he tried to help someone out.

"Gil's marriage was turning bad around then, and he had to deal with some personal business. So I spent the day working alone. I was looking for information on a suspect in a case we had, and I went to talk to Elijah Johnson, a skip tracer who was also looking for him. Skip tracers are like bounty hunters who don't bring fugitives in; they just find out where they are and leave the rest to the cops.

"Elijah was heading out of his office as I walked in, so I tagged along with him, talking about my case as he worked on his. He thought he had a lead on a woman he'd been looking for named Rosie Pratt. It didn't seem like anything to be concerned about. The only thing Rosie was charged with was petty theft, so if she was there, I figured I'd grab her myself."

Rosie was there, all right. But so was her husband, Josiah Pratt, a drug dealer and small-time hood who had a habit of getting violent when he drank. That night, he was juiced to the gills.

"We got Rosie easy," Sanders says as he recalls what happened, pausing as he thinks about what followed, and letting a small sigh before continuing. "Then Pratt came out of the bedroom. He might have been passed out, because we didn't even know he was there at first. He started screaming when he saw us, yelling at us to let her go. I told him I was a cop and showed him my badge, but all he said to that was, 'I don't give a fuck.'"

Josiah Pratt reached for a gun he had tucked in the front of his pants, and Sanders reached for his.

"I used to have a saying: 'They don't pay me enough on this job to be slow with my gun.' I wasn't slow then, I'll tell you that."

Sanders fired first. The bullet hit Pratt in the forehead from only a few feet away. He was dead by the time he hit the ground.

"Everybody thinks that the toughest thing a cop has to face is death. They're right. But it's not your death. It's someone else's. When you die, you die. Whatever you had to deal with is done. But when someone else dies, there's no end to it. I don't mean bureaucratic stuff. I mean emotions. No matter who you kill, or how right you were in doing it, the memories haunt you in ways you never expect."

Because of the shooting, Sanders was put on temporary leave. Rosie hid Pratt's gun in the confusion that followed his death and tried to sue the department, claiming Sanders fired without cause. Eventually the gun was found, and the investigation cleared Sanders of any wrongdoing. Yet, as Sanders says, the memories lingered.

"I couldn't get the shooting out of my head. It made me tentative. Before then, if trouble started I was always ready to get into it. But afterward, I kept thinking about having blood on my hands. People kept telling me I couldn't blame myself, but it's easier said than done.

"I don't think I was over it until sometime in summer. Gil and I were arresting a female suspect who shot some guy in a bar. But she started to resist when he tried to cuff her, and they got in a fistfight. She was giving it to Gil good, and he started to yell for me to help. Normally, I'd jump right in, but this time I held back. And finally he started yelling, 'Hit the bitch, School! Hit the bitch, or I'll kick your ass when I'm done with hers!'

"Finally I dove in to help. And the moment she started to smack me in the face, all hesitation was gone."

It was early in the summer of 1973 when Sanders returned to active duty. The rest of the summer was filled with increasing racial tension as the Officers for Justice lawsuit began to be argued in court and the debate and recriminations over it raged inside the Hall of Justice. Then, as the dog days of summer blended into a blistering early fall, Quita Hague's murder underscored those tensions and cast them in stark relief.

4

The .32-Caliber Killings

ONLY A FEW DAYS AFTER THE MURDER OF Quita Hague, a police officer from Berkeley paid a visit to Bill Armstrong. Unlike Sanders, Armstrong hadn't attended the California Homicide Investigators Association meeting in Oakland, where the speaker had discussed the "motiveless killings" plaguing the West Coast. So he was taken aback when the Berkeley cop, referring to wounds caused by a machete-like weapon, made that connection with the Hague assault, theorizing, just as Sanders had done privately at Quita's autopsy, that her death might be linked to these others. The Berkeley cop went even further, taking the connection as a matter of fact and predicting that sooner or later the link would be proven.

However, all he had to support his theory was speculation based on circumstantial evidence, and Armstrong needed something more solid than that. Weeks of trying to develop leads had resulted in little progress in the case. During this time, Armstrong developed great respect for Quita's husband, Richard, who, though brutally injured, never gave in to bitterness or despair. Spurred on by the image of his loss, Armstrong kept plugging away, determined to find the killers.

Just a little more than a month after the Hague attack, on November 26, 1973, Judge Robert F. Peckham handed down a preliminary ruling in the Officers for Justice lawsuit, finding that the SFPD was guilty of discriminatory practices and ordering both the city's Civil Service Commission and the SFPD to begin immediately to redress them — in his words, "to alleviate, with due speed, the past effects of discrimination and prevent any future discrimination." As good as that sounded to Sanders, Gilford, and the others in the Officers for Justice, their lead attorney, Robert Gnaizda, made sure they realized that this was merely the first round in a long battle. Among the remedies, Peckman directed that entry-level patrolmen be hired at a ratio of three minorities for every two nonminorities until the proportion of minorities in the department reached 30 percent. In addition, minorities must make up at least 30 percent of all sergeants in the SFPD. Peckham also imposed a temporary freeze on promotions, demanding that he be given final approval over all examination and selection procedures in the promoting of police personnel. The decision constituted the largest quota hiring ever ordered in the United States up until then, making it a landmark case in affirmative action. But merely stating a set of goals was no guarantee that any would be reached. The question remained of how each goal might be accomplished, and when. As Gnaizda warned, these preliminary findings could be subject to stalls and appeals without end.

It wasn't long before his words of caution were borne out. Less than twenty-four hours after the ruling, Sergeant Gerald Crowley, head of the Police Officers Association, announced that he would begin the first of a series of legal appeals against the ruling, which he termed "a slap in the face of every policeman in San Francisco and throughout the country," claiming that "the profession has been sold out." He vowed to do everything he could to reverse it, adding that he would also be relentless in lobbying San Francisco's Civil Service Commission to file an appeal of their own. In short order, the POA had successfully petitioned to be named an intervenor in the lawsuit, becoming a full party to it and as able to bring an appeal as the SFPD or the OFJ. Chief of Police Donald Scott also belittled the decision, saying that the department was considering a separate appeal. Bernard Orsi, the head of the Civil Service Commission, though noncommittal as to whether or not the commission would appeal the ruling, implied that it might in fact be illegal, as it directed the city of San Francisco to violate its own charter, which requires the civil service to chose, in Orsi's words, "the highest ranking eligible" for any city job.

The response of many of the white officers on the force mirrored the resentment expressed by Crowley.

"There'd been tension growing ever since the suit was filed," Sanders recalls. "But as angry as the reaction had been, it grew even more bitter after Peckham gave his first ruling. I think a lot of the officers who were against the lawsuit didn't take it seriously until that preliminary decision was handed down. From then on, they knew they had a fight on their hands. The resentment was so thick you could cut it with a knife. Sometimes it'd come out in racist jokes, people calling you 'boy' and then acting like it was an accident, saying they meant to call you 'Roy.' But sometimes it was just flat-out hate, people talking about blacks trying to take over. And 'black' wasn't always the word they used."

The reaction to the ruling underscored what Sanders had known implicitly the moment he entered the SFPD: the white Irish old-boys' network ran the department with two sets of rules. White cops lived by one, but imposed another on black cops. The rules weren't written; they were understood. As blacks lobbied for more power in the department, this double standard became starker than ever.

A case in point was Percy Cooksey. Cooksey was a fair-skinned black officer in his late thirties who had come on the force shortly after Sanders. Although his record couldn't compare with that of Sanders, who had reached the rank of inspector in the unprecedented span of only three years, Cooksey was an effective officer, and in April 1972 he became the first African American to be assigned to plainclothes duty with Chinatown's vice squad.

To Sanders, this was a dubious honor. Chinatown duty was what's known among cops as a "paying detail," a place where the payoffs could equal or surpass one's regular earnings. This was especially true of Vice, which was supposed to police the gambling endemic to the neighborhood but all too often protected it instead. Ever since the gold rush days, when the Chinese of San Francisco were forced into the impoverished three-block-wide hillside stretch that surrounded what was known as Dupont Street before the Civil War and Grant Avenue afterward, the area was rife with gambling and corruption. By the 1970s, pai gow and fan-tan had become the games of choice, and while the neighborhood was still poor, the gambling was not. Some games required a bankroll of up to $25,000 just for a seat at the table, drawing players all the way from Hong Kong and Taiwan. Pots in games like those were massive. And when the pots are large, so are the payoffs.

One evening not long after being assigned to Chinatown, Cooksey showed up at Gilford's apartment on Ashbury Street in the Upper Haight along with two veteran white officers from the Chinatown squad. Sanders was there that night as well, and relates what happened.

"Gil and I made it a point to stay away from crooked cops. We had plenty of opportunities. Back when I was working downtown Vice, a pimp named Pedro Swinger offered Willie Johnson and me each nine hundred dollars a night to look the other way while his girls turned tricks. That was a lot of money then, especially for a young cop. But two things stopped me. One, I knew black cops had different rules. White cops might get their hands slapped if they were caught, but I'd get slapped upside the head. And two, I promised my mother on her deathbed that I'd finish school and stay out of jail. I'd already done one, and I was determined to do the other.

"So when he made the offer I nodded and said, 'I'll tell you how I'll handle this. I'm going to pay special attention to your girls.' He smiled, 'cause he thought I was hooked. I wasn't. 'They'll be my personal business. In fact, I'll make sure they can't even lie down without getting busted. So they can forget turning tricks. See, they're my business now. And your business just dried up.'

"Gil and I didn't even want to look dirty, let alone *be* dirty. So when Cooksey walked into his place with two cops who we knew were crooked, Gil took him in the kitchen and let him have it.

"'What're you doing bringing those motherfuckers into my house?' Gil was pissed. Cooksey tried to calm him down. 'No, no, man, they're cool, they're cool.' Then he took out his wallet and showed us a thousand in cash that he had just gotten from his part of the take. Gil looked at it, called him a fool, and walked out of the kitchen. He didn't want to hear another word. That was the last time Cooksey came over."

In November 1973, within a week of Judge Peckham's first ruling on the Officers for Justice lawsuit and just over a year after Percy Cooksey came onto the Chinatown detail, Cooksey was busted by the FBI, having been set up by the same cops he had thought were his friends.

The veteran white officers who had worked with the Chinatown detail avoided any disciplinary action, while Cooksey, the newest man on the squad, went to jail and never worked as a cop again.

Different races; different rules.

The Greeks, Gus Coreris and John Fotinos, were oblivious to such distinctions. They lived by one rule and one rule only: getting the job done. "Gus and John were hard-nosed but fair," Sanders recalls. "We never talked about the OFJ suit back then, but I have a feeling that we probably would have disagreed, with them saying it wasn't necessary. But it wasn't a malicious thing with them, the way it was with the POA. I think they figured everybody was as color-blind as they were. I only wish that had been the case."

When, the same week that Judge Peckham's decision was announced, a case fell to the Greeks that they thought Sanders and Gilford could help them solve, they turned to their two black colleagues without a second thought. Not one of them had any inkling how significant the case would become, forming one link in the chain that would eventually take them back to the killing of Quita Hague.

Saleem Erakat was a fifty-three-year-old Palestinian Arab who had come with his family from Jordan to the United States in the late 1950s. Since 1960 he had owned and operated a small family grocery at 452 Larkin, right near Turk Street, at the edge of the Tenderloin. The Tenderloin was a neighborhood in transition. It had earned its name in the nineteenth century, when it lay at the western edge of the waterfront district known as the Barbary Coast, an area rife with crime. "Tenderloin" referred to the quality of graft that cops working there could expect. This wasn't the sort of place where all you could hope to get was salt pork and soup bones for your payoffs. Here, you got tenderloin.

In the first half of the twentieth century, the Tenderloin lost its rough-and-tumble reputation, becoming a working-class neighborhood where the streets were more likely to be filled with kids playing ball than with criminals looking for a score. After World War II, it began to change again. Flophouses replaced the more legitimate hotels in the area. Soon it became known as San Quentin North, and as the crooks moved in, families moved out. During its working-class days, most of the grocers in the Tenderloin had been Chinese. When the families left, the Chinese sold off their stores to newer immigrants who were more willing to put up with a rougher element. More often than not these new store owners were Arabs who, displaced by the turmoil in the Middle East, were flooding into San Francisco.

Saleem Erakat's murder took place early Sunday morning, November 25, just after he opened for business. What baffled the Greeks about the killing was the way it was carried out. The safe and cash register had both been emptied, just as one would expect, netting the killer some $1,300. Yet Erakat was killed execution-style, kneeling on the floor, hands tied behind his back, shot in the head with a .32-caliber gun. A quilt, of the sort used by movers, was found at the scene pierced with bullet holes and had evidently been used to muffle the gunshots. The few witnesses they located had mentioned seeing a black man with an attaché case outside the store around the time of the shooting. With little else to go on, apart from a bloody palm print that couldn't be positively identified, Coreris and Fotinos turned to Sanders and Gilford to ask around and see if there was any word on the street as to who the killer or killers might be.

By 1973, Sanders and Gilford's reputation for cracking murder cases in the black community was well established. A big part of the reason for their success was the sources both had developed inside the community over the years, which they considered "insurance policies." It was Gilford who had coined the phrase, meaning that sooner or later each source would pay off with dividends, just as an insurance policy does. Only these dividends didn't come in cash — they came in information.

As Sanders recalls, "Our informers knew that if they passed on information when it came their way, we'd do what we could to help when they got in trouble. But if they didn't, the 'insurance policies' they had with us would lapse, and they'd be on their own."

For Sanders, the concept of establishing sources and making connections in all aspects of a community is not simply a matter of good detective work but goes further than that. The relationship between an officer and the public that surrounds him is the essence of what has become known as "community policing," which Sanders believes is the only way to effectively police a city.

"People talk about community policing like it's something with good intentions but no practical application. That's crazy. The fact that Gil and I were part of the community is what made us effective in it. We were trusted. And trust translates into information. Say there're two guys on a street who've been going at it for years, and finally one shoots the other. Everybody on the street knows who did it. Half the folks there probably saw it actually happen. But you put a white cop into that, and all he'll get is a lot of 'I don't knows' and 'I didn't see nothings' and 'I was watering my lawn, man, and didn't look up till after it all went down.' In other words, a lot of bullshit. But you put me in that, and people won't be so afraid to talk. Or if they are, I'll call them on it, look them in the eye, and say: 'When you die and go to heaven, you're gonna meet your maker. Now are you telling me that you're ready to stand there like some fool and have him ask you why you let so-and-so get away with murder — or are you gonna tell me the truth?' That's the kind of thing a white cop can't get away with. And it doesn't just impact a single case. It carries over from one case to the next, creating an openness that facilitates policing in general."

But despite their network of contacts, none of Sanders and Gilford's sources could turn up a thing about the Erakat killing. There wasn't a whisper of information to be had, which meant one of two things: "Either whoever did it came from somewhere outside the city, or else they were staying very, very quiet."

Hitting a dead end in the Tenderloin, Sanders and Gilford left the Erakat case to the Greeks and brought their focus back to one of their own, the murder of a wealthy dowager on Lombard Street. Gilford and Charlie Ellis, the lieutenant who headed up Homicide, thought the main motive was robbery and that the killing was just something that happened in the course of the crime. Sanders didn't buy that. In his mind, the killing had been personal, and almost certainly committed by someone who knew the old woman. For one thing, there was no sign of a break-in. Even more significant was the fact that she had been stabbed over forty times. That kind of attack didn't evolve out of a robbery. It was deliberate, determined, and had to be the reason the assailant entered the house. The robbery must be a cover. Gilford and Ellis balked at Sanders's theory. So did the victim's son, a respected physician who resisted any implication that another family member might be involved. In the end, though, Sanders was right. The killer was the victim's grandson, a 1960s burnout who had done so many drugs over the years that he had become a borderline psychopath.

As Sanders and Gilford wrapped up the Lombard case a week or so later, the irrational brutality of that killing added to a general sense of the craziness infiltrating their lives. Events in the larger world, too, seemed to be spinning out of control.

On the morning of Friday, December 7, as Sanders sipped his coffee and lit his first cigarette of the day while scanning the front page of the *Chronicle,* his eyes lingered on the lead story. The previous day, Gerald Ford had taken the oath of office to become the fortieth vice president in the nation's history. He replaced the disgraced Spiro Agnew, who had resigned in October, little more than a week before the Quita Hague killing, to plead no contest to a charge of income tax evasion committed while he was governor of Maryland. The picture of Ford standing beside Nixon brought to mind something that George Sing Louie, the greatest con man Sanders had ever met, had said to him not long after Agnew's resignation.

Louie was an enormous man, half African American and half Chinese, who weighed well over three hundred pounds and crushed stereotypes with every step. A man of equally large appetites, he loved Jewish deli food and could often be found devouring half the menu at David's, in the theater district on Geary. Yet he never let his girth get in the way of his appreciation of women. He employed an array of beautiful females, some of whom were his lovers, to help pull off his scams, figuring their beauty would blind those he was conning and help to make them willing marks. Louie was the architect of some of the biggest cons San Francisco had ever seen, and on more than one occasion he pulled off scams that were like real-life versions of the movie *The Sting,* targeting the crooks who lorded over the rackets in both the Fillmore and Hunters Point. Still, he was slick enough always to keep himself out of jail. Smooth and stylish, Louie cultivated an understated tone, speaking with a deference that his actions never matched.

"The VP's a player, Inspector," Louie told Sanders just after Agnew's resignation in October. Sanders had gone to Louie to ask about a fence in the Fillmore whose murder he and Gilford thought Louie might know something about. But part of what kept Louie alive was knowing when to keep his own counsel. He didn't want to talk about the fence. He wanted to talk about politics, although Sanders soon realized that he was actually talking about both.

"Nixon, too. Look at the paper, all that Watergate shit. People say Nixon did this, Nixon did that. He don't care. 'Cause he ain't saying." Louie smiled, knowing he had both made his point and avoided the queries. "Works for the president. Works for me."

Right below the photograph of Ford, Sanders took in an article about Alexander Haig, Nixon's chief of staff, who claimed that a "sinister force" was responsible for the infamous eighteen-and-a-half-minute gap in the so-called Watergate tapes Nixon had made in his office, recording every word that was said there. The fact that Haig couldn't say what that sinister force was, or why anyone other than Nixon and his aides would have a motive to destroy potentially damaging evidence, didn't matter to Haig. His mission was clear: evade. He did it, Sanders mused, with a deftness that would have made George Sing Louie proud.

The whole front page was a testament to how unhinged the world had become. Ford replacing the disgraced VP. Haig, H. R. Haldeman's replacement, spewing lies. In addition, leftist guerrillas had kidnapped an American businessman in Argentina. An escape attempt at San Quentin by a small group of black nationalists had ended in a shootout with prison guards. And a young African-American teenager from Hunters Point trying to enter the Federal Building for a job-training program was shot in the back by an FBI agent after he and the agent got in a shoving match over whether or not the agent had sought to stop the young man from going through the front door.

Among these stories, it was the escape attempt that held Sanders's interest, if only for its irony. Those who took part most likely belonged to one of the far left splinter groups that had broken away from the Black Panther Party. Organizations like the Black Guerrilla Family, formed by George Jackson in Soledad Prison, and the Black Liberation Army, begun by Eldridge Cleaver during a feud with Huey Newton, espoused doctrines of what they termed "righteous violence." The people they targeted most were the police, and, as with Herman George a few years earlier, the officers they went after more than any others were African Americans. "It was like the saying goes," Sanders says ruefully, reflecting on the irony that the hatred displayed by white racists inside the department was equaled only by that of the black radicals outside it, "we were smack in the middle of a rock and a hard place. Crackers and Panthers and no rest in between."

When his coffee was gone, Sanders stubbed out his cigarette, folded the paper, and took it with him as he prepared to leave for the Hall of Justice. He made a point of cutting out articles that were of interest, and the prison escape story seemed worth keeping. It was still early when he started out. He heard his wife in the shower and called out good-bye, looked in on his two children as they slept, then headed to his car.

The story about George Session, the kid from Hunters Point who was shot in the back by a federal agent in an incident that began with a white man refusing to tell a black man he was sorry, would be all over the news for the next few days as a debate raged over who was at fault, and whether or not Session, who was in the hospital with a bullet in his back, was unfairly being charged with assault.

Sanders gave the story little thought at first. Later he would wonder whether others had paid far more attention to it than he — and if it had been not merely a portent of the times but a spark for what followed. Yet it was another shooting early the following week, one in which race at first seemed to play little part, that would open a door to the killing of Saleem Erakat.

Paul Dancik was your basic garden-variety junkie. Twenty-six years old. White. Recently out of Quentin on a possession charge, Dancik lived up north in Sonoma, in the little town of Monte Rio. However, San Francisco was the place to score, and only one week earlier Dancik had been arrested in a violent confrontation with Greg Corrales, an undercover SFPD officer working in Narcotics. Now he was out on the street once again, looking, as always, for a fix. There was nothing special about Dancik, except for the fact that his "jones" was heroin, rather than the drug most junkies were falling prey to in the early 1970s: crystal meth, the street name for methamphetamine.

The shooting took place at a phone booth on Haight Street, across from the projects between Webster and Buchanan, in the heart of the Fillmore. Dancik had stopped by the apartment of a dealer who lived in the projects. But the dealer was out, so Dancik headed to the phone booth to make a call. Accounts of what happened next varied. One, or possibly two, African-American men walked up to him and fired at point-blank range, then fled, disappearing into the projects.

The Homicide inspectors on call on December 11, the night Dancik was shot, were Al Podesta and Ronald Schneider. Both Podesta and Schneider were excellent investigators, especially Podesta, who had made a name for himself while teamed with Charlie Ellis, before the latter was promoted to head of Homicide. At the crime scene the evidence was so scant, and the cause for the killing so indecipherable, that they had little to go on. There had been no robbery, no argument, no obvious motive. Although witnesses claimed the shooter was black, they provided little else in the way of identification. This was the sort of killing homicide cops dread, a murder wrapped in mystery that, on the surface at least, seemed arbitrary.

Subsequently, the criminalists who pored over the crime scene found the shell casings from three .32-caliber bullets, which they submitted to Mitch Luksich in the crime lab. In addition three .32-caliber slugs were taken from Dancik's body, which were also sent to the crime lab. Luksich, a twenty-nine-year-old expert on guns and ballistics, was known among the cops on the SFPD as "Big Mitch." As Sanders says, the name was appropriate.

"Big Mitch was built like an armoire, about six-foot-seven and wide enough for a big-screen TV. But he was like a lot of big guys you meet. Big, but sweet. As sweet a guy as you'll ever find."

He was also unparalleled at identifying a bullet or shell casing. It was painstaking work, but Mitch was a patient man who seemed to enjoy hunching his huge frame over a double-lens comparison microscope and gazing for hours at the tiny marks and scratches left on slugs and casings by the firing of a weapon. Sometimes the hours spent paid off; sometimes they didn't. This time, they did.

Because the bullets that killed Dancik were .32s, Mitch compared the casings he had to those of some other .32-caliber bullets that had recently crossed his desk. They had been collected from the crime scene of Saleem Erakat, the grocer shot in the Tenderloin about two weeks earlier. They were a perfect match. The slugs would be too.

The link thus established between the two crimes drew Coreris and Fotinos into the Dancik investigation. The fact that witnesses on the scene claimed the shooter was black brought in Sanders and Gilford as well.

That there had been two killings with the same gun within a week or so of each other wasn't that unusual. What was, though, was the gun involved. Most criminals know better than to use a .32, which has little stopping power and often doesn't kill its victim. A .32 is for amateurs, a "lady's gun" that can be tucked safely into a handbag without taking up too much space. But whoever these killers were, that's what they were using.

Thinking the two killings might be just run-of-the-mill homicides, perhaps no more complicated than a couple of stickups turned bad, the following day Sanders and Gilford began asking around the Fillmore about Dancik. Their queries soon bore fruit, as a beautician they often used as a source told them about an African-American woman in her thirties she had worked on, who claimed to have "seen somethin'" that night.

The woman lived on the second floor of the projects, right across the street from where the shooting took place. But though she had talked freely with the beautician, she was uncomfortable speaking to the police, agreeing only to speak off the record with Sanders and Gilford. The reason, it turned out, was that she was having an affair with one of the few other black inspectors on the SFPD, Wendell Tyree. Tyree was a tall, good-looking African American in his forties who worked in General Works, a catchall bureau that investigated crimes like assaults and domestic violence. He was married, so the woman feared she might get him in trouble if she was drawn into an investigation and word got out they were involved with each other. Sanders assured her that Tyree, who was a compulsive womanizer, could get into plenty of trouble all on his own, with or without her help, but she remained reluctant. All the woman would say was that she thought she recognized the person she saw running through the projects from the high school she had gone to in Berkeley. Yet she claimed she couldn't remember his name. Sanders and Gilford suspected she knew more than she was saying, but try as they might, they couldn't get her to say more. That's where the lead left them, though they never knew for sure whether it was their colleague's careless dalliance that frustrated them, or the woman's unstated fear of the person she recognized.

The following day, after wrapping up work at the Hall of Justice, Sanders and Gilford piled into Sanders's blue Ford Fairlane and headed for Gilford's apartment on Ashbury.

It was a Thursday night. Cops are used to working weeks that never end, but for homicide cops it is even worse: for them the job is 24/7. Adding these strange motiveless killings to his and Gilford's own caseload made Sanders feel more drained than usual, and he just wanted to drop Gilford off and go home, for once arriving while dinner was warm and his wife and children were awake. However, Gilford needed company. He and his wife had been cyclically breaking up and getting back together for more than a year. Yet despite all the breakups, and the fact that Gilford was seeing other women, every time he moved out of the house he shared with his wife and kids and set up digs as a bachelor, he felt racked by loneliness.

As usual, Gilford wanted Sanders to come upstairs to drink and play dominoes. The talk would hit all topics: work, politics, the progress or lack thereof of the Officers for Justice lawsuit. But the subject talked about, or more accurately talked around, the most, was the ill health of Gilford's oldest son, Michael.

"Gil used to call his oldest son 'Big Mike,'" Sanders recalls. "And he was *big*. Went to the Naval Academy in Annapolis and started as a lineman with the football team. Mike was smart, athletic, with the kind of future you dream of for your kids. Then he had a car accident that just tore up his body. Had to drop out of school and go in and out of the hospital for treatment. Mike was never the same. And neither was Gil."

While Sanders and Gilford unwound and traded stories, two other San Franciscans began their evening with the kind of unthinking ease with which most people live the little unguarded moments of their lives, never imagining what was about to occur.

Art Agnos was walking to his car. It was December 13, less than two weeks before Christmas. At thirty-five, Agnos had already spent a decade working in politics. A sturdy dark-haired man with a warm, open smile, he was a Kennedy-era liberal who had been shaped by the student movement of the 1960s. Now Agnos was a consultant with the California legislature's Joint Commission on Aging and had just finished a meeting with residents at a public housing development in the largely African-American neighborhood of Potrero Hill. Other local activists, such as Jim Queen, were there as well.

The situation might have been uncomfortable for some legislative aides, who as often as not showed up in African-American neighborhoods to explain why things couldn't get done rather than how they could. But Agnos was different. His concern was genuine, and the people who worked with him, like Jim Queen, who'd go to war with anyone he thought was trying to pass off a lot of jive as compassion, could see it. They trusted him. And it paid off. Agnos came to assure everyone that the new health-care clinic the community hoped for had gained support in the state legislature. It was the kind of meeting Agnos liked to attend, one where he could prove to himself and others that the system worked, and that change, which both he and the underprivileged people he tried to represent so desperately wanted, could occur from within.

Marietta DiGirolamo was looking for her boyfriend.

At thirty-one, Marietta had long defined herself more by the pursuit of simple pleasures than by anything else. She lived at 651 Scott, a few blocks from the Panhandle of Golden Gate Park, on the border between Haight-Ashbury and the Fillmore. In a way, those neighborhoods encapsulated Marietta's life. She was part of a generation who came of age in the 1960s, and moved from her home in New York City to San Francisco at a time when both psychedelia and black power rose like twin suns above a street called Divisadero, with the hippie ghetto of Haight-Ashbury on one side and the black ghetto of the Fillmore on the other. A pretty woman of Italian descent who was just over five feet tall, with long dark hair and a shapely figure, Marietta easily inhabited both worlds.

Her boyfriend did the same, though in a different way. A handsome African-American man in his thirties, he was one of a number of blacks in the Fillmore who had found a rich vein of opportunity in the drug culture of nearby Haight-Ashbury. Young white hippies who loved to get high often found a kind of romance in going to the ghetto to score, and he was happy to give them what they wanted, becoming one of the more successful cocaine dealers in the Fillmore, and something of a catch for a young woman like Marietta, whose life revolved around a party scene of clubs and bars, even on a Thursday night like tonight.

Marietta and her boyfriend shared the apartment she lived in on Scott. Their relationship was an intense one, which often flared up and down but always kept them tightly bound. Marietta didn't know where he was. This was his working time now, the nighttime hours when scores were made and product moved. So she headed toward the bars and clubs that lined Divisadero, figuring she might find him drinking, partying, or maybe doing some business. And if she didn't find him, well, at least she'd be where she could do some drinking and partying herself.

Art Agnos had parked close to the meeting on Wisconsin Street. But it was taking him a while to get there. His friend Jim Queen talked to him for a bit, then two women who had also been at the meeting stopped to talk as well. In the middle of their discussion, Agnos suddenly saw the women look past him. He wasn't sure why, and was about to turn to look as well when he heard a sound that he thought was firecrackers. Agnos felt something hit him in the back, like an elbow or someone bumping into him. But he ignored it, because the women immediately turned and ran, terrified. So Agnos took off after them, calling out to them not to worry, that it was only firecrackers.

That's when they stopped and pointed at him, saying it wasn't fire-crackers, it was a gun, and he had been shot.

Agnos turned to see who had done it. Some fifteen feet away stood an African-American man staring at him, his features unreadable in the darkness, a gun held in one hand. Then the man pivoted and ran, and Agnos began to feel the dampness of the blood that was soaking through the back of his shirt, pouring out of him. It had been bullets that hit him from behind, not an elbow. The damage they had done inside him started to cause a deep, searing pain.

People who had been at the meeting rushed to Agnos, helping him into a nearby home where he could be taken care of while an ambulance was called. The home he was in, like most in Potrero Hill, and like the majority of people who helped him, belonged to African Americans, like the man who shot him.

Marietta DiGirolamo was walking south on Divisadero, toward Haight Street, in a relatively unlit area as an African-American man came toward her. Some whites might have taken notice of a black man approaching them on a rough, dark urban street at night. Not Marietta. In her mind this was as much her world as his. So when the man suddenly grabbed her as they crossed paths and shoved her into the doorway of a barbershop, her reaction was one of anger. She yelled at him, asking him what he thought he was doing. The few onlookers thought they were arguing and paid them scant attention.

Until the man answered Marietta with a gun.

He shot her twice in the chest, then a third time in the back as her body turned from the impact of the first two bullets. She died before any of the passersby on the street could even call an ambulance.

Sanders was back in his blue Ford Fairlane, heading home from Gilford's, when he heard the report over the police radio. Two more whites had been shot in black neighborhoods, and once again the assailants in both shootings were African American. No one was sure of the weapons that had used, but they were definitely on the small side, which meant that .32-caliber was a distinct possibility. One detail distinguished these shootings from the others.

Art Agnos was still alive.

That night, a young CSI officer named Ken Moses collected what he hoped would be promising pieces of evidence at the two murder scenes. One was a quarter with a thumbprint on it, near where Agnos had been shot. Unfortunately, the print turned out to be that of Agnos himself. The rest of what was collected was mostly shell casings, .32-caliber, with markings that, even to the naked eye, Moses thought bore a striking resemblance to the casings found at the murder scene of Paul Dancik.

The following day Coreris and Fotinos let Sanders and Gilford know that Big Mitch Luksich had verified Ken Moses's suspicion, matching the bullets from both the Agnos and the DiGirolamo shootings to the same gun that killed Erakat and Dancik. Suddenly there was a clear, evidentiary link between four separate shootings, in four different locations, spread over less than two weeks. Word of the connection quickly made its way through the Hall of Justice. Cops stopped talking about the shootings individually and instead referred to them generically with a single phrase, "the .32-Caliber killings."

Sanders, who always tried to stay abreast of the latest developments in forensic science and homicide investigation, knew more than most of his colleagues about the recently named phenomenon of serial killers. The creatures themselves had been around for years. The concept, however, and the understanding of these killers as having a specific fixation that fueled their murderous impulses, was relatively new. In the late 1960s and early '70s, the Bay Area became a kind of ground zero for serial killers, with Edmund Kemper and Herbert Mullins both operating in Santa Cruz and the Zodiac Killer conducting his reign of terror in San Francisco. Sanders recalls wondering at the time whether the .32-Caliber killings might be the beginning of something similar.

"The thing about these shootings was that all we had to link them was the weapon and the issue of race. The only pattern was, the victims were white and the suspects black. But there was nothing else to indicate a motive. Usually killers like this are driven by something sexual, like Kemper and Mullins down in Santa Cruz, or some crazy kind of pathology, like the Zodiac. But we couldn't put our finger on anything here yet. Even Agnos couldn't say why he'd been shot. It was as much a mystery to him as to us. The few people who saw DiGirolamo get shot said the same thing. It just happened, out of the blue, for no reason."

If the shootings were linked, there had to be a reason. Sanders thought of the little they had to go on: bullets and race. In many of the "motiveless killings" he had heard about at the Oakland meeting — in fact, the vast majority of them — the suspects had also been black and the victims white. The theory that had been proposed was that the perpetrators might be a radical group of some sort attacking whites with a specific, if unclear, political agenda. This case, Sanders felt, could very well be the same. As the most junior inspector in Homicide, though, he knew he was expected to let those senior to him take the lead. So for now he kept his thoughts to himself.

In the days that followed, Sanders and Gilford coordinated with the other inspectors investigating the .32-Caliber killings, especially Coreris and Fotinos, who were the lead investigators on Erakat, the first of the now four shootings that could be linked to the same weapon. Sanders and Gilford took as their primary interest the murders of Dancik and DiGirolamo, both of which had occurred in the Fillmore. Helpfully, Sanders already knew something about DiGirolamo's boyfriend from his time in Vice, before he became an inspector with the Robbery Bureau.

"This gentleman had more class than a lot of the guys in the Fillmore who dealt drugs in the Haight. Most were like a pint-sized punk I knew who barely reached five feet and got his start by pushing catnip to hippies and calling it pot. He was the sort who would deal, or do, anything to anyone. Not the boyfriend. He dealt in cocaine. Period. And not just to hippies, either. He had clients all over, even in the financial district. This was back when cocaine was just becoming fashionable, and people started wearing chains with silver spoons around their necks as jewelry, like it was something to be proud of, and a dealer with some style and smarts could make some real money."

DiGirolamo's boyfriend was picked up early in the morning after the shootings. The few people who witnessed the DiGirolamo shooting described a man a bit like him, and given the possibility of a domestic dispute and his own involvement in the drug scene, he briefly became a suspect. However, he had a solid alibi for the evening and was clearly distraught over the shooting. It was clear he had nothing to do with his girlfriend's death, so he was released. That wasn't the end of Sanders and Gilford's interest in him, though. As Sanders explains:

"Dealers are just that — 'dealers.' They deal in all sorts of ways and for all sorts of things. Some trade drugs for sex. Or clothes. Or cars. Or just protection. The smartest, though, trade for information. It's like any business, you use your assets to strengthen your position and find out about product, or competition, or snitches. Word we heard on the streets was that he had decided to take what you might call a dealer's initiative and run his own investigation into the shooting, in his own way. He set up what Gil and I called 'the ghetto reward,' sending word all over the Fillmore that he'd give three ounces of pure cocaine and five thousand dollars in cash to anyone who came to him with information about whoever it was that shot DiGirolamo.

"The street price for a gram of coke was about fifty bucks back then. This was pure, so you could step on it five or six times, easy, before it hit the streets. That meant each ounce was worth from five to eight thousand dollars. You add the cash to that, and he was putting up between twenty and thirty thousand dollars for information. That was serious money. Hell, I only made about sixteen a year before overtime, and I had to pay taxes. He was offering what amounted to a fortune in the ghetto. Gil and I figured something had to come from that. It was too much money for people to walk away from. Someone had to turn on someone else. Someone had to snitch."

At least, that was what Sanders hoped.

The weekend after the DiGirolamo and Agnos shootings, a group called the August 7th Black Guerrilla Movement — named in honor of George Jackson's younger brother, Jonathan, who died while trying to free Jackson from a Marin County courtroom — took credit for the recent murder of a San Quentin prison guard. The San Quentin killing was the latest of a number of bloody assaults the group had taken credit for since an October communiqué claimed they had shot down an Oakland police helicopter. Little was known about the group, but their potential for danger was underscored by a $40,000 reward that the

Oakland Police Department offered to anyone who had information on them.

That Monday, December 17, the *Chronicle* ran a page-long article about the growing political violence in the area, listing a string of crimes that included everything from the Black Liberation Army's murder of SFPD sergeant John Young to the killing on November 6, 1973, of Oakland school superintendent Marcus Foster by another new group shrouded in mystery, the Symbionese Liberation Army. On the surface, there seemed little similarity between the attacks listed in the article and the .32-Caliber shootings. Assaults on people like Foster and Young were targeted assassinations directed at figures of authority. By contrast, the .32-Caliber shootings appeared to be just random attacks, without any sense of being political. Yet a bloody chain of events that began that same Monday made Sanders wonder if random death hadn't become as much a part of political violence as any assassination.

The day the article on political violence appeared in the *Chronicle,* members of the Palestinian Liberation Front attacked the Pan American lounge at Fiumicino airport in Rome. The terrorists then assaulted both a Pan American and a Lufthansa airliner, going at them with gunfire and grenades. Between the attacks on the lounge and those on the two planes, they killed thirty-two people and wounded almost double that number. The Pan American plane was crippled. The terrorists managed to take off in the Lufthansa jet, hijacking it and taking fourteen passengers as hostages. The plane landed in Athens, where the terrorists tried to use their hostages to gain the freedom of guerrillas belonging to another organization, Black September, who were imprisoned there, threatening to kill a hostage every hour until the prisoners were released. After a few hours, however, and four more executions, the terrorists gave up on their comrades and decided to save their own skins, continuing on to Damascus. From there they went to Kuwait, where only five of the more than a dozen terrorists who had started the operation were finally taken into custody, leaving a total of thirty-six dead and scores more injured in their wake. The day after the hijacking in Rome, a similar sort of random violence erupted in London, where sixty-five innocent people were injured during a string of IRA bombings around the city.

Thinking back about the growing spiral of violence, Sanders recalls, "I remember reading about the craziness spreading all over the
world and thinking of something H. Rap Brown said a few years earlier, when he was still the head of SNCC: 'Violence is as American as
cherry pie.' A lot of people got upset when he said it. But no one for-
got it. Because of the phrasing. The metaphor. And looking around
back then, at the madness in the Middle East and Ireland and everywhere else, I thought of that line, and it occurred to me that random
violence was becoming as political as bumper stickers. Except these
bumper stickers were written in blood."

The day after the IRA bombings, exactly one week after the attacks on DiGirolamo and Agnos, the .32-Caliber killer struck again. If
the shootings were bumper stickers, they were multiplying fast.

Ilario Bertuccio was walking home from work.

It was December 20, just a few days from Christmas. At eighty-
one years of age, Ilario Bertuccio was like a short stretch of old knotted
twine, tough, indefatigable, and seemingly unbreakable. He was only
five-foot-three and weighed barely over 130 pounds. Yet despite his age
and his slight stature, Bertuccio worked as a handyman at the 7-Up
bottling plant in the Bayview district, just east of Hunters Point. Still
married, the crusty old Italian American lived less than a mile from the
plant, on the other side of the 101 Freeway, in an area that was largely
Italian when he moved in years earlier but now was becoming more black
than white. The changes meant nothing to him. He walked home from
work every night, regardless of the hour, never thinking he had a reason to fear anyone.

As Bertuccio neared the corner of Bancroft and Phelps, a half mile
from his home, he may or may not have taken notice of the black man
walking toward him. What was probably of more importance to the thin
old man was keeping his windbreaker zipped up tight against the chill
night air and holding on to the bottle of 7-Up that he had in a brown
paper bag. That, and getting home to the little house on Goettingen that
he shared with his wife. The world he inhabited was an uncomplicated

one, without guile and from another time. But it was about to come crashing down.

The first bullet shot by the black man as he neared Bertuccio hit the bone of his right shoulder and ricocheted sideways through his chest, causing the old man to turn toward his killer. Three more bullets followed, each one entering Bertuccio's chest and exiting his back.

Hearing the gunfire, a neighbor looked out of his window to see an African-American man running to a car, where another African-American man sat waiting. It is doubtful that the crusty old Bertuccio was aware of any of that. By the time he lost his grip on the bottle of 7-Up and fell to the street, blood pooling around him, Ilario Bertuccio had most likely already died, and the simple, trusting world he inhabited had ended.

Theresa DeMartini was driving home.

At twenty years old, Teri, as her friends called her, had a look that so perfectly captured the image of a 1970s coed she might as well have been picked by central casting. A sophomore at San Francisco State College, Teri was attractive, with long hair flowing past her shoulders and styled in the straight, shapeless fashion of the time. It was a style without style, fitting for a generation of young people who arrived on the scene as the passion of the 1960s dissipated into the ennui of the '70s.

Christmas was only a few days away, and Teri was coming home from a party with friends near campus, in the Sunset district. The semester was over, and most of those still at school were planning to party late and hard, but Teri left early, deciding to head out before things got too crazy, driving across town to the apartment she and a girlfriend shared near the panhandle of Golden Gate Park, at the border of Haight-Ashbury and the Fillmore.

Teri arrived a little before 10:00 P.M. and found a parking space for her beat-up 1965 Mustang on the 600 block of Central, near Grove, just a short walk from where she lived. As she looked for the space, Teri passed a car that was double-parked on Central with a black man sitting at the wheel. She had trouble fitting her car in the space she found, and Teri noticed another black man walk up to the man in the car as she maneuvered her Mustang. Finally she was done, and as she got out of her car she glanced in her rearview mirror and saw the second black man start toward her.

Living in places like the Haight or Fillmore makes you learn to put on your game face when you head out on the street. The best way to handle anyone who might be trouble is to ignore them. This guy, with his long camel-hair coat, may have been flashier than most but seemed no more scary than hundreds of other people she saw, both black and white, every day she ventured out. He had his hand in his pocket as he approached her. Then as he reached her gas tank, he took his hand out. It was holding a gun.

The man fired without saying a word. The first bullet hit before Teri knew what was happening. The second bullet hit her as she saw the gun, and the third struck her spine, paralyzing her and causing her to collapse. Which meant that the fourth bullet the man fired, the one aimed at her head and meant to kill, missed.

It was then that Teri started screaming, pain and fear finally taking hold of her. The man turned and ran to a nearby car, speeding off into the night. Then suddenly another car sped toward her, as if intending to finish her off, and despite being paralyzed Teri managed to push herself off the blacktop and roll under her Mustang, causing the car to miss her as it raced by and leaving her there, paralyzed and in agony, but alive.

This time it didn't take a match by Big Mike Luksich to generate alarm inside the SFPD. All it took was for the cops at the crime scenes to identify the shell casings that were left near the bodies.

They were .32-caliber. That said it all.

Sanders was at Gilford's when they heard about the latest shootings. After learning that these too were committed with a .32, they took it on themselves to drive out to Hunters Point and check with their "insurance policies," hoping for information. Just as before, no one knew or would say a thing. Sometimes information gathered from such sources would be indirect, clues rather than solutions, especially if a snitch felt he could be endangering himself by talking. But there was nothing even that vague to be had. It was as if the shootings had taken place in a vacuum, with all clues about their perpetrators sealed off from the world.

Sanders barely slept that night. The next morning Espanola, his wife, had to be at the bank where she worked earlier than usual, and Sanders agreed to see that his son and daughter got off to school on time. Because of work, Sanders was only rarely able to spend the time he wanted with his children, ten-year-old Marcus and eight-year-old Marguerite. Dinnertime appearances were so rare, in fact, that when Sanders came home early one evening to pick up something he had left behind, Marguerite ran upstairs and changed into a dress, saying she knew that "if Daddy's home, we're going out to dinner." Not wanting to disappoint his little girl, Sanders put aside work for the evening and took his family out.

Now Sanders's concern about his children was more serious. Marcus was having a hard time adjusting to the new neighborhood, where he and Marguerite were the only black kids on the block and he was often taunted. As Sanders recounts, "It hurt me to see the distress the taunting caused Marcus. He was only ten years old. I felt like I wanted to wipe his pain away and make it all better. But I knew he had to go through it. I'd gone through the same and worse, growing up in Texas. Now, San Francisco wasn't Texas. And the seventies weren't the nineteen forties. But racism was still real. And the only way to learn about it was by going through it."

A story about the Bertuccio and DeMartini shootings appeared that morning on page 3 of the *Chronicle,* eclipsed by John Dean's testimony before Congress about an "enemies list" compiled by Nixon and the assassination of Luis Carrero Blanco, the Spanish prime minister and second-in-command under General Franco, who had been murdered in a car bomb attack by Basque separatists. Even though the shootings were only page 3, the Hall of Justice was already buzzing with talk about them when Sanders arrived there. He and Gilford were sitting at the desk they shared, going over details on some of their unsolved cases, when Charlie Ellis, the lieutenant who headed up Homicide, told them to come into his office.

Most of the office space taken up by the Homicide Bureau was the large central room where the eight teams of inspectors had their desks, one desk to each team, with a chair on either side. In a corner of the bureau stood Lieutenant Ellis's office, really just a glass cubicle, set off from the rest of Homicide by glass panes from ceiling to floor. Charlie Ellis was about Gilford's age, but although the two had worked alongside each other for years, having been in Robbery together before Sanders made inspector, they didn't get along. Gilford never talked specifically about the reason for their friction, but Sanders always felt he had a sense of what caused it.

"Charlie Ellis was more of an administrator than a real investigator, and political in an 'office politics' sort of way. He was also Irish, which made him part of the whole ruling clique that ran the department. It may be that Gil was a little jealous. In most ways Gil was a better cop than Charlie was. He was a better investigator, I'll tell you that. A better interrogator, too. And he had a better record when it came to collars and convictions. But it was Charlie who was lieutenant, and Gil who was inspector. And we both knew it came down to this: no matter how good Gil and I might get at being cops, there were two things we'd never be any good at — being white, and being Irish."

Neither Sanders nor Gilford had a clue what Ellis wanted. Sanders recalls going in to see him.

"Charlie looked up from some papers on his desk as we sat down and told us to stop work on all our outstanding cases. He wanted us to start working full-time on the .32-Caliber killings. Then he told us that we'd be working with Coreris and Fotinos. He was putting them on it full-time, too. I was excited. This was a big case, and to me it seemed fascinating. I'd studied the kinds of cases that today we'd call serial killings. We didn't know nearly as much about them then as we do now. But I had read about Gilles de Rais, the killer the Bluebeard character was based on, who confessed to killing over a hundred children in fifteenth-century France, and Victorian London's Jack the Ripper, and the Cleveland Torso murderer, who eluded Eliot Ness in the 1930s. So I was primed for something like this. But I looked at Gil before talking. He was the senior partner. I was supposed to be seen and not heard.

"Gil was cool as could be. He fixed Charlie with one of the poker stares he always kept in his hip pocket and asked, 'Just us?' Charlie said other inspectors would be involved as needed. From Homicide and all other bureaus. But the Greeks and Gil and I were the only ones on it full-time. Gil still didn't react. He just kept his eyes on Charlie and asked, 'Is this coming from you or somewhere else?' Charlie stared back at Gil, just as cool, and said, 'It's coming from Barca.'

"I looked back at Gil, and there was a little smile on his face. I knew why. Barca was Charlie Barca. Captain over all the inspector bureaus. Barca was a good guy. But he was still part of the brass, the guys with scrambled eggs on their hats and stars on their shoulders who ruled over the department. We knew that, because of the Officers for Justice lawsuit, most of the brass hated our guts.

"Now, they needed us."

5

The Ghetto Reward

ON MARCH 7, 1973, Lubos Kohoutek, a thirty-five-year-old Czech astronomer who had defected to Germany only a few years earlier, stared up into the night sky through the telescope of his Hamburg observatory and saw the first faraway glimpse of a celestial body he recognized as a comet, and which would come to bear his name.

Kohoutek had left his homeland after the economic and intellectual reforms introduced by Czech leader Alexander Dubcek ended in a wave of fury, when the Soviet Union invaded their Communist "friend" and neighbor in August 1968 and overran Prague with tanks and troops. Kohoutek was one of a number of Czech scientists, artists, and academics who fled the repression that ensued. Less than five years after a shroud of intellectual darkness descended on his homeland, he discovered the glimmer of light that would make him famous.

The coming of Kohoutek caught the attention of those weary souls seeking an escape from the cares and conflict that seemed to envelope the globe then. They latched onto it the way others would latch onto the Hale-Bopp comet a generation later. Predictions were made that Kohoutek would blaze across the firmament with a holy fire.

The night of December 21, 1973, was when the comet would pass closest to Earth. It would be blinding, some claimed, lighting up the night sky as a harbinger of the apocalypse, harkening the end of days. Things didn't quite work out that way. In astronomical terms, Kohoutek was a bust. It didn't light up the sky or blaze across the firmament. If all you had was the unaided eye, you could have missed the whole thing.

That didn't stop the diehards from demonstrating on the streets of San Francisco, of course. Early on the cold, cloudy morning of December 22, 1973, the SFPD had to deal with a few dozen of the still-faithful who gathered to celebrate the comet, competing with Christmas carolers and the ringing bells of the Salvation Army to claim that the last days would begin when Kohoutek reached its perihelion — the point where it came closest to the sun — on the twenty-sixth and twenty-seventh, just after Christmas Day. By then, claimed the faithful, Kohoutek would prove to be the new North Star. Just such a celestial spark had announced the first coming of the Messiah, and now a second Christmas vision would presage His return and bring at last the Kingdom of God.

Earl Sanders only half listened to the general call on his police radio about the bizarre downtown celebration as he drove to the Hall of Justice that morning. Cops in the area were being advised of the situation just in case. However, he had his own "end of days" to deal with, the kind of personal apocalypse that comes to an individual rather than a world and is harkened not by a comet moving across the sky but by a .32-caliber bullet traveling from a gun barrel into flesh.

Sanders was on his way to a fourth-floor briefing for those who had been assigned to the .32-Caliber shootings, especially Coreris, Fotinos, Gilford, and himself, along with others who had already worked some of the assaults and would be available to fill out a nighttime squad dedicated to stopping the violence. Charlie Barca, the captain of detectives, ran the meeting with Bunky Cummings, the highest-ranking captain on the force and one of the closest in the SFPD hierarchy to Donald Scott, the chief of police. Cummings, Irish Catholic and staunchly conservative, ran the day-to-day operations of the department. The lieutenants who led the inspector bureaus were also there. Barca sat at a table with a file open in front of him. Bunky Cummings sat next to Barca.

That morning the *Chronicle* had run a story culled mostly from an interview that Barca had given reporter Duffy Jennings the day before, stating that the shootings of Paul Dancik, Marietta DiGirolamo, Ilario Bertuccio, and Teri DeMartini were definitely linked, though he wouldn't say how. In addition, he noted that there had been a number of other motiveless murders in recent months, coming with a frequency far greater than normal. Some of these, like the young woman who was beaten to death with her own roller skates by a patient from a psychiatric hospital, appeared unrelated to these latest attacks. Yet there were others, like the murder of Quita Hague, for which no direct link could be found, but which couldn't be ruled out as being somehow connected.

Sanders describes the edginess that pervaded the meeting: "Barca went over with us what he wouldn't tell the media — that the shootings were linked by markings on the bullets that indicated they were shot from the same gun. But there was something else besides just the bullets that linked them. Barca didn't say much about it to the press, but he had to talk about it here. In every assault, the shooters were black, and the victims were white. And those were the details that made everyone's heart skip a beat."

It was just over five years since the assassination of Martin Luther King and the riots that followed his murder, which ravaged more than a hundred cities. Most of the damage those riots caused hadn't even begun to be repaired yet. Parts of Detroit, Washington, D.C., and Philadelphia looked as if wars had been fought in them. San Francisco wasn't affected to the same degree, but it wasn't unscathed. There were buildings in Bayview and Hunters Point that were still burned-out shells, standing like scars cut into an already barren landscape. The ghettos had become the urban equivalent of dry brush. They weren't on fire, but all it would take to light them was a single spark. No one wanted this to be it.

While the resentment of the brass toward Gilford and Sanders was palpable because of the OFJ suit, the specter of blacks killing whites and the fear it might cause a panic in the city outweighed any other consideration. As Gilford said, "the sons of bitches" needed them.

Nor was this an instance of appearance over substance — that in the wake of the lawsuit the SFPD wanted to appease the black community during a case that could easily heighten racial tensions. Sanders doesn't deny that both Gilford and he were friends of Willie Brown, who in 1973 was already one of the most powerful figures in San Francisco's black community. Gilford's ties with Brown went back to their days in college, but Gilford didn't have half as much "juice" — cop slang for political pull — as people thought. As Sanders tells it, "People liked Gil. They liked me, too. But we didn't have anything to trade, and that's what politics and power are all about. You give and you get. If you can't give, you ain't gonna get much of anything besides a smile and a slap on the back."

Not "juice" but contacts on the street made them indispensable. They had the connections and knew the area in which the killings were taking place better than anyone else on the force. Even so, Barca and Cummings made it clear that Coreris and Fotinos would be the lead team. All four inspectors were being assigned to the case full-time. They would all be equal in terms of work and the initiative they could take in investigating leads. Inspectors from all the bureaus were being made available to help all of them. However, Coreris and Fotinos had seniority, so when it came to running things, whether it was making assignments or talking to the press, who were sure to be all over this, it would fall to the Greeks.

Sanders was fine with that. He was a decade younger than Coreris and Fotinos, who had both joined the SFPD some seventeen years before he did. But Gilford was the same age as the Greeks. He considered the years of seniority they had over him less meaningful than others did, since the department wasn't even hiring blacks at that time. The edge of resentment Gilford felt over not getting what he thought was his due wasn't something he often talked about. According to Sanders, though, whether Gilford talked about it or not, he couldn't hide it.

"I could understand, too. If things had been different in the forties and fifties, Gil would have had the same seniority as any cop his age. But it wasn't just about seniority. People forget what the early seventies were like. It was only twenty years since *Brown v. Board of Education,* just ten since the March on Washington, and less than that since the Voting Rights Act. There were inroads, but only a few. And the way it was back then, you had to be better just to be equal."

So Gilford held in check whatever resentment he felt, and channeled his anger into doing his job — and doing it better than anyone else.

*   *   *

That afternoon began a pattern that would be repeated many times over, as Sanders and Gilford started making the rounds to talk with their "insurance policies" from Hunters Point to the Fillmore, to see if anyone knew anything about the shootings. Nothing had changed since the DiGirolamo slaying. No one knew a thing.

While it wasn't uncommon to hit a brick wall in an investigation, with so many shootings in so short a time Sanders and Gilford expected at least one of the informants they worked with to have heard something about the attacks. But "the streets" — as Sanders calls the buzz of gossip, rumor, and truth that serves as an information network for the dealers, hookers, junkies, cabbies, and pimps who populate the nighttime world of the city — were strangely silent.

Even more surprising than the silence of their own sources was that the "ghetto reward" offered by the cocaine-dealing boyfriend of Marietta DiGirolamo had still gone unclaimed.

Sanders and Gilford looked for the boyfriend as they made their way through the Fillmore. The bars were already filled by midday, the regulars having gathered to watch Kenny Stabler and the Raiders beat Terry Bradshaw's Pittsburgh Steelers in a play-off game. He was nowhere to be found. The word they got from those who knew him was that he was probably hidden away somewhere, still broken up over the death of Marietta.

The offer of the reward was only a week old, so Sanders and Gilford remained hopeful that someone would find the lure of three ounces of pure cocaine and five thousand dollars in cash too good to pass up and come forward with a lead. But that hadn't happened yet, and the fact that it hadn't was beginning to disturb them.

By evening, both Sanders and Gilford were back home, hoping to spend at least a little time with their families during the Christmas holiday. For Gilford, because of the divorce, this was a time of conflicting emotions.

Sanders's wife, Espanola, came from a big family that included nine siblings, most of whom had by now moved from Texas to the Bay

Area. With dozens of children between them, every Christmas season they threw a flock of parties, each sibling taking a night somewhere between December 15 and January 1. On that night one of Espanola's brothers was hosting a dinner.

The procedure in 1973 for officers listed as on call was to phone in to the SFPD Operations Center when they arrived somewhere and leave a number where they could be reached. Normally, Homicide inspectors were on call only one week out of every eight, during their team's regular shift in the rotation, but Sanders, Gilford, Coreris, and Fotinos would all be on call constantly from now on, until further notice. This meant they could be taken away from anything, no matter what the occasion, on a moment's notice. Their families would just have to deal with it.

That night, Sanders's call came just after eight. There had been another shooting. Once again, the victim was white. And according to a witness on the scene, the shooter was black.

Neal Moynihan was holding on to a teddy bear.

Moynihan had bought the toy earlier in the day as a Christmas present for his ten-year-old sister, and the slender, boyish-looking young man carried it with him as he stepped out of a bar on Market Street and headed up Twelfth. The bear was tucked inside a paper bag that didn't quite cover it, leaving the top of its furry head and ears peeking out over the edge and giving the young man an almost comical look, like an actor ready to play one of the Lost Boys in *Peter Pan,* grown up in size but not in spirit.

At nineteen, Neal Moynihan was a perfect example of what police in the early 1970s described in their written reports as "a hippie-type," with long dark hair framing a Botticelli face that was round and angelic, and dressed in the classic Haight-Ashbury attire of a flannel shirt, faded jeans, and heavy, thick-soled boots. In a way, the bear almost made sense in Neal's arms. Although he lived on his own and was able to drink in Market Street bars well before he was twenty-one, Moynihan was still more a kid than a man. He navigated his way through the rough neighborhoods he frequented as much by his seeming innocence as anything else. Neal's life hadn't been easy. His mother died when he was young, after which his father remarried and started a new family, forcing Neal to pretty much support himself by the time he was seventeen. Hardship never seemed to make an impact on him, though. No matter what he went through, on the surface he remained the sort of sweet-faced Irish-American lad who never meant anyone harm and therefore seldom, if ever, found it headed his way.

Until tonight.

There's no way to know whether Neal was looking at the lean young man coming toward him on Twelfth Street. Even if he was, he may have had a hard time discerning the man's race. It was a night watchman across the street at the old Pacific Gas & Electric building who ultimately identified him as black. Yet even he said that the man's skin was fair and that his long, straight, dark hair looked more like that of a Mexican American than an African American. Maybe the question of the man's ethnicity was what caused Neal to turn toward him slightly as they passed each other on the sidewalk, as if stealing a glance at him. Whatever the reason, it was a move he never completed.

The first bullet hit Neal in the face right as he started to turn. The second hit him in the neck. The third hit him flush in the chest. A fourth shot missed as Neal's turn became a fall, gravity starting to pull him to the ground. The strange young man with long dark hair and a nebulous complexion had raised his arm up like a picador as he passed Neal, firing downward and bringing his arm lower with each shot. By the time Neal hit the sidewalk, dead, with the teddy bear lying beside him, the shooter was already running off into the night.

Gilford was at the wheel in the unmarked car as he and Sanders raced to the murder scene. Sanders, who almost always let Gilford drive when they were together, tried to picture the location in his mind as they sped toward Twelfth Street, working through possibilities of where the shooter might have come from or in which direction he might have fled. Gilford's focus was entirely on the road, so he could run red lights and swerve past other vehicles as safely as possible. Yet something nagged at them both, something neither said aloud. If this shooting followed the same pattern as the others, there would probably be more than one victim.

The moment they reached the crime scene, they learned that their fears were true.

Mildred Hosler was walking to a bus stop.

Mildred appeared older than her fifty years, her features worn by a lifetime of hard work and obesity. Walking wasn't easy for her, but she didn't have the money for a car. As good as the public transit system was in San Francisco, there always seemed to be a few blocks that she had to walk to catch a bus or a streetcar. She had been at work earlier in the day and now was headed up Gough to Van Ness, where she could catch a bus to Ellis, only a few blocks from where she lived. Then, at last, she could rest from Saturday night until Monday morning, when it all would have to start again.

The testimony of witnesses indicated that, unlike the other shooting victims, Mildred saw her killer well before he saw her, and that a streetwise wariness may have caused her to start away from him the moment she did. Yet if she was trying to evade him, she failed.

Coming toward her from across the street, the strange, thin man with long, dark hair approached Mildred from her left side, shooting her five times in the upper half of her body. Witnesses said the bullets were fired fast — pop, pop, pop, pop, pop — with barely a second between each blast. Mildred's body told a similar tale, showing five bullet wounds in a tight semicircle, fired at almost point-blank range.

Word of the shootings spread within minutes, prompting an onslaught of looky-loos to pour out of nearby bars and hotels, joining the police, press, paramedics, and forensic officers already there. The Moynihan scene was teeming with people by the time Gilford and Sanders pulled up. They wouldn't stay long. A sergeant informed them about the second shooting as soon as they arrived, and after making sure the scene was secure, they jumped back in their car and sped the two blocks to where Mildred Hosler's body lay. Sanders still recalls sharply his first impressions when they got there.

"The first thing I noticed was the blood. It gets to where you're around murder enough that you can smell it before you even see the body. That's the way it was at the Hosler scene. But then something else struck me. I knew that whoever did it couldn't be much more than a few blocks away. Maybe closer. We had cops all over the area. But I could sense we weren't going to find him. Not that night. Whoever did it knew how to slip into the dark and disappear. I knew that the way I knew the bullets were .32-caliber, without even having to look. And it was that sense of knowing — knowing about the bullets, knowing he was close, knowing we couldn't stop it — that chilled Gil and me both like no killing ever had before."

Sanders and Gilford remained out on the street investigating until early the next morning. Sanders's instincts turned out to be correct. The killer had disappeared into the night without a trace.

The witnesses at the two scenes all described a similar assailant: a thin young man with long black hair and the kind of washed-out, sallow complexion that could have made him Latin, Asian, Native American, Pacific Islander, Middle Eastern, or black. The only witness who seemed certain of the killer's race was Eugene Tracey, the night watchman at the Pacific Gas & Electric building across the street from where Moynihan was shot. Tracey is the only part of that night that Sanders remembers with a smile.

"He was an older guy, and was up on the second floor when he heard the shots. Then he looked out the window and saw the killer just as he took off running. The first time he described him he said he had pale skin and seemed kind of 'Latin-looking.' But later, when I asked if he could tell what race the killer was, the watchman, who was white, immediately said, 'Black,' without a moment's hesitation. So I said, 'Wait a minute. You just told me he was Latin-looking. How can you be so sure now that he's black?'

"He glanced at me with a kind of sheepish smile. Like he was embarrassed. I guess because I'm black. Then he said that he knew the killer was black because he 'ran black.'

"I stared at the old guy like he was nuts. 'He *ran* black? You're telling me you can tell if a person is black or not by the way they run?'

"He nodded his head and said, Yep, he could. Then he did a little move that tried to show what he meant. That's when I had to laugh. The old guy couldn't run black, I'll tell you that. But I had to admit that I knew what he meant. Not every black 'runs black.' But there can be a way that some blacks move or run that has a very specific rhythm or cadence to it. And that night watchman was absolutely certain that the killer he saw run away from the Moynihan shooting 'ran black.'"

Despite his laughter, the description added to Sanders's unease. The killer the witnesses described may have "run black," but the details they recalled differed from those given by witnesses at other shootings. That could mean that the killer had taken to wearing a disguise. Or that there was more than one, using the same gun and working together as some sort of horrifying team.

Between the crime scenes and the paperwork, neither Sanders nor Gilford got much sleep that weekend.

In 1973, a cop could live up on the fourth floor of the Hall of Justice if he had to. As Sanders recalls, there were times when he practically felt like he did.

"Things weren't quite as 'by the book' back then. There's a kitchen area where people store lunches now and use the microwaves, but then we had a full stove and a refrigerator that we kept stocked with meat and chicken and fish, and there were people cooking up all sorts of things any time of the day. There was an interrogation room where we had a cabinet with a full stock of liquor. We had locker rooms where you could shower, shave, and keep a change of clothes or two. And we had beds, too, and rooms where you could catch a few hours' sleep.

"In today's mindset all that sounds wrong somehow, like we were getting perks we shouldn't have had. But the truth is, it enabled us to do more work than we probably would have otherwise. You could be in that building round the clock, and still have yourself a good steak dinner and a fresh shirt when you wanted them. And if you were up all night and needed a little 'fortification,' you didn't have to take a break and go find a bar on Bryant Street. You could just pour yourself a shot right there and then get back to work. I don't remember if Gil and I did any 'fortifying' after the Hosler and Moynihan shootings. But I can't say it would have been out of character."

Fortified or not, they kept working through that night and into the next day, the twenty-third, the final Sunday before Christmas. Most Sunday mornings would find Sanders attending services either at Third Baptist Church, the oldest African-American congregation on the West Coast, founded in 1852, where he and Espanola were married, or at United Methodist in Daly City, which they joined when they moved into their new home. Church attendance was even more important around the holidays, when Espanola would see that Sanders and their two children were dressed in their finest for services that were almost as much a social event as a religious one. But this season Christmas was put on hold.

Sanders remembers Coreris and Fotinos both coming to the Hall of Justice that Sunday, along with Charlie Ellis and some of the others who had been at the meeting the day before, as well as some of the inspectors from Homicide and other bureaus, to be briefed by Sanders and Gilford on the murders of the night before. Later that day Mitch Luksich, the crime lab's expert on guns who had identified the other bullets, came in with the results from the comparison microscope on the latest slugs.

Same markings, same gun. A perfect match.

It was what everyone expected. But the certainty of Big Mitch's results underscored the gravity of what was going on. This was the real thing. Like Bluebeard or Jack the Ripper, like Zodiac, or Mullins, or Kemper. This was a serial killing. But unlike the others, it wasn't sexual.

What drove these killers was something harder to define. And even more unnerving because of it.

That night Sanders and Gilford went back to the scene of the shootings to talk again to people who frequented the area and see if there was anything they might have missed the night before.

Driving with them was Herman Clark, a friend of both men, who at the time was an inspector in Robbery and was helping out. A number of automobiles had been described by witnesses as being in the vicinity of the various shootings. The car most commonly mentioned, seen near both the Bertuccio and DeMartini shootings as well as the Hosler and Moynihan crime scenes, was a light-colored four-door sedan described as being either a Plymouth Valiant or Dodge Dart, cars that were almost identical save for a few cosmetic details. So when Gilford noticed a car that matched the description near the crime scenes, he didn't miss a beat, starting after the sedan as soon as he saw it.

The moment Gilford sped up, the other car seemed to realize it was being followed and turned into an alley near where Twelfth meets Market. Sanders describes what followed:

"Herman and I held on as Gil raced after the other car. We thought it was a Dodge, but it was hard to tell. It was dark, and those alleys were a maze, so every time our headlights washed over the other car's license plate, it turned down another corner. We couldn't see well enough to get anything down, not the license or the make."

The San Francisco streets of Twelfth, Market, Gough, Otis, and McCoppin all come together in a tangle of oblique angles and three-way intersections. The triangle at Twelfth and Market has changed over the years, its insides getting fenced off to become parking lots and industrial yards. Back in 1973, it was a warren of narrow alleys that cross-cut the area between the warehouses and businesses lining both streets.

"For a while we lost the other car. Then Gil made a turn, and we saw it again. But then it was gone. And when Gil turned where he thought it went, we were back on Market, and the Dodge was nowhere in sight. We were close enough behind that if it had gone onto Market we would've seen it. But it didn't. It was like it made a turn and then just vanished."

Neither Sanders, Gilford, nor Herman Clark knew where the other car had gone. But they realized that whoever was driving it knew those alleyways even better than they did.

Later that evening, as the three men canvassed the bars and restaurants that catered to the locals in the neighborhood, Sanders noticed that among the buildings along the maze of alleys was a two-story warehouse that housed a moving and storage company called Black Self-Help, which Sanders knew was connected to the Nation of Islam.

"I'd driven by there countless times, so it wasn't like I'd never seen it before. But that night it stood out to me. I noted the building. Noted that it was in the vicinity of the shootings. And that its backside faced the alleys where we lost the other car."

It was a mental note that Sanders would soon draw upon again.

Christmas Eve was supposed to be the day Sanders would finally catch up on the shopping he had to do. Espanola had taken care of most of the presents, but it was up to him to get ten-year-old Marcus a bicycle at Whitman's, a little family-owned bicycle shop in Daly City. This would be Marcus's first real bike, and Sanders knew there'd be hell to pay if he didn't get it. He headed out after only a couple of hours of sleep, making sure to use the unmarked police car that had been issued to him and Gilford.

"It got to where you were so on edge, every time the phone rang you thought it was the operations center calling about another killing. Christmas Eve or not, I wanted a car with a police radio in it. Just in case."

The call came in before noon.

There had been another killing. But this wasn't a shooting. This was something that could only be described as butchery, a slaying so grue-some, so clearly a product of torture, that it seemed to spring from the time of Torquemada and the Spanish Inquisition rather than twentieth-century San Francisco.

In police records, the victim was identified as Unknown Body #169. Among the cops, he became known as the Christmas Turkey.

The body was found where Pacheco Street meets the Great High-way, out in San Francisco's Sunset district. Dorene Racouilla, a young nurse at Presidio Hospital, spotted it as she was walking her dog on the beach. The dog caught the smell first, barking as they neared the bundle. Then Doreen saw it: something human and bloody was wrapped up in canvas and plastic. She couldn't see much more than that, but she didn't want to. The smell alone was enough to keep her away and make her call the police.

Morning fog still lingered by the time Sanders had picked up Gil-ford and they made their way out to the beach. The medical crew on the scene had pulled away a bit of the plastic from the body, enough to

allow them to make a pronouncement of death. The odds of this Dead
Jones, as Sanders calls unidentified male bodies, being anything other
than dead were nonexistent; but rules were rules.

"It was a little rocky at that part of the beach," Sanders recalls.
"And you had to go down a slope to get to it. But Gil wouldn't come
anywhere close. He hated stiffs. Just getting near them made him sick.
And by the time we got there, you could smell this Dead Jones all the
way up on the road. So I went down alone.

"The closer you got, the worse that smell got. I don't think it was
in the water long, because the tissue hadn't deteriorated much. You
could see sand had collected inside the plastic and was stuck to the flesh
in places. With some stiffs you have to make yourself look for the little
things, because it's the details that matter. But here I found myself focusing on the details right away, because every time you looked at the
body as a whole it was like an electric jolt went up and down your spine.

"The body wasn't completely unwrapped until we were back at
the Hall of Justice. But what you could see here was enough. The head
had been hacked off where the neck meets the shoulders, and the hands
and feet were gone. All that was left was the torso. And it was all bound
up in wire like one of the frozen birds we got each year from Charlie Ellis. Like a Christmas turkey."

The SFPD searched the beach and coastline for days, looking for
the severed head, hands, and feet, checking the currents to see if they
might have been carried into the bay, hoping to be able to use them to
identify the body. They never could. Whoever the poor soul was, he
remained anonymous, his identity defined only by the horror of his
death.

There are two kinds of homicide cops: those who view corpses as
a challenge, the inspection of which they either have to endure or avoid
altogether, and those who see them as an opportunity, where every
morbid detail equals pages of testimony. Sanders was the latter. It usually was as easy for him to spend time with a corpse as with a witness.
This Dead Jones was different.

"Maybe it was that I'd barely slept, or that there'd been so many
deaths in so short a time. But that one time I was as bad off as Gil. It
was like a fever hit me. I felt dizzy. Like there was no up or down, just

gray everywhere I looked — clouds, sea, fog, everything. And right in the middle was this thing that had once been a man but whose skin was now as gray as the rest, dead gray, the way flesh gets when the blood drains out and takes the life with it."

When the body reached the Hall of Justice autopsy room, where Dr. Boyd Stephens led the examination, the plastic was fully removed. In addition to the hands and feet being hacked off at the wrists and ankles, the knees had been pulled up against the chest and held in place by thin-gauge wire. A hole had also been cut in the man's stomach, from which organs spilled as the plastic was peeled away. As if that wasn't enough, the man had been castrated as well.

There were no bullet wounds, so this killing could not be directly connected to the .32-caliber attacks. However, there was another link to be made.

"Those of us who saw Quita Hague couldn't look at this body without making a connection. It wasn't just the kinds of wounds. It was the violence of them. Looking at him I thought the same thing as when I looked at Quita. Whoever did it was fueled either by madness, or by something so deep and powerful it made them that way. Not many things can do that to a person. But hate can. And rage can."

Even though it was Christmas Eve, Sanders and Gilford headed to the Fillmore from the Hall of Justice to call on more of their "insurance policies" and check again if the streets had anything to say about the killings. They wanted more than ever to talk to DiGirolamo's boyfriend about the "ghetto reward," hoping he might have had a response.

The holidays are usually a boon to hookers and pimps, who find that Christmas cheer often leads to yuletide lust. But the string of shootings had sent a chill through the city, and street trade had slowed down to almost nothing. The reason was simple: fear. Yet as Sanders explains, it wasn't just the whites who were afraid.

"People in the Fillmore were as scared as anyone. Part of the reason was the fear of a white backlash. They knew that if anybody went out looking for revenge, they wouldn't waste time trying to find out who it was that did the shooting. They'd just head to the ghetto and wreak the same kind of havoc that was coming their way."

That wasn't the only thing causing uneasiness. Something else about the shootings did even more to put people in the ghetto on edge: the mystery that surrounded them.

"When stuff goes down in the ghetto, you hear things. This time, we didn't. And neither did anyone else. And that silence was starting to scare the shit out of people."

Sanders and Gilford caught up with the boyfriend that evening in the Fillmore. It had been ten days since he spread word about the "ghetto reward," yet still no one had come forward with even a scrap of information. More than anything else, that continued lack of response troubled Sanders, Gilford, and everyone in the ghetto who knew about it.

"People who kill aren't loyal. Not when the money's on the table. And neither are their friends. But this was different. It was like the whole 'ghetto reward' meant nothing. And if they wouldn't turn on each other for something like that, they were unlike any killer anybody in the ghetto had ever seen."

It was late by the time Sanders and Gilford drove out of the Fillmore. Sanders knew he wouldn't get any sleep before Christmas morning, then only hours away. He still had presents to wrap, and one — the bicycle he had picked up for Marcus that morning — to assemble out in his garage. Even so, he and Gilford swung back by Twelfth and Market before they ventured home for one last glimpse of the Moynihan and Hosler crime scenes. As Sanders explains:

"A crime scene isn't just brick and concrete. It's a living thing, filled with all kinds of people — mamas, kiddies, daddies, lovers, workers — you never know who was there when the crime took place. Or when they'll come back. And the more times you go, the better chance you'll have of finding someone who knows something."

Gilford drove them back toward Twelfth and Market using side streets; he traveled on Webster rather than Fillmore, Page rather than Fell, Octavia rather than Gough. It was at Octavia and Haight that they saw it — a light-colored Dodge Dart that looked enough like the car they'd lost in the alleys to send a shot of adrenaline coursing through both men's veins.

Gilford turned onto Haight and started after it, following as it crossed Divisadero and passed by Buena Vista Park. This time, though, instead of speeding up, the driver of the other car slowed down. He seemed determined not to attract attention, but it was too late for that. By the time they reached Masonic, Sanders had the flashing red light on the dash. The driver quickly pulled over. By then they were almost at the corner of Haight and Ashbury, the center of the hippie district, surrounded by head shops, coffeehouses, teenagers out late on a holiday night, and wasted speed freaks spare-changing for another fix.

The driver of the Dodge stepped out of the car as soon he parked it and stood on the street, facing Gilford and Sanders as they walked toward him, Gilford approaching on the left side of the Dodge and Sanders approaching on the right. Even now, after thirty years, Sanders describes the encounter with a clarity that speaks to the way it burned itself into his memory.

"He was about twenty years old, and thin, maybe six feet or so. He had on a dark sweatshirt and chinos. But what struck you most was his color. He was a pale, fair-skinned black man, with reddish, short-cropped hair."

In the front seat on the passenger's side was an African-American man, a little older than the driver and edgier, with a cold, unmoving gaze that he kept glued straight ahead and a face that seemed frozen in a scowl, whom Sanders would eventually come to know as J. C. Simon.

"The man in the passenger seat didn't get out. He was black, too, with short hair, but darker and bigger, more muscular. I told him to put his hands up on the dash where I could see them. There was a hard hat there, and he put his hands up just below it. But he never turned to look at me. Just kept staring straight ahead, a look of outright rage on his face. Like he'd take me apart if he could. I kept one eye on him, and one on the driver standing with Gilford on the other side of the car."

The driver put on a show of politeness. However, as Sanders recalls, it was just a show.

"He did everything he could to act like he wanted to assist us, but he did it in a way that made it clear it was the last thing he wanted in the world. He had his license out before Gilford could even ask for it. And every time he finished a sentence he ended it with 'sir.' It was 'Yes, sir' and 'No, sir' and 'Absolutely not, sir.' But the way he said it, it wasn't respect. It was a slap in the face. It got to the point where I wanted to tell him that if the word 'sir' came out of his mouth one more time, I was going to shove it back down his goddamn throat."

The driver identified himself as Larry Green, a twenty-one-year-old living in an apartment at 844 Grove Street in the Fillmore district and working at Black Self-Help Moving and Storage, on Market Street, near Twelfth. The mention of Black Self-Help caught Sanders's attention.

"Sometimes working a case is like turning a lock. You reach a point where you hear all the little tumblers fall into place. That was what it was like talking to Green. He was familiar with the area where Hosler and Moynihan were killed. He knew the alleyways where we lost the car. His own car was similar to one that had been seen at some of the shootings. And it looked like the spitting image of the one that outsmarted us the night before. On top of that, the fact that he worked with Black Self-Help meant he was a member of the Nation of Islam.

"The Nation helped a friend of mine get off heroin, so I knew the good they did. But I knew the anger that fueled them, too. The Nation of Islam was breaking apart back then. Elijah Muhammad was dying, and it was like a lot of radical groups at the time, riddled with violent factions. And I knew the discipline that kept members of the Nation bound together. It was exactly the kind of discipline that would be needed to keep the identities of those involved in the killings so secret for so long.

"But there was something else that seemed to tie Green in. It was a connection I made as I stood there staring at him. It wasn't the car. Or where he worked. Or lived. Or even his faith. It was something very simple, but also not so simple at all. It was the color of his skin."

Green's complexion was what Sanders refers to as "high yaller," a skin so pale that it might be hard for a witness to be sure that a person was black.

"He had the kind of skin tone where if you saw him in passing, or at night, you might say he was Mexican, or Asian, or almost anything. And if you put a wig on him, with long dark hair that hung down straight and framed his face, he would have looked exactly like what the witnesses at the Hosler and Moynihan shootings described."

Tumbler after tumbler seemed to be falling in place.

"Both Gil and I could sense that Green was guilty. We talked about it later. It was his look, his manner, everything. It was in the air. You could smell it."

But hunches are not enough to nab a killer. They needed evidence, so Gilford asked Green if they could look in his trunk. The Fourth Amendment makes illegal any search of a vehicle that is unauthorized. However, that constraint is moot if an officer is given permission.

"Green didn't know what to say at first. He'd been putting on this act of cooperating, but you could see him tense up when we asked for something real. Finally, he agreed. We were hoping to find physical evidence — a gun, bullets, a wig — anything that might give us a reason to bring him in. But we got nothing. All there was in that trunk were stacks of copies of *Muhammad Speaks*."

Green said he was on his way to hand out the latest issue of the Nation of Islam's newspaper and smiled as he offered a free copy to Sanders and Gilford. They declined. Then, having no other choice, they told Green he was free to go.

"Gil and I had talked earlier that night about the possibility that whoever was behind the killings was part of some sort of radical group, and how that would explain the silence on the streets. And we knew the Nation of Islam might fit the bill. But it was conjecture. We couldn't take it to a judge or the DA. We couldn't get a search warrant or make an arrest. We were officers of the law, faced with a horror like nothing we'd seen before. But we couldn't do a thing. We were powerless. And it felt like getting kicked in the gut.

"The 'bad guys' aren't bound by anything. They can do whatever they want, whatever their rage or desire demands. But a cop has to live by the law. That's how it has to be. How it *should* be. I know that. But when you're faced with having to let someone go who you believe is guilty, it tears you up. And that night, it made me wonder what the hell I was doing being a cop."

It is impossible to know what Green or his passenger, J. C. Simon, talked about as they drove off into the night, but as Green got back in the car, Sanders saw him smile, happy with himself. Seeing that sickened the detective. It was like pouring gasoline onto the fire already burning inside him.

"I knew the son of a bitch thought he was getting away with something. What I wanted was to grab the key out of the ignition, rip Green out of the driver's seat, throw him on the ground, and cuff the s.o.b. right then and there."

Sanders knew that he couldn't, so he didn't. But he wouldn't forget him.

6

Revenge

"Lesson Number Ten: Why does Muhammad and any Muslim murder the devil? What is the duty of each Muslim in regards to four devils? What reward does a Muslim receive by presenting the four devils at one time?"
—The lessons of Elijah Muhammad

NUMEROUS LESSONS WERE GIVEN BY ELIJAH MUHAMMAD, the leader of the Nation of Islam, to be memorized by the faithful. Lesson Number Seven asked why the devil kept American blacks, whom Elijah Muhammad called the Lost-Found Tribe of Shabazz, illiterate. Lesson No. 8 asked why the devil kept blacks unequal. Perhaps the most famous, provocative, and misunderstood of all the lessons, both by believers and nonbelievers, is No. 10, the meditation on the relationship between the believer and the infidel, which, like many of the others, has little if anything to do with traditional Islam.

The answers to the questions posed in the epigraph above are: "Because he [the devil] is 100 percent wicked and will not keep and obey the laws of Islam. His ways and actions are like a snake of the grafted type. So Muhammad learned that he could not reform the devils, so they had to be murdered. All Muslims will murder the devil because they know he is a snake and also if he be allowed to live, he would sting someone else. Each Muslim is required to bring four devils, and by bringing and presenting four at one time his reward is a button to wear on the lapel of his coat. Also a free transportation to the Holy City, Mecca, to see Brother Muhammad."

As taught in the schools run by the Nation of Islam, Lesson No. 10

was a metaphor about killing the devil inside the devil and turning the infidel toward faith. Years earlier, when the Nation's founder, Wallace D. Fard, was still leading the religion that was the precursor to the Nation of Islam, the Allah Temple of Islam, similar teachings were misinterpreted with tragic results. During Thanksgiving week of 1932, nearly thirty-nine years to the day before the murder of Saleem Erakat, a Detroit member of Fard's temple named Robert Karriem construed his *Secret Rituals,* which had wording almost identical to that in Lesson No. 10, as inspiration for the brutal slaughter of his neighbor. The neighbor was an African American who was not a temple member, and therefore was looked on by Karriem as an infidel and, in the words of the *Secret Rituals,* a devil. The temple leaders denied any connection between the *Secret Rituals* and the murder. Nevertheless, the killing created a crisis that led to Fard's disbanding of the temple and founding of the Nation, control of which he would cede to Elijah Muhammad in the mid-1930s. Looking back, that killing seems an anomaly. Nothing like it had previously occurred among Fard's followers, or under the leadership of Elijah Muhammad during the several decades that followed. In the early 1970s, however, the Nation of Islam was shaken again by a series of crises, and Lesson No. 10 was once more being pushed from the metaphoric toward the literal and into the tragic.

Although only those in his inner circle knew it, by 1973 Elijah Muhammad was already seriously ill with the cancer that would kill him, setting off a power struggle that echoed in various ways down through the ranks of the entire organization. Tensions inside the Nation of Islam had begun to build a decade earlier, when Malcolm X left the church to form his own organization. The Nation, which nourishes a set of beliefs that cannot be found in the Koran, was strictly African American, claiming to reject the "White Man's God" and establish a faith-based system of values for what Elijah termed "the so-called Negroes." Malcolm, who had been Elijah Muhammad's closest aide and served as the Nation of Islam's spokesman, wanted a more inclusive organization, embracing traditional Islam and all races. He also began to speak out about the failings of the man he had once exalted as "the Messenger," using his own disillusionment to induce other followers of

Elijah Muhammad to turn away from his leadership. Reaction within the Nation was strong and swift. Malcolm was denounced widely, and less than a year after he left, members of the Nation assassinated him in Manhattan's Audubon Ballroom while Malcolm was speaking before his new group.

In the aftermath of Malcolm's death, infighting within the Nation increased. As the 1960s flowed into the '70s, the internecine struggle grew ever more violent, and competing factions vied for power and influence. A Washington, D.C., center for the Hanafi Muslims, a more traditional Islamic group whose leader had left the Nation and counted among his followers basketball star Kareem Abdul-Jabbar, was attacked by men from the Nation's Philadelphia temple in a brutal assault that left seven dead. Shootings in Los Angeles, Atlanta, and Brooklyn were also tied to divisions within the Nation. During this period, the FBI was actively working to break the Nation apart with its covert counter-intelligence program, COINTELPRO. Meanwhile, the heightened aggressiveness evidenced by many radical groups at the time showed in the Nation as well, which began to have ongoing confrontations with police in various cities across the country.

It would be unfair to catalog the problems of the Nation of Islam and not at the same time acknowledge the sense of values and self-reliance the Nation offered African Americans, especially men, known in the Nation as the "Fruit of Islam." While the concept of "black is beautiful" did not begin in the Nation, until the late 1960s perhaps no group communicated the concept as fully or as effectively as the Nation of Islam did, demanding for instance that their members wear their hair in a way that was "natural" and, though often close-cropped, never with the processed look they felt was merely aping whites. The Nation did as much as any group to nurture a groundwork of black capitalism and encourage African Americans to look to each other for help rather than depend on the whites who had once enslaved them. The belief that may have been most prescient, however, was the conviction that, long before Lewis Leakey hit upon his "out of Africa" theory of evolution, they were the "original man" who, after generations of being "lost," was now "found." Such concepts appealed to a growing number of African Americans at a time when they, like so many young people in that era, were trying to "find" themselves — people like Larry Green.

Larry Craig Green was born in Berkeley, California, in 1953, the son of middle-class parents who were part of one of the most well established African-American communities in the Bay Area. His father worked as a maintenance engineer with the University of California, and Larry, like his sisters, did well at Berkeley High, excelling in sports, especially basketball, and going on to study at two East Bay community colleges, first Laney and then Merritt. Green's ambition was to play with the NBA someday. But when he realized how long, and how uncertain, the journey would be, he quit playing basketball and soon afterward dropped out of college.

The early 1970s was a time when much of America's privileged youth questioned, and in some cases rebelled against, the roles expected of them. Most often they were white, like Bernardine Dohrn, who grew up well-off and graduated from the University of Chicago. Instead of following the path laid out before her, Dohrn helped form the most radical offshoot of the Students for a Democratic Society (SDS), the Weathermen, in June 1969, helping to orchestrate their Days of Rage in Chicago that October, later setting off bombs, and becoming one of the FBI's Ten Most Wanted. Dohrn also made what may be one of the most inflammatory statements ever to come out of the American Left, glorifying the bloody murders of Charles Manson by rhapsodizing, "Dig it. First they killed those pigs, then they ate dinner in the same room with them. They even shoved a fork into the victim's stomach! Wild!" Radicals like Dohrn blamed their rage in part on Vietnam. They were "bringing the war home," and the violence that resulted was, in their minds, a just response to an unjust war. Well-off black radicals were affected by the same stimuli as whites: the war, the music, the drugs, and the spirit of excess that infused every aspect of the era. As Sanders points out, something else moved them as well.

"Just because you grew up well-off didn't mean you were immune to racism. In the 1970s, any privileges that a black might have were usually no older than a generation. Even if the kids didn't have the bit-ter taste of Jim Crow in their mouths, their parents did, and they handed it down to their children with story after story.

"The early 1960s were filled with hope and progress. But some-thing happened in the second half of the decade. Instead of more, there became less. The riots began. Then King was killed. There's a saying about the civil rights movement: 'We asked for freedom and they gave us integration.' We started with hope. But we ended with disappoint-ment. And that was when African Americans coming out of the uni-versities began to embrace groups like the Panthers and the Black Liberation Army."

For Larry Green it was the Nation of Islam.

Despite the anger Sanders sensed simmering beneath Green's fake politeness, his younger sister believed that the impulse that drove Green was not rage but what she termed the desire to be "a man." Yet in a culture where a common racist affront is being called "boy," the desire to be a man, and treated with respect, is far from simple. A note-book Green began to keep in the fall of 1973 points to the youthful sense of searching that he felt, as well as a preoccupation with under-standing what it is to be a man.

"A man lives to be known," Green wrote.

"What greater pleasure can a man get out of life than to know himself?"

Green shows a curious sense of fate in the journal for a young man just barely over twenty-one, quoting James 4:14 from the New Testament: "What is your life? For you are a mist that appears for a little time and then vanishes." He goes on to define his goal in life with messianic fervor, taking the burden of African-American history onto his own back, referencing the number of Africans estimated by some to have been sold into slavery and claiming that his sole purpose was to "deliver the 17 million dead to the Lamb of God, the Honorable Elijah Muhammad."

In choosing the Nation of Islam as his path to self-knowledge, Green acquiesced to a program that forced him to turn his back on the part of his past that fostered any sense of privilege. Vilbert White Jr., an academic who entered the Nation as a young man in the mid-1970s and then left it some years later for traditional Islam, recalls in his memoir *Inside the Nation of Islam* being asked what his skills were when he joined. White replied that he had a liberal arts education and was told by his interviewer that the Nation needed individuals with real ability, like engineers and electricians, not "college niggers."

Green dropped out of college when he joined the Nation, taking the name Larry 9X to replace his "slave name." He attended services at Temple No. 26 at Fillmore and Geary, in the heart of San Francisco's historic black neighborhood, and embraced what was perhaps the central tenet of the Nation's message, the importance of black enterprise.

Green had previously worked for various white-owned businesses. When he became Fruit of Islam, that changed. He quit his job at Berkeley and started to work for the business in San Francisco that he mentioned to Sanders, Black Self-Help Moving and Storage. Black Self-Help Moving and Storage was owned by another member of the Nation of Islam, Thomas Manney, who provided jobs to men who were either already members of the Nation or interested in joining. Part of the business's purpose was to serve as a conduit and refuge for those deemed unemployable. Often Manney would hire men fresh out of San Quentin and give them a way to fashion a life for themselves outside the prison walls. Like Green, Thomas Manney was a child of relative privilege and a graduate of one of San Francisco's most prestigious high schools. Though one can debate whether his goal was matched by results, there is no doubt that part of what drew people like Green to his business was its idealism and the way it incarnated the Nation's creed of self-reliance among blacks in a world dominated by whites. Initially Manney opened two businesses, a storefront on Hayes in the Fillmore where he planned to sell used furniture as well as the warehouse on Market. The economic success he envisioned, however, did not materialize, and by January of 1974 only the warehouse remained open.

There was another way in which Manney's life paralleled Green's: both had been star athletes in college and had dreamed of playing professionally. Thomas Manney got even closer to that dream than Green did, having been drafted by the Pittsburgh Steelers after excelling as a running back at San Francisco State. Manney didn't make the team, however, and not long after returning to San Francisco he became a member of the Nation of Islam, his aspirations channeled into the larger movement.

The passions and aspirations driving the men of Black Self-Help Moving and Storage involved not only racial pride and the love of Islam but also the desire, as Malcolm X put it, to change the system "by any means necessary." Speakers would often come to Black Self-Help to give talks in the warehouselike storage area on the second floor. Usually these related specifically to the Nation of Islam, but often they were expressly political, as was a talk on the Watts riots of 1965 that included a film showing the beating of blacks by police and National Guard troops invading the ghetto. Some speakers addressed "revolutionary" topics, like how to make a homemade bomb. There is no proof that the Nation of Islam formally endorsed any sort of violent revolution. However, among many radical groups at the time, there was a sense that the violence that had swelled during the 1960s would grow even more in the 1970s, fostering a belief among some of a coming revolution for which they had to prepare. Many texts from the period, including the writing of Abbie Hoffman and others, provided advice on how to both foment and survive such a rebellion. Some texts even went so far as to provide instructions on how to make anything from a Molotov cocktail to a pipe bomb.

The sense of impending violence, even of a race war, contributed to the insularity of the Nation. Courses in self-defense were integral to its educational program. Certain practices of the Nation, such as rigorous discipline in regard to food and learning to eat lightly, so that one could subsist on meager rations of beans and vegetables in case of a food shortage, were intended to teach members how to survive during just such a violent upheaval.

As with many groups, both radical and religious, which hold apocalyptic visions of the future, the Nation of that era created an expectation among its members that better days would follow the upheaval that lay ahead. They were, in the language of their liturgy, the "original Black man" to whom "the Earth belongs," and, as befit the "Lost-Found" people, what had been lost would soon be renewed. Within the wider organization, this anticipation of an ultimate conflagration was little

different than the traditional Christian belief in Armageddon and the
Second Coming, a doctrine of faith rather than a call to action. In the
smaller circle of Black Self-Help, however, as with many other extrem-
ist factions, these beliefs took a violent turn. Adding to that more violent
spin was the fact that the political passions and religious zeal of those
who worked at Black Self-Help mixed with another element in many
of the men: a prison-hardened belief that they had nothing to lose.

The Nation of Islam did much of its recruiting inside prisons.
Malcolm X became a member while in prison, and Eldridge Cleaver
joined the Nation for a time before he left prison and became the Black
Panthers' minister of Defense. For the inmates, the effect was for the
most part positive, giving them a sense of racial identity beyond the violent prison gangs and offering an avenue for reform. But prison has a
way of sticking with people, and sometimes these new members would
bring their criminal ways with them when they got out.

For Larry Green, working alongside the ex-cons who were part of
Black Self-Help offered an opportunity he embraced with an almost
missionary zeal. Though far more educated than them, Green treated
these men like brothers, sometimes loaning them his car, finding them
places to live, even inviting some over for dinner at his parents' home
in Berkeley.

Green co-managed Black Self-Help for Tom Manney, along with
J. C. Simon, the passenger in his car when he was stopped by Gilford
and Sanders. A handsome young African-American man in his late
twenties, Simon was originally from Opelousas, Louisiana, just across
the border from Beaumont, Texas. Ironically, he went to college for a
short while in Tyler, Texas, right next to Nacogdoches, where Sanders
was born. Even though Simon had had a year or so of college, his background could not have been more different from Green's. Since before
moving out west, Simon had lived a gypsylike life, dropping out of college, roaming around Texas, marrying, fathering a child, then abandoning both wife and child to come to California. In San Francisco he
had married another woman, then left her and got involved with someone else. Throughout all the changes there was one constant: a bitter
dissatisfaction with life that fueled the transformations and often came
out as a rage-filled, controlling anger. A telling example of how that

anger manifested itself can be found not in something Simon said but rather in something said to him.

Not long after Simon broke up with Ada Dison, the woman he had married and lived with in San Francisco, she wrote him an almost servile letter asking to get back together. What is so telling about the letter are the many apologies she makes for being too "rebellious" and not knowing how "to submit." Over and over she assures Simon that she would "like now to submit" and that she "knows how to submit." Her words make it clear that he had little patience for or understanding of her wishes or needs, and her assurances imply there had been an explosive and bitter end to their relationship. Yet in her total contrition, she takes the blame for everything, including Simon's hurt pride, and though he never did take up with her again, Simon kept her abject appeal tucked away among his possessions.

Shortly after Simon's separation from Ada, he and Green both rented apartments at 844 Grove, halfway between Temple No. 26, at Fillmore and Geary, and Black Self-Help, at Twelfth and Market. Both had keys to Black Self-Help and were able to open up in the morning and close at night. While Simon took an authoritative foremanlike attitude to the work, Green seemed interested in far more than power. More than Simon, Green reached out in supportive ways to the ex-cons who worked there, making friends with several.

Probably the closest friendship Green formed was with Anthony Harris, an ex-con from San Quentin who had spent much of his adult life shuffling in and out of prison. Green met Harris at Temple No. 26, where Harris went hoping to find work soon after he was released from San Quentin in summer of 1973. After conferring with a captain at the temple who counseled the younger members, Green brought Harris to Black Self-Help and got him a job there. Later, according to Green's younger sister, he practically adopted the older, more experienced, but far less educated man, inviting him again and again to his parents' home, teaching him about both Islam and secular subjects, like reading and writing, which Harris never fully learned, having dropped out of school at a young age. Green would even accompany Harris when he visited his girlfriend, Carolyn Patton. The visits with Carolyn led to Green himself finding a girlfriend, an acquaintance of hers who also belonged to the Nation of Islam. When he eventually married the woman at a ceremony in City Hall, Harris served as their witness.

Among those Green befriended, Jesse Lee Cooks demonstrated the greatest propensity to violence. Cooks had multiple convictions on major felonies that included bank robbery, and a history of violence in the commission of his crimes. He was released from San Quentin in June 1973, just a few weeks before Harris. Four months later, he was back in prison on a homicide conviction. The murder occurred just ten days after the killing of Quita Hague, and took place just a few blocks from Black Self-Help, where Cooks, who worked at Shabazz Bakery in Ingleside, often spent time along with Green, Simon, and Harris. Like the .32-Caliber shootings that came later, the crime seemed to have no motive, but since it was committed with a .22-caliber gun instead of a .32, it had not been linked to the others.

The victim was Frances Rose, a twenty-eight-year-old woman who, like the other victims, was white. But unlike them, Frances Rose got in an argument with her killer before being slain. Seconds after the argument began, Cooks shot Rose three times as she sat in her 1967 Ford Mustang, once in her chest and twice in the face, then fled as the life bled out of her. By coincidence, Homicide inspectors Frank Falzon and Jack Cleary were close enough to the assault to hear the gunshots, and rushed to the scene so quickly that Frances Rose literally died in Jack Cleary's arms. Cooks, still holding the murder weapon, was caught by the detectives minutes later and confessed to the killing that same night.

A week before the murder of Frances Rose and only two nights after the attack on the Hagues, Cooks had also committed a rape. The victim was about the same age as Frances Rose, but more petite. It was a Tuesday night, and she was walking home from a meeting at a church she attended when Cooks grabbed her near where he later killed Rose, and forced her to a vacant lot. There, hidden in the bushes, he argued with the woman, threatening to kill her. Somehow she managed to navigate a delicate psychological line, talking to her assailant in an effort to calm him and drawing him out, prompting him to vent about how the oppression of blacks had to end and how "people were going to be killed and the streets would be lined with blood." The killing,

Cooks said, would be indiscriminate, and "there was no use to be afraid or upset." Cooks then took the woman to her apartment, raped her, and finally left after a grueling two-hour ordeal.

Nothing in Green's record was in any way comparable to Cooks's demeanor. By his own admission, Cooks was a street tough brought up with little parenting or guidance, and his behavior toward others was nothing short of psychopathic. Green, on the other hand, was cool and polished and had been raised in a caring family. He was a son who kissed his mother every time he saw her. Despite their differences, though, they shared a sense of hate centered on the Nation of Islam's concept that whites were "devils" to be blamed for all ills and all evil besetting black men. They were joined not only in friendship but in a fellowship of shared rage.

In the days after Christmas, Sanders, Gilford, and other inspectors working on the growing number of motiveless killings tried desperately to identify Unknown Body #169, although the lack of hands or a head prevented the usual means of identification through fingerprints, facial features, or dental records. They searched through the rolls of missing persons and talked with the family and friends of the missing, hoping somehow to produce a lead. Although a number of times they thought they had one, the IDs never panned out. The nameless, faceless corpse known as Unknown Body #169 remained just that.

At the same time as they tried to track down the identity of the body, Sanders and Gilford also followed up on their stop of Larry Green, running his driver's license number through the department's computer system and checking to see if he had a rap sheet. He didn't. Green's record was spotless. They checked on Simon as well, but although he had pleaded no contest to possessing a stolen gun some years earlier, Simon had served no time, and the limited research tools available then turned up nothing more on him, either. Even so, the sense Sanders had of Green's guilt and the impression of his barely suppressed rage or resentment lingered, as did the suspicion that members of the Nation of Islam might somehow be involved in the shootings.

Sanders and Gilford were not alone in their suspicions. Coreris and Fotinos also believed that members of the Nation might be involved, especially Fotinos, who felt that the clean-cut description given by some of the witnesses matched the general look of men who belonged to the Nation. When Fotinos brought up the possibility to Charlie Ellis, though, Ellis balked at the notion.

"Charlie was ambitious," Sanders recalls. "He had reason to be. When it came to administration, he was one of the best cops around. But he wanted to be chief. And back then you didn't get to the top job by making waves. So as far as Charlie was concerned, the shootings were bad enough without dragging in politics and religion and God knows what else."

An incident shortly after Christmas roiled Sanders's private life and brought home, in an indirect way, the role that racism played in the lives of blacks who might be considered privileged. This was never something Sanders had given much thought to when he was younger. "Growing up poor," he says, "you tend to identify discrimination with poverty. But when you're black and you get a little something for yourself, you realize that poverty's only part of it." Intellectually, he came to understand that truth as soon as he began to move up in the world, and he felt it when, as an inspector in the SFPD with a working wife and two young children, he moved to the previously all-white development in suburban South San Francisco where he now lived. However, it was only when his son, Marcus, began to experience the kind of hate from which even privilege is no protection that it hit Sanders with an emotional power he would never forget.

"One day not long after we found the body on the beach, Gil and I spent hours talking to people out on the Great Highway and in the Fillmore, where a number of the shootings occurred. But it was one of those days where you get nothing, and finally we packed it in and went to blow off some steam at the Half Note, a jazz club on Divisadero we used to hang at. We had a drink or two, then Gil stayed to talk to a woman he met and I went home to shower, shave, and see if I could get at least a bit of sleep before it all started up again.

"I must have stood in that shower for over half an hour. I usually don't mind stiffs. Dead Janes and Dead Joneses tell you things you'd never learn anywhere else. But that body on the beach was different. Three or four days had gone by, but I still couldn't get rid of the smell. I don't know if it was in my nose or my mind, but I couldn't get rid of it. I let that water pour over me, wishing it would just wash it all away.

"Finally Espanola came in, pissed off about how late it was. We started arguing, with her yelling about me being gone all the time, knowing Gil was probably off with some girl somewhere and saying she wondered when I was 'gonna get a blond of my own.'

"After a while, she cooled off, and the fighting stopped. Then I told her about the body. How it stuck with me. And how I couldn't shake it. I don't know when we got to bed. But before we did, she told me about Marcus, how he'd been riding his new bike around the neighborhood and this older white kid up the hill kept messing with him. Marcus was no more than eight or nine and didn't have a mean drop of blood in his body. There was no reason in the world for that other kid to mess with him. Except one: that kid was white, and Marcus was black.

"That morning Marcus and I had a talk. His mother always told him not to get in fights. I told him, Your mother's right. You shouldn't fight. But sometimes you have to. I told him that he should never forget he's black. Because nobody else would. That he should be proud of who he is no matter what anyone says. That he should only fight when there's no other way. And that even then, he should never fight angry. Because a man enraged is a man out of control."

A few days later Marcus and the older kid had it out, with little damage between them except a bloody nose and some scraped knuckles. Sanders made sure it was their last battle, however. He paid a visit to the kid's father and told him straight out that if it ever happened again, it would be the two of them who were fighting instead of their children. Not long after that, the other father put his house up for sale.

The worst cold spell in twenty years hit San Francisco during the first few days of 1974. Mountain areas all the way from Tamalpais in the north to Santa Cruz in the south were blanketed with snow. Cars got stuck in snowdrifts, bus riders were stranded, and a thin white veil of frost began to cover the city each night, making the rolling hills and towering buildings seem crystalline to Sanders as he drove to work in the morning light.

Within the Hall of Justice, tensions between the black cops supporting the Officers for Justice lawsuit and the white cops who supported the POA continued to run high. The POA's appeal of the preliminary decision was ongoing, and the department still held out the possibility of contesting the ruling with a parallel suit. In union elections, the POA had voted in a reactionary group of leaders who styled themselves as the "Bluecoats." The name referred to the fact that most were patrolmen, cops who had never traded in their uniforms for the plain clothes of an inspector. The express implication was an avowal of their working-class persona. But in a place as politically charged as San Francisco in the early 1970s, the similarity between the name Bluecoats and the Nazi militia known as the brownshirts was hard to miss.

"The Bluecoats had a 'screw you' attitude about everything the OFJ was trying to do," Sanders recalls. "There was no debate. And not much respect."

An example of the POA's derisive tone can be seen in the January 1974 issue of the periodical they published, the *Notebook*. In one cartoon, a graduating class from the police academy is depicted as including the Frito Bandito, Frankenstein, and a gorilla, and beneath it the caption reads, "I've heard of minority hiring, but this is ridiculous!"

Sanders recalls the effect the cartoon had on black officers. "Back then, being characterized as an ape or gorilla wasn't any different than being called a nigger. We'd heard it all our lives. So we didn't like it. And we sure as hell didn't like seeing it in print."

The cold spell outside the Hall of Justice spread into the Homicide Bureau as well. But this was less about the temperature in the room than about cases going cold. Throughout December the shootings seemed to come every few days or so. That pattern changed in January, as suddenly the shooting stopped and the trail vanished. Yet despite the pause in the attacks, anxiety in black neighborhoods persisted. The "ghetto reward" had still produced no clues into Marietta DiGirolamo's murder, nor had any of Sanders and Gilford's usual street sources come up with information about any of the assaults.

"The ghetto," as Sanders recalls, "was cold, dark, and silent. That's what made Gil and me certain it had to be radicals. They were the only ones who'd be disciplined enough to keep things that quiet. Because of Green, and the motiveless killings we'd been briefed about in Oakland that October, I thought they [the Nation of Islam] were the most likely group. But there were others. The Black Liberation Army, the Weather Underground, even the Panthers, who were going crazy over in Oakland, with Huey Newton getting wilder and wilder."

Gus Coreris was so convinced that a radical group might be behind the shootings that when he went to the hospital to talk to Art Agnos, one of the two survivors of the December shootings and whom Coreris knew to be the son of Greek immigrants, he spoke to him in Greek.

Agnos couldn't figure out what was going on at first. For one thing, he had no idea how Coreris knew that he spoke Greek. He had even less of an idea why the detective would be so circumspect. Coreris, still speaking Greek, explained that the shootings might have been politically motivated, and while they didn't know the identity of the perpetrator yet, they couldn't be sure who they could trust, or who might be listening. When Agnos found that paranoid-sounding claim hard to take seriously, Coreris assured him with an urgency that left a lasting impression that he absolutely should.

Not long after that conversation, still another possibility emerged, in the form of the SLA.

On November 6, just a few weeks prior to the slaying of Palestinian grocer Saleem Erakat, Marcus Foster, the superintendent of the Oakland school system, was gunned down in the parking lot behind where he worked in the East Bay. Foster was one of the rising stars of Bay Area politics, a highly educated man who was successful in bringing together diverse communities and looked on as someone with tremendous potential.

Initial statements by witnesses concurred that three young black men were responsible for Foster's shooting. To many, the idea of blacks attacking a rising star in the African-American community seemed baffling. To those like Sanders, who knew that some black radical groups were targeting African Americans they deemed part of the "establishment," it made a sad and regrettable kind of sense.

"They didn't want reform. They wanted revolution. And the shortest way to it was to go after people like Marcus Foster, who were trying to change things from the inside."

For two months, the investigation into the Foster killing went nowhere, despite the Symbionese Liberation Army's claim of responsibility. The problem was that the police knew next to nothing about the SLA and still less about its membership. Then the chance stop of a van on January 10, 1974, broke the case wide open.

The van contained two young white men, Joseph Remiro and Russell Little, rather than blacks, and was driving through the East Bay suburb of Concord on a quiet early morning when it was stopped by a Concord officer. Remiro panicked, pulling out a gun and exchanging fire with the officer before being subdued and arrested along with Little. Propaganda found inside the van tied them to the Symbionese Liberation Army, the group that had laid claim to the Foster shooting. In addition, among the many weapons found in their possession was a classic Walther PP automatic carried by Remiro, which the Oakland police identified as one of the guns used to kill Foster. Both Remiro and Little were charged with his murder.

Yet because witnesses reported seeing blacks at the scene of the Foster shooting, the suspicion remained that others involved might remain at large. That feeling was validated when a string of communiqués began to appear in the press after the Remiro and Little arrest, adding to the notoriety of the still mysterious SLA, a group unheard of before Foster and commanding the attention of police forces across the West Coast, including the SFPD.

Like many police departments in the 1960s and '70s, the SFPD had an intelligence unit that gathered information in much the same way national organizations like the FBI did, focusing their efforts on the radical, politically based groups that had become so prevalent. Paul Lawler ran the SFPD's unit. Lawler's background in the SFPD was stellar, with a history of high-level work almost as soon as he entered the force. Sanders knew him from the Robbery Bureau, where Lawler had once demonstrated his toughness and fairness by refusing to allow the otherwise all-white bureau to cancel the yearly Christmas party because blacks were now working with them. Lawler was known as an excellent administrator. As in most police intelligence departments of the time, though, the personnel he had to work with only rarely seemed to have the street savvy needed to understand the new breed of political revolutionaries. Moreover, there were never enough officers, let alone enough competent ones, to keep tabs on and successfully infiltrate all those groups.

"People used to call them Red Squads," Sanders says as he talks about the bureau. "Sometimes the information they gathered was all right, but sometimes Gil and I would laugh at the intelligence they sent out. Half the people they said were revolutionaries were just street thugs. It was the same problem a lot of the bureaus had. If you couldn't relate to the people you were policing, you couldn't do the job. It's not that being able to relate is some 'feel good' kind of thing. It's that it's the only way to gain access."

It was Paul Lawler's job to determine who among the many revolutionary groups in the Bay Area might be behind any crime that smacked of radical violence. As far as Lawler was concerned, the .32-Caliber shootings were high on that list. Yet, with little access, he and his investigators could only draw inferences from scant evidence, making most theories little more than hunches and leaving them to scramble after whatever organization seemed most active. Like Sanders and Gilford, Lawler had harbored suspicions about the Nation of Islam, but in the wake of the Marcus Foster shooting and the arrests of Little and Remiro, the SLA loomed larger as a likely candidate. As January drew to a close, however, a sequence of events began that would make Sanders and Gilford's feelings about the Nation of Islam seem prescient. It started with a shooting, not by a radical bent on revolution but by a cop.

The incident began almost like a replay of the arrest of Joseph Remiro and Russell Little a week earlier for the killing of Marcus Foster. Once again, an East Bay cop stopped a van. This time the van, which had the words *Nation of Islam* stenciled on its side and *Fresh Fish* on its back, happened to be in the ghetto, not the suburbs, at Sixty-third and Baker, just south of Alcatraz Avenue, where Berkeley, Oakland, and the little industrial town of Emeryville all come together. And it was filled with blacks, not whites.

Relations had never been good between the Oakland Police Department and Oakland's African-American community, and in the early 1970s tensions were on the increase. The Panthers had grown factionalized and violent, leading to a marked rise in their confrontations with police. Out of concern that cops were targeting blacks and provoking the confrontations, members of the Nation of Islam's Oakland Temple No. 73 began to use police scanners to monitor law enforcement activities.

On the afternoon of January 25, forty-four-year-old Nation of Islam member Herbert Tucker and three younger Nation of Islam members who worked with him in a fish business owned by the Nation were pulled over by a Berkeley cop for reasons that were not quite clear. Tucker thought the stop was harassment and refused to identify himself. Later, the Berkeley police would claim that the reason for the stop was that there had been rapes in the area by someone selling eggs or fish door-to-door. However, nothing was said about that at the time, and to Tucker it seemed an obvious case of white cops jacking up blacks.

William Cooper, the Berkeley patrolman who had stopped the van, reacted angrily. What followed was an escalating altercation that snowballed into tragedy. First, the other men in the van, Larry Crosby, Donald Craig, and Robert Wright, piled out to come to Tucker's aid. That caused Cooper to call for backup, and two more cops arrived in a squad car, which led to the argument heating up even further, and a scuffle broke out.

During the fight, Cooper's gun fell to the ground, and, according to the police, Larry Crosby picked it up and pistol-whipped him. Then Crosby tossed the gun down, and he and the others took off running. Cooper picked up the gun and fired at them, hitting Crosby in the back with one bullet. At twenty-four, Larry Crosby, also known as Larry C. 3X, lay on the blacktop on the border between Oakland and Berkeley, his own blood pooling around him and a policeman's bullet lodged in his spine, paralyzing him for life.

When he was brought to Berkeley's Herrick Hospital, Crosby was declared to be in critical condition and placed on life support. News of what had happened resounded among the members of the Nation of Islam's Oakland and San Francisco temples like a gun's report, registering in the minds of many as a call to action.

On Saturday morning, January 26, Earl Sanders woke to find the news of the shooting of Larry Crosby in the *San Francisco Chronicle.* It had been more than a month since the last .32-Caliber shooting, and the investigation had apparently come to a dead end. So, even though it was a Saturday, Sanders and Gilford had a series of appointments to keep in order to follow up on the few tenuous leads they still had. After that, they would head to the Hall of Justice, where they, Coreris, Fotinos, and the other inspectors working on the shootings would compare notes and try to spin all they knew about the crimes on its axis, to examine them from every conceivable point of view and search for any detail or possibly crucial insight they might have missed. If the session ran late enough, they would probably open up the interrogation-room bar, pour themselves some drinks, and get out the dominoes and cards.

Anyone who happened upon the men of Homicide at times like that might have concluded that they did nothing but booze and play games. However, the cops in Homicide knew different. While they relaxed and played, they talked about cases, their minds collating clues even as their hands shuffled cards, and more than once after a domino was laid or a hand was played something emerged that changed an investigation and brought a bad guy to justice.

That was the day that lay ahead of Sanders as he prepared to head out, lingering over the story about Larry Crosby. He didn't have time to cut the article out, but he put it aside with the intention of doing so later, as he had with most of the other articles he had read about the Nation of Islam over the past year or so, tracking the tensions that had been tearing the organization apart and, more recently, seeking connections that might help provide a solution to the motiveless killings that had been plaguing the Bay Area.

Minister John Muhammad, head of San Francisco's Temple

No. 26 and spiritual leader to most of the Bay Area members of the Nation of Islam, learned of the shooting soon after it had occurred and lodged protests about it with both the Berkeley police and the local papers. A broad-shouldered, charismatic man who was always immaculately dressed, Minister Muhammad announced a public meeting on the shooting to be held that Sunday at Temple No. 26, hoping for an audience that might reach into the thousands.

Simply by virtue of its location, San Francisco's Nation of Islam temple formed an integral part of the city's history. Located at 1805 Geary, at the corner of Fillmore Street, the distinctive yellow brick building that contained the temple began life in 1912 as the Majestic Hall, an auditorium devoted to dancing and music. Later it showed movies under various names, including the Temple Theater, and then, in the 1960s, it became the original Fillmore Auditorium, home to impresario Bill Graham's weekly rock-and-roll extravaganzas. As the 1960s waned, Graham grew disenchanted with the declining neighborhood and sold the building to the Nation of Islam, moving his operations to Fillmore West, at the corner of Market and Van Ness. From then on, the place that had witnessed the birth of such icons as the Jefferson Airplane, Janis Joplin, Santana, and others became host to the Lost-Found Tribe of Shabazz: instead of the wailing of a Joplin or the feedback of a Hendrix, one could hear the wisdom of the Messenger.

Minister Muhammad certainly knew that the meeting at the temple would be significant. He must also have been aware that not just the Nation of Islam would draw the crowd, but the event itself. Regardless of who had started the altercation, a man shot in the back and lying paralyzed in a hospital bed was the kind of tragedy that highlighted the adversarial relationship of the police with not only the Nation but also the entire African-American community.

In fact, the crowd that showed up numbered well over two thousand and included as many nonmembers as it did members of the Nation. A line of people waiting to get inside snaked around the block, just as other crowds had done when the building was the domain of Bill Graham rather than John Muhammad. Once inside, the audience listened to Minister Muhammad's urgent appeal for money to bail out the men involved in the incident, including the paralyzed Crosby, for all had been charged with assaulting the police. He also called upon all blacks, Muslim and non-Muslim, to come together, saying they "should be tired of having their black brothers shot down in the street."

Among those listening in the audience were a number of the men who worked at Black Self-Help, including Green, Simon, Manuel Moore, and Harris. Like everyone else, they had endured a long wait to get in, but they were determined to hear what the minister had to say. Unlike many, though, they felt a meeting alone would not be enough. Something else was needed, something not merely to mourn the tragedy or even protest it, but to avenge it.

Until the publication of this book, information about the assaults referred to as the .32-Caliber shootings or murders, which would soon become known as the Zebra murders, was largely based on the court record. However, evidence presented in court is rarely, if ever, all of the evidence developed by the police and prosecution. While this book was being researched, material developed as evidence but never presented in court or made public came to light that has provided crucial insight into the crimes.

While chief of the San Francisco Police Department in 2003, Earl Sanders had the extant police files on the cases covered in this book removed from storage for his review. A short while later, he was forced into an early retirement for health reasons, after suffering two strokes in quick succession. Between the time he left his job and when he first returned to the Hall of Justice following his retirement, Sanders had his personal effects packed up by assistants and shipped to his home in northern California. At the same time, the boxes of police files he requested were returned to storage — all, that is, except one, which was mistakenly shipped with his personal effects to Folsom.

Earl Sanders did not ask for these files or play any role in their delivery to him. However, once the files were in his possession, he and his coauthor began to pore over them and soon found that they opened up a new window on the crimes and the motivations of those involved, as well as their political implications. Among the documentation are both handwritten and dictated confessions by Anthony Harris, which reveal not only details of some of the crimes but also what was discussed on the evening of January 27, when plans were made for what would become the bloodiest night in the spree, during which at least five victims were shot. The box contains notebooks and personal effects belonging to Anthony Harris, as well as evidence about Harris's and J. C. Simon's work with the Nation, and about Simon's personal life, including the letter from Ada Dison mentioned earlier. Personal effects of Larry Green, among them his journal, are also included, as is a notebook that belonged to Clarence Jamerson, a suspect who was later arrested but never indicted, enclosing instructional material connected to both Black Self-Help Moving and Storage and the Nation of Islam, including Lesson No. 10, the controversial passage about why Muslims must "murder the devil." Jamerson's notebook bears the Swahili word *bishana*, meaning "dispute" or, perhaps in this instance, "uprising," on its cover. There are files of tips about possible leads that were sent to the SFPD by various sources, including police agencies and individuals, as well as police surveillance records, information gathered about the movements of the suspects, and photographs of Temple No. 26, Black Self-Help Moving and Storage, and lineups of the suspects.

The files in that box, along with Earl Sanders's personal files, notes, recollections, and interviews with many of those involved in the cases who are still alive, form the basis for what follows.

The meeting took place in the apartment of J. C. Simon, at 844 Grove. Besides Simon, also participating was Manuel Moore, who was living with Simon at the time and was the newest addition to the group. Moore had done time in San Quentin for burglary while Jesse Lee Cooks was there and had been released from prison only two months earlier. Larry Green, who resided in the same building, was there too, along with Anthony Harris. In addition, there were four other members of the Nation of Islam whom Harris, who would eventually give the police an account of the meeting, claimed not to know.

Born and raised in southern California, Anthony Cornelius Harris was in his late twenties in January 1974 and had handsome features and a lean, athletic frame. He had dropped out of school in the ninth grade, and soon afterward Harris's mother had him committed to a state mental hospital, claiming she couldn't control him. A year later he was out. Though he attempted to support himself by teaching kung fu, which he had begun to study as a youth, for the most part Harris seemed to live a life of crime. He was arrested at various times for burglary, assaulting an officer, and the illegal possession of a gun. He married a white woman in southern California, fathered two children by her, then left her. After serving time in San Quentin from 1971 to 1973 for yet another burglary conviction, he was helped by Larry Green following his release and became involved in Black Self-Help. Settling in San Francisco, he married Carolyn Patton, a member of Temple No. 26, in a union that lasted less than a month, then moved in with Deborah Turner, another Temple member, who had begun to use the name Deborah Sue 7X.

Despite the disorder of Anthony's life, he had about him an engaging, almost playful quality that led many, like Larry Green and others at Black Self-Help, to be drawn to him and welcome him into their lives. According to Harris, though, the meeting to discuss the shooting of Larry Crosby and what to do about it was when he began to question the wisdom of getting caught up in lives such as these.

In October 1973 there had been earlier meetings at Simon's apartment, to which Harris had been brought by Larry Green and where others from Black Self-Help, such as Clarence Jamerson and Dwight Stallings, were also present. At those meetings, according to Harris, Simon had quoted Lesson No. 10, interpreting it as a directive about, in Harris's words, "killing white people" and asking Harris if he was ready to "destroy the enemy." This time, however, he went even further. Harris would recount how those present were furious over the shooting, and how their outrage incited what he termed the "vicious thoughts" that "crossed their minds." They discussed various options for revenge. One idea was to blow up school buses. The plan would be to get up early the next day, Monday morning, go to the garage where the buses were kept, and place dynamite in some of the exhaust pipes, on the theory that the dynamite wouldn't explode until the exhaust caused it to sweat, by which time the buses would be filled with children. The explosion would kill not only the children in the buses but also people in the cars around them. Another idea was to procure a high-powered rifle, drive to a road near the airport, and attempt to shoot down an airliner as it took off.

Harris claimed that he argued against these ideas, pointing out that Muslims might be in the plane and that black kids might be among the schoolchildren on the buses. That was when J. C. Simon leapt up angrily from his chair and unleashed a torrent of abuse at him, according to Harris, complaining that he was critical of every plan they devised to deal with what Simon called the "disease-carrying, blue-eyed grafted devils" and ordering him to get out of his apartment.

But then Simon softened, saying that he understood it took time for someone to be ready to kill. No sane person would want to make killing a habit. But this was something that they had to do, because whites were evil, and getting even with them was necessary not only as revenge for Larry Crosby but because of generations of wickedness. His anger spent, Simon told Harris he was sure that when Harris was ready to get even with whites, he would rise to the challenge, adding that they would never force him to do something against his will. Then Harris claimed that he left the meeting to spend the night with his girlfriend while the others continued talking, discussing outside his presence how to best avenge the shooting.

A few hours after the meeting at Simon's apartment ended, Sanders woke and padded downstairs for his early-morning ritual of coffee and the *Chronicle*.

Over the weekend, the world had seen chaos descend on Cambodia, where terrified residents fled Phnom Penh, abandoning the capital as Pol Pot and his Khmer Rouge rebels overran it. Thus began the process that would lead to Pol Pot's assumption of power and declaration that the following year, 1975, would be "Year Zero," initiating an era of genocidal horror that would become known as the time of the "killing fields."

In Chile, photographs of the last days of Salvador Allende were finally released to the world media. Some images depicted President Al-

Inspector Earl Sanders, aka "School," at his desk in the San Francisco Police Department's Homicide Bureau, 1976.

Photograph by Bob Bryant. Used by permission of the *San Francisco Examiner*.

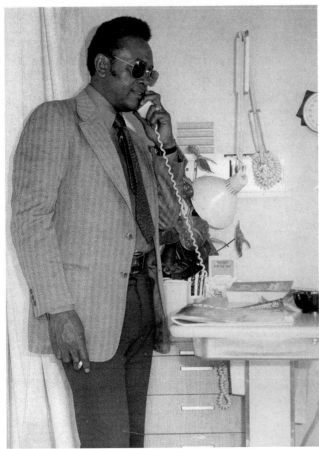

Inspector Rotea Gilford, Sanders's partner and mentor, 1972.

Kissie Lacy née Baxter née Sanders, with Earl on her left and Earl's younger brother, William, on her right, in Texas in the 1940s.

Henry Baxter, Earl Sanders's maternal grandfather and the man who raised him during his earliest years. Date unknown.

Earl Sanders as a teen. He lived alone and supported himself in San Francisco, unbeknownst to school authorities.

John Fotinos (left) and Gus Coreris (right), the lead investigators on the Zebra murders, 1969.
Courtesy Gus Coreris.

Willie Johnson, Sanders's partner before he entered Homicide and teamed with Gilford, shown with his wife, Ruby, in the 1960s.

Earl Sanders and his wife, Espanola, out on the town in November 1973.

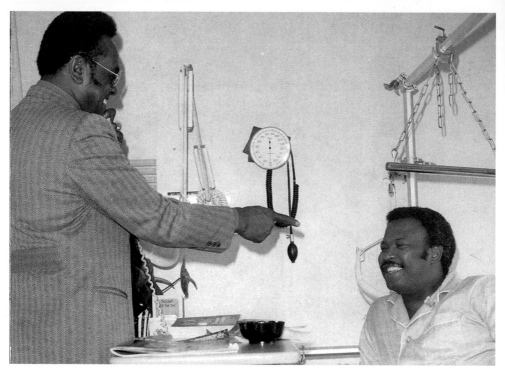

ABOVE: Rotea Gilford cheering up his partner as Sanders recovered in the hospital from an automobile accident, 1972.

BELOW LEFT: A .32 pistol cartridge. John Fotinos and Carl Klotz retrieved this cartridge, which has a nickel-plated bullet, from the home of Michael Armstrong, who purchased it for his own use in the Beretta that later became one of the two Zebra murder weapons.

Zebra victim and later San Francisco mayor Art Agnos, who was shot on December 13, 1973, sitting in the audience of the Zebra lineups on the morning of May 1, 1974, immediately after the arrests. SFPD file photograph.

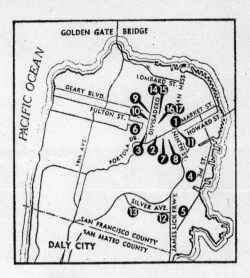

Shootings

Where the 17 random shooting incidents have occurred:

(1) Nov. 25, 1973 — Saleem Erakat killed at 452 Larkin street.

(2) December 11 — Paul Dancik killed at Haight and Buchanan streets.

(3) December 13 — Marietta DiGirolamo killed at Haight and Divisadero streets.

(4) December 13 — Arthur Agnos, wounded at 991 Wisconsin street.

(5) December 20 — Ilario Bertuccio killed at Bancroft avenue and Phelps street.

(6) December 21 — Terri de Martini wounded on 600 block of Central avenue.

(7) December 23 — Mildred Hosler killed at Gough and McCoppin streets.

(8) December 23 — Neal Moynihan killed at 40 12th street.

(9) January 28 — Tana Smith killed at Geary boulevard and Divisadero street.

(10) January 28 — Vincent Wollin killed at Fulton and Divisadero streets.

(11) January 28 — John Bambic killed at Ninth and Howard streets.

(12) January 28 — Jane Holly killed at Silver avenue and Brussells street.

(13) January 28 — Roxanne McMillan wounded at 102 Edinburgh street.

(14) April 2 — Thomas Rainwater killed at Geary boulevard and Webster street.

(15) April 2 — Linda Story wounded at Geary and Webster.

(16) April 14 — Terry White wounded at Hayes and Fillmore streets.

(17) April 14 — Ward Anderson wounded at Hayes and Fillmore.

A map of the Zebra shootings printed in the *San Francisco Chronicle* on April 16, 1974, on the same day that Nelson Shields III, the last of the Zebra victims, would be murdered in the Ingleside district. Also absent from the list are Richard and Quita Hague, Frances Rose, and Unknown Body #169.

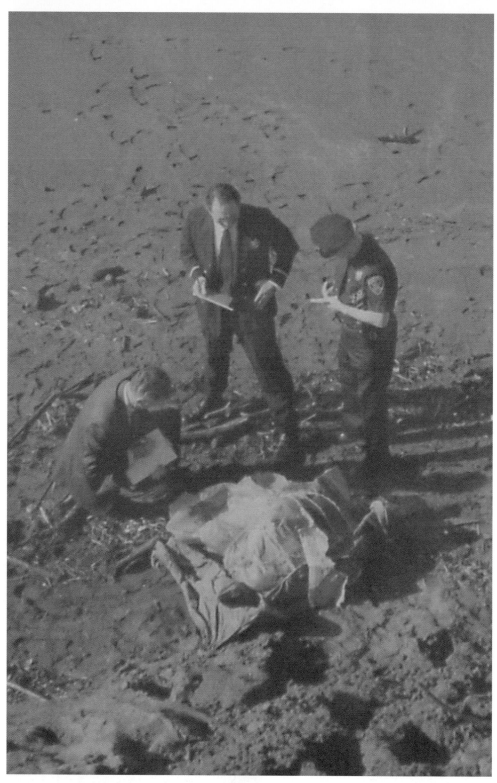

The Zebra victim known as Unknown Body #169, where he was discovered on the beach near the Great Highway, December 24, 1973. Looking on are SFPD officers and inspectors.
SFPD file photograph.

ABOVE: Surveillance photograph of the Dodge Dart owned by Larry Green, parked behind Black Self-Help Moving and Storage on April 26, 1974, three days after Anthony Harris turned himself in. Photograph taken by SFPD officers staked out in the Bradmar Apartments. SFPD file photograph.

BELOW: Surveillance photograph of the Cadillac owned by Clarence Jamerson, parked behind Black Self-Help Moving and Storage on April 27, 1974. Photograph taken by SFPD officers staked out in the Bradmar Apartments. SFPD file photograph.

Anthony Harris standing in line outside Nation of Islam Temple No. 26, at Fillmore and Geary, on the January 27, 1974, rally in support of Larry Crosby. Harris is looking toward the right of the frame.

Photograph by Dave Randolph. Used by permission of the *San Francisco Chronicle*.

The murder scene of John Bambic, one of the Zebra cases for which Rotea Gilford and Earl Sanders were the official lead officers, on the night of January 28, 1974. CSI officer Ken Moses is kneeling by the body at the right of the frame, smoking a pipe.

Photograph by Jim Domke. Used by permission of the *San Francisco Examiner*.

Random Attacks

S.F. Killing Spree---
5 Shot on Streets

Pat Says Nixon Sleeps Well

Two-Hour 'Death Drive'

Washington

ABOVE: Headlines the morning after the shooting spree of January 28, 1974.
Used by permission of the *San Francisco Chronicle*.

BELOW: A photograph found in Anthony Harris's Oakland apartment after he turned himself in to the SFPD, showing him holding his child. A gun can be seen on the coffee table.

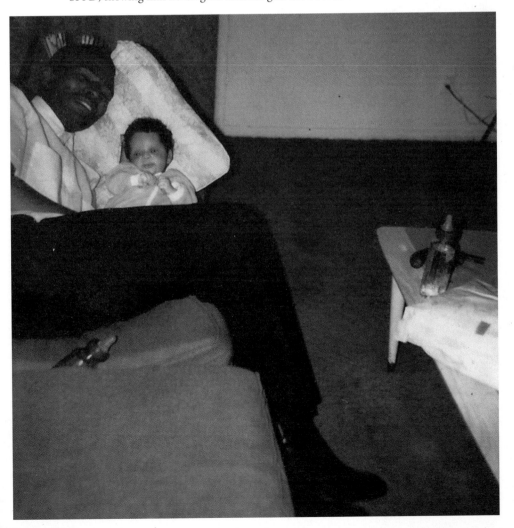

Sketch of a Zebra suspect made by SFPD Homicide inspector Hobart Nelson, under the direction of Gus Coreris and John Fotinos. Seeing this sketch convinced Anthony Harris he had been identified by the police, leading him to turn himself in.

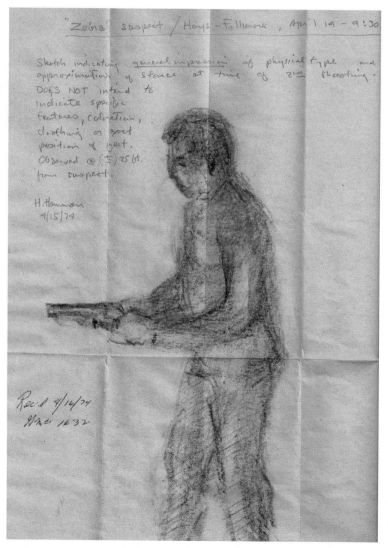

Sketch of one of the Zebra suspects drawn by a witness of the shooting of Ward Anderson and Terry White, April 14, 1974.

J. C. Simon sometime before the Zebra shootings.

Memo from Rotea Gilford to Chief of Detectives Charlie Barca, proposing a special Zebra squad of mostly minority officers. Gilford sought a more effective way to deal with the shooting than the draconian Zebra sweeps.

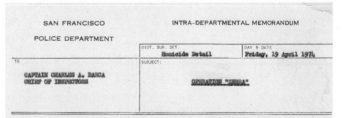

SAN FRANCISCO
POLICE DEPARTMENT

INTRA-DEPARTMENTAL MEMORANDUM

DIST. BUR. DET. **Homicide Detail** DAY & DATE **Friday, 19 April 1974**

TO
CAPTAIN CHARLES A. BARCA
CHIEF OF INSPECTORS

SUBJECT:
OPERATION "ZEBRA"

Sir:

A Squad of 30 men, most of whom will be Black Officers, specially selected from all Districts and Details within the department will be utilized to form 2 Teams.

One team will operate as an intelligence gathering unit. It will be in operation in areas of the city predominately populated by black people, and on a person to person and house to house basis, gathering information on people who fix the profile and description of the Zebra suspect, and on automatic pistols that may be .32 caliber. In the event of a Zebra case occurring, will go into the area and literally knock on every door in the immediate area to locate witnesses for the purpose of turning said information over to the Officer in Charge of the investigation.

Team #2 will act as a Strike Force to act upon intelligence information gathered. This team will take such action as seizure of suspected weapons and observation of possible suspects and pass suspected weapons and information on possible suspects on to the Officer-In-Charge of the investigation.

The entire unit will be under the direction of Chief of Inspectors Charles A. Barca and will consolidate some of its' activities with the efforts of the Community Relations Unit, so as not to duplicate effort. The Unit expects some aid from Community Organizations in gathering intelligence. It is further proposed that this squad be in operation between the hours of 12 Noon to mid-night daily.

Attached is a list of men proposed for this Unit. The men have been contacted and have expressed a willingness to work this detail.

FROM **INSP. ROTEA GILFORD** #592 APPROVED BY **CHARLES F. ELLIS** REFER TO

RANK STAR RANK **LIEUTENANT** STAR A-718

SFPD - 68 (9 - 70)

San Francisco Chronicle

The Largest Daily Circulation in Northern California

| 110th Year   No. 113 | ★★★★ | TUESDAY, APRIL 23, 1974 | GArfield 1-1111   15 CENTS |

| More Nixon Tapes Sought On 3 Topics | **Mayor Spat On** | **Angry Crowd Protests Police 'Zebra' Dragnet** |

Headlines at the height of the Zebra sweeps, when protestors attacked Mayor Alioto.
Used by permission of the *San Francisco Chronicle*.

Mayor Joseph Alioto fighting his way through a crowd of protestors outside City Hall
on April 22, 1974. The photograph was published on April 23, the same day
Anthony Harris turned himself in to the SFPD.

Photograph by Susan Ehmer. Used by permission of the *San Francisco Chronicle*.

Mug shot of Anthony Harris, taken soon after his arrests on May 1, 1974, along with a mug shot of Jesse Cooks taken at an earlier date.
SFPD file photographs.

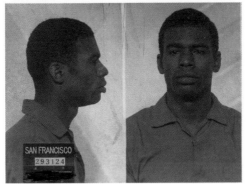

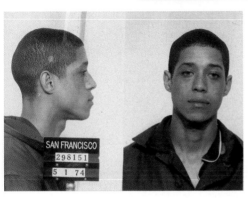
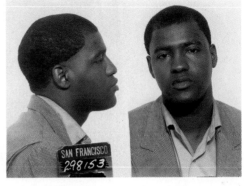

Mug shots of Larry Green, J. C. Simon and Manuel Moore, taken soon after their arrests on May 1, 1974.
SFPD file photographs.

FACING PAGE FAR LEFT: Larry Green shown in a full-body mug shot taken the morning of his arrest, May 1, 1974.
SFPD file photograph.

FACING PAGE RIGHT: J. C. Simon shown in a full-body mug shot taken the morning of his arrest, May 1, 1974.
SFPD file photograph.

LEFT: Manuel Moore shown in a full-body mug shot taken the morning of his arrest, May 1, 1974.
SFPD file photograph.

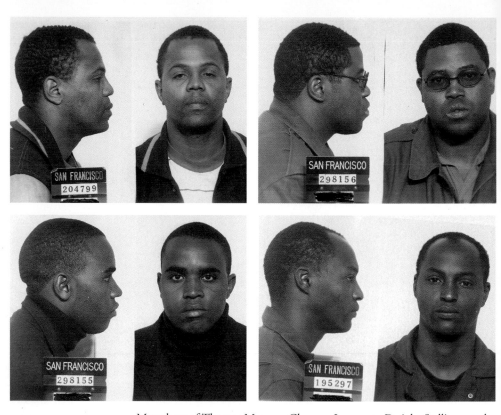

CLOCKWISE FROM TOP LEFT: Mug shots of Thomas Manney, Clarence Jamerson, Dwight Stallings, and Douglas Burton, all of whom were arrested on May 1, 1974, but were never identified in lineups and never indicted. SFPD file photographs.

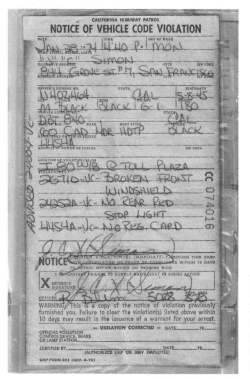

The traffic ticket issued to J. C. Simon on January 28, 1974, while he was driving Thomas Manney's Cadillac across the Bay Bridge with Manuel Moore, returning to San Francisco just a few hours before the wave of shootings began.

DATE June 18 1974
TIME 7:30 P.M.
Tuesday

TO WHO IT MAY CONCERN, AT THIS "TIME"

I, ANTHONY C. HARRIS,
THOUGHT IT WOULD BE BEST TO WRITE THESE FEW LINES NOW BEFORE IT IS TO LATE, FOR I FEEL A VERY STRONG TYPE OF UNKNOWN POWER TO MANKIND SLOWLY POSSESSING MY PHYSICAL MIND, AND FORCEING ME TO REVEL THAT WHICH HAS NEVER BEFOR NOW BEEN REVISE, IT IS SO STINGENING TO THE IMAGINATION! THAT I CAN NOT LIVE WITH IT ALONG.
YOU MAY, F.C.C., ERIN, OR SMILE OR EVEN MAKE MARKET, BUT IS IS YOU TO WHO ARE LIVING WITHIN A VERY DARK CAGE OF FEAR.
AND NOW IT THIS YOUR TARN TO LEARN OF THE SECRETS OF WHAT IS NOW KNOWN AS A VERY SECRETTY OREINIZATION CALLED THE DEATH — ANGELES —
IT MAINLY CONSIST OF A VERY LARG NUMBER OF BLACK MEN OF THE AGE WHO AT ONE TIME OR ANOTHER HAVE BEEN PLACED BEHIND PRISON BAR'S ON JUICE (I.Y. OR JUSTLY.) EATHER
AND NOW THESE MEN HAVE BEEN BRING WASHED. EN DOCTRINATED, OR HUPMNTIZE UNDER A FAKEN POWER.
AND NOW HAVE BECOME PERFESSIONAL KILLERS FROM WITHIN THEMSELFS AGAINST THE FRI FACE OF A WHITE MAN, WOMAN, OR CHILDEN!

NOTE.

THE ENNUCEN KILLING OF WHITE PEOPLE UPON ORDER FROM HEADQORE HAS BEEN TAKEING PLACE FOR A FREI PERIOD OF TIME.
ONE DAY UNEXPECTEDLY I WAS TAKEN OUT FROM SANFRANCISCO TO A FRIEND FATHER 'MOTHER HOME IN BERKELY
AFTER LVEING HIS MOTHER HOME I WAS TAKEN TO A COLLEDG CAMPUS WHERE I WIATNESS, THE FRIST KILLING OR AN ENNUCEN MAN BY LARRY GRIGG GREEN WITH A WHAT A PEAKED TO BE SOME SORT OF LARGE KNITE.
AS I STOD THERE WATCHING HEITLESS IN A VERY DEET STATE OF CHLOCK AND LISONING TO THE VICTOM CRIMIE STOP - PLEASE STOP WHAT HAVE I DONE!
THE VICTOM THEN FELL TO HIS NEEDS SLOWLY GETTING UP AND BEGAN RUNNING ACROSS THE STREET
I STOD THEIR FOR A FEW SECONDS, THEN I HEARD THIS VOICE SAYING COME ON COME ON BROTHER ANTHONY I DIDN'T QUIET UNDERSTANT WHAT WAS REALLY GOING ON UNTIL SOME

202

THAT NIGHT AFTER WORK LARRY GREEN, MANUEL MOORE, J.C. SIMMON, ME, AND FOUR UNKNOWN BLACK MUSLIMS WERE STANDING DOWN UP STAIR'S IN J.C. APARTMENT DISCUSSING WHAT SHOULD, AND WILL BE DONE ABOUT GETTING AVENAGE FOR THE SHOOTING OF LARRY 3X.
SO VERY MANY DIFFERENT VICIOUS THOUGHTS CROSSED THEIR MINDS THAT THEY BROUGHT FORWARD TO EACH OTHER ATTENTION. SUCH AS GETTING UP EARLY THE NEXT DAY AT 5:00 A.M., AND GOING DOWN TO THE GARAGE WHERE THE SCHOOL BUSS ARE BEING KEPT, AND PUTTING FOUR STICKS OF DYNAMITE INTO THE MUFFLER OF AT LEAST FIVE BUSS, SO THAT WHEN THE BUS DRIVER MAKES HIS ROUND TO PICK UP THE CHILDREN, AND START BRINGING THEM BACK TO SCHOOL THE HEAT FROM THE MOTOR WOULD MAKE THE DYNAMITE AUTOMATICLY START SWEATING, AND BLOW UP KILLING ALL OF THE CHILDREN IN THE SCHOOL BUS ALONG WITH WHO EVER AROUND THE SCHOOL BUS WHEN IT BLOW UP, BECAUSE THE HOT SCHOOL BUS WILL TURN INTO A FRAGMENTATION BOMB THAT WILL KILL ANY, AND EVERYONE THAT IS IN AT LEAST 98 YARDS OF THE BLAST. IT HAD EVEN CROSSED THEIR MINDS OF BUYING HIGH POWER RIFLE, AND GOING DOWN TO THE SAN FRANCISCO AIRPORT, AND HIDING AND COMING OUT AT NIGHTTIME, AND SHOOTING THE T.W.A. AIR PLANE, DOWN OUT OF THE SKY AS THEY WERE TAKING OFF FROM THE RUNWAY. ALSO SHOOTING THE ONE'S DOWN THAT WERE IN THE PROCESS OF LANDING, BUT I HAD CONVINCED THEM THAT IF THEY DID SHOOT THE PLANE DOWN THAT THERE JUST MIGHT BE SOME BLACK MUSLIMS WOMEN OR MEN ON THE PLANE, OR IF THEY WERE SUCCESSFUL IN PUTTING DYNAMITE INTO THE BUS MUFFLER, THE BUSES JUST MIGHT HAVE A LARGE NUMBERS OF BLACK CHILDREN ON IT. BUT THEIR ANSWER WAS, WE DON'T GIVE A DAM IF THEY ARE ON THERE. THEY'LL JUST HAVE TO BE SACRIFICE FOR THE CAUSE OF FREEDOM FOR

Prentice Earl Sanders, the first African-American chief of police in the history of the San Francisco Police Department. Photograph by Inspector Matt Perez, courtesy SFPD.

lende and members of his government armed and attempting to defend themselves while soldiers from the Chilean military fired on them
and jets strafed them from the air, seeming to back up the contention
that Allende and his men were killed by attackers and did not commit
suicide, as the junta that overthrew him claimed.

In San Francisco on Sunday, while thousands gathered at Temple
No. 26, another set of apparently motiveless murders were solved when
Inspectors Frank Falzon and Jack Cleary arrested William Hanson, the
twenty-four-year-old son of a respected psychiatrist who became known
as the Paper Bag killer because he carried a shotgun to his murders in a
paper bag. Despite the weapon used, police had wondered for a time if
the attacks might be linked to the .32-Caliber shootings. However, the
descriptions given by witnesses of a tall, hippie-like young man with
long blond hair ruled that out. The explanation ultimately given for
the crimes was that Hanson had become delusional after the rape of a
girlfriend and shotgunned his victims in the confused belief that he was
killing her rapist.

It was, as Sanders says, "a crazy time."

That morning, the paper reported that the Israelis were fighting
again with the Syrians along the Golan Heights. Muhammad Ali was
preparing for the second in his series of bouts with Joe Frazier, scheduled to take place at Madison Square Garden that night. But the story
that most took Sanders's attention was on page 2, concerning the rally
held the previous day at Temple No. 26 to protest the shooting of Larry
Crosby.

As with the other articles about the Nation of Islam, he began to
cut it out with kitchen scissors. There was a large photograph above the
article, showing a group of men waiting to get into the rally, and
Sanders cut that out, too, stapling both clippings onto a lined yellow
sheet of paper torn from a legal pad, making sure the date was still attached. Then he slipped it in a folder with the other articles he saved,
never noticing a curious detail in the image.

Although everyone else in the photograph is looking ahead
toward the entrance of Temple No. 26, one man is looking to the side,
staring off at something unseen and unknown. That man was Anthony

Harris, pictured on page 2 of the *San Francisco Chronicle,* January 28, 1974.

Sanders closed the folder on Harris's photo and headed out to begin his day, never suspecting that, as he put it later, "the gates of hell were about to open."

7

Operation Zebra

MOST OF THE BUZZ IN HOMICIDE on the morning of January 28 was about William Hanson, the drug-addled Paper Bag murderer whom Falzon and Cleary had busted that weekend. A topic that garnered almost as much discussion was the Ali/Frazier fight, scheduled for that night. Cops tend to be fight fans, and the men of Homicide were no different. Ali had lost his first fight with Frazier in Madison Square Garden in 1971. It was his first loss as a pro, and many of the white cops, who still referred to Ali as "Clay" and considered him to be a draft dodger, were pulling for him to lose again. The black cops tended to feel just the opposite. They may not have thought much of Ali's boastfulness, his flashy style of fighting, or even his membership in the Nation of Islam. Yet the fact that he had stood up against the war in Vietnam and refused to kowtow to white America, incurring its wrath, made him a hero to blacks across the country. The majority felt that they had to support him, even if some of them really preferred Frazier.

"Whites can't always understand that," Sanders explains. "I loved to watch Ali fight. But even if I didn't, I would've had his back if someone put him down. Especially if that person was white. It's not that blacks can't see the faults of other blacks. It's that they see the whole context. What might seem 'boastful' to whites could just be a brother 'signifying' to blacks, doing the same thing rappers do today. But even if I hadn't seen Ali that way, I would have stood up for him. Because I knew what he had to go through to get to where he was.

"I felt the same way about the African Americans I had to deal with on the street. If I could, I'd be there for them. Up until the moment they screwed up so bad I had to arrest them. Then I'd bust their ass so fast, they wouldn't know what happened. But once they paid the price, I'd try to be there for them again if they could get themselves straight and start doing right instead of wrong."

Some acts, however, were so monstrous and so vile, Sanders could never forgive the person who committed them, even if he was able to understand the context in which the urge to commit those acts was born.

The day started slowly at Black Self-Help. Not many workers were there that Monday morning: some, like J. C. Simon and Manuel Moore, still preoccupied by the shooting of Larry Crosby, never even came in. For those who were there, the Ali/Frazier fight was almost certainly as popular a topic as it was in the Hall of Justice. Ali had been a hero to the members of the Nation of Islam ever since he went public with his conversion following his victory against Sonny Liston in February of 1964, and his stature as a hero had risen ever since, bolstered not only by his success in the ring but also by his refusal to fight in Vietnam, making him a figure of such importance inside the Nation that he was perhaps second only to the Messenger himself.

The fight was going to be shown on closed-circuit TV in Winterland Auditorium, at Post and Steiner, just around the corner from Temple No. 26. Tom Manney made sure that everyone who worked at Black Self-Help was able to get a ticket, advancing the money for them if they needed it.

The fight began at 6:30 P.M., and the plan was to stop work early, go to Winterland in a group, and sell copies of Nation of Islam's newspaper, *Muhammad Speaks,* outside the auditorium before the doors opened. For some, though, the idea of attending the fight was displaced by a very different plan, with a far different purpose.

Early that afternoon, J. C. Simon and Manuel Moore drove Tom Manney's 1959 Cadillac to the East Bay, returning across the Bay Bridge just after 4:30 P.M. On the way back, they were stopped by a highway patrolman at the toll plaza and cited for three violations: a cracked windshield, nonfunctional brake lights, and no registration. What they had been doing in between has never been proven, but some investigators believe a meeting was held in Oakland to further discuss how to avenge the shooting of Crosby, who was, it should be recalled, a member of the Nation of Islam's Oakland temple. After Simon and Moore made it back to the city, they could have easily attended the fight if they had wanted to, but they didn't.

Sanders and Gilford also left work early that night. Ever since they had teamed with Coreris and Fotinos on the .32-Caliber killings, they had been working what amounted to an around-the-clock schedule. Now, however, after a month without a shooting, the investigation at a near standstill, and Ali about to take on Joe Frazier, it finally seemed time for an early night.

It was too late to get tickets by the time they left the Hall of Justice, so instead of heading for Winterland, which was about three miles from the Hall of Justice, they went to the Half Note, in the same direction on Divisadero but about a mile closer. They knew the round-by-round results of the fight would be relayed to the club as soon as the round bell rang, and to occupy themselves in the meantime they had music, liquor, and, in Gilford's case, the parade of women who came from all over to take in the famous Fillmore jazz joint.

"Gil liked women, there was no doubt about that," Sanders says with a smile, recalling his friend's charms and weaknesses. "But it'd be wrong to think of him as a womanizer. The truth is, Gil never went looking; women searched him out."

According to Anthony Harris, Simon and Moore showed up at Black Self-Help around 5:00 P.M., just as Harris was leaving to go to Larry Green's apartment on Grove. Green had left early, and Harris thought he would meet up with him. However, Simon told Harris that Green wasn't home but was either at the temple or at the home of Dinah, the woman he had recently married and who lived near it.

Harris was feeling a little hazy. He had been heavily into drugs as a young man and never completely gave them up. The day at Black Self-Help had been so slow that, after Green left, he'd popped a couple of "reds," the street name for the barbiturate Seconal, and though two were not enough to knock him out, he was experiencing their effect. One would think that the meeting of the night before would have given Harris pause when it came to accompanying Simon anywhere.

However, Harris was not one to think things through, and when Simon and Moore offered him a ride in Manney's Cadillac, he accepted.

They drove up Market to Divisadero, then turned right onto "Diviz," as the street is known among locals, and continued north, driving by the Half Note, where Sanders and Gilford were still relaxing with the other regulars, waiting for the bartender to convey phone reports of the fight. Simon continued past Geary to Sutter, where the Temple's Fruit of Islam House, a residence for young men who had joined the temple, was located and where he and Moore thought Green might be. After Simon parked, Harris entered the FOI House while Simon and Moore went in the opposite direction, going on foot toward Geary.

Tana Smith was waiting for a bus.

At thirty-two, Tana had made a new home for herself in San Francisco, having moved to the city from her native Kentucky. As pleasant as the South had been, San Francisco was a whole other world. Tana worked at Bechtel as a secretary. But work was not what had lured her west. It was the place itself. San Francisco was a city with culture, like the opera house where she did volunteer work, and it was vibrantly alive, even on a Monday night when most towns in the South would have already rolled up the sidewalks. In San Francisco, Tana could step out of her apartment in the evening and shop, or go out, or do whatever she wanted and then grab a bus from wherever it was she ended up and make her way home, as she was doing now. Only a week earlier, a mugger had tried to grab her purse, but that didn't deter Tana. San Francisco made her feel welcome. Until suddenly the welcome ran out.

David Benveniste was driving slowly behind a city bus, heading north on Divisadero and nearing Geary, when he heard a sound he didn't recognize. David was an enterprising young florist who, at twenty-three, already owned a shop a few blocks down the street. The only experience David had with murders was that they inevitably led to funerals, and funerals led to flowers. When he looked toward where he heard the sound, though, he had an uneasy sense that something terrible had happened.

A black man was standing at the corner, no more than fifteen feet away. He was about six feet tall, wearing a hat, scarf, and a long coat, and was standing over a woman lying on the sidewalk. David also noticed that the man was holding something in his hand. That was when he finally put it all together. The man was holding a gun; the sound he had heard was gunshots. The woman, David realized, might be dying.

David watched as the man ran east, toward where Temple No. 26 was located. The person he would later identify as holding the gun was J. C. Simon.

Sanders and Gilford were working on their second drinks by the time the fight reached the middle rounds. During the early rounds it seemed that Ali might make quick work of Frazier. But Frazier came back strong, and as the fight reached its midpoint it had grown close, with the outcome wide open.

That's when the call came.

"We thought it was another round being relayed to the bartender. But then he told the person on the line to hold on and brought the phone to Gil. We always called in to work and left a number where we could be reached. Normally, if the Hall of Justice called back, it could be about anything. But this time, Gil and I knew instantly. We could feel it. There had been another shooting."

Gilford learned that the assault had taken place at Divisadero and Geary, barely five blocks away. He and Sanders took off without another word, rushing from the club, dashing to their car, and racing down Divisadero to the crime scene.

Ken Moses heard about the shooting not long after he started his night shift at the Hall of Justice. Some criminalists at the SFPD, like Soji Horikoshi, who grew up in the Fillmore with both Gilford and Coreris and eventually became the head of the crime lab, were civilians. However, criminalists dispatched to the scenes of crimes were sworn SFPD officers with the title of crime scene investigator.

Ken Moses was the SFPD's youngest CSI officer and one of its best, more versed in the science of forensics than most of his other colleagues on the force. It was Moses, who had graduated from Berkeley only a few years earlier, who first saw the similarity in the casings of the bullets that hit Art Agnos and Marietta DiGirolamo, and tipped Mike Luksich to the fact. A trained cop with a detective's instincts, he felt sure this was another of the .32-Caliber shootings, which meant the murder spree had resumed. The sense of gravity this elicited was mixed with a jolt of excitement.

It only took a few minutes for Sanders and Gilford to reach the corner of Divisadero and Geary. The Fillmore still had not lost the edge of fear that followed the December attacks, and news of this latest shooting quickly made its way around the neighborhood, attracting the looky-loos who are drawn to crime scenes the way iron filings are drawn to a magnet. Patrolmen on the scene were having trouble controlling the crowd by the time Sanders and Gilford got there, so they lent a hand in holding back the onlookers even as they tried to help with the investigation by canvassing for potential witnesses.

"I'm very jealous of my crime scene," Sanders says, pointing out what to him is the foremost rule of Homicide. "And if I'm not the investigator in charge, the first way I try to help is to make sure that the crime scene stays pure. There's no telling what kind of damage people walking through can do. It can be the difference between a dead-bang conviction and an unsolved case."

Though Sanders and Gilford did what they could to protect the crime scene, looky-loos kept coming. When the fight ended and Winterland let out only a few blocks away, their numbers would increase exponentially. By then Tana Smith would be officially declared dead at San Francisco's General Hospital and Sanders and Gilford would be gone, pulled away by another call.

Anthony Harris met up again with J. C. Simon and Manuel Moore outside the Nation of Islam's Temple No. 26, at the Shabazz Bakery near the corner of Fillmore and Geary. He still had not found Larry Green. So when Simon offered to give him another ride, Harris, who had heard the gunshots but claims he was oblivious to what was going on, agreed to go, buying a cup of coffee from the bakery, popping two more reds, and then sliding into the back of Manney's black Cadillac as Simon drove off.

*   *   *

Vincent Wollin was heading home.

Wollin, who had turned sixty-nine that day, had retired a few years earlier, having worked both as a cabinetmaker and a sailor with the Coast Guard, and now lived in a rest home by Alamo Square, near the corner of Scott and Grove, not far from Temple No. 26 and only two blocks from the apartment building where Simon, Green, and Moore all lived.

Even though it was his birthday, Wollin kept busy with his usual daily routine, going out to scavenge for things he thought he could use somehow to supplement his fixed income. What he found might be clothes or a toy or an old broken transistor radio that he could fix up and sell. The daily strolls were like a job to Wollin, who left the home each day at 10:00 A.M. and sometimes did not return until late at night. That night he did not return at all.

The shooter was dressed like Tana Smith's killer. But this time there would be no stopping, no staring, no lingering over the kill. He merely approached Wollin on Scott Street between McAllister and Fulton, shot him twice, and ran. One bullet pierced the aging pensioner's heart, killing him almost instantly.

Two more blocks, and he would have been home.

Sanders and Gilford took off from the Tana Smith crime scene as soon as they heard about the second shooting, driving back down Divisadero and turning east on Grove. This was a quieter scene than the one on Divisadero and easier to control. That allowed Sanders and Gilford to help the others there inspect the area, searching for the .32 shell casings they knew would be there somewhere.

Calls over the radio began to multiply between all the investigators involved in the case. Coreris and Fotinos coordinated the response, first from the Hall of Justice and later from the streets as they began to speed from one scene to the next, keeping in contact not only with the inspectors working the scenes with them but also with their superiors, Charlie Ellis and Charlie Barca. Both Ellis and Barca were concerned about the effect these latest shootings could have on an already anxious city. It was for Barca to brief Chief Scott. That high up, the chain of command got into the kind of rarefied political air the Greeks preferred to leave to others, unless forced by necessity to venture there too.

*   *   *

John Bambic existed at the lonely edges of life.

Although he was eighty-four years old, whatever history he had accumulated over the years seemed to have been forgotten by all but him. He lived on Ninth near Folsom, in the shabby run-down area south of Market that in 1974 made up the heart of San Francisco's skid row. Though he shared a room with another old man, no one knew a thing about him, except that he liked to wear a funny hat. Old, sad, and almost anonymous, John Bambic nevertheless did something that no other victim was able to do. He fought for his life.

Bambic was shot in the back, once at waist level and once higher up. The second bullet hit his heart, leaving a centimeter-sized hole in it. Yet the eighty-four-year-old still turned around and grabbed the man who shot him, clutching him in his arms and refusing to let go.

Richard Williams was walking on Howard Street, near Ninth, when he heard two gunshots. Turning the corner, he saw Bambic struggling with a man about six feet tall and wearing a long coat. Unlike the witnesses at the other shootings, Williams could not be sure if the man was black, but he was certain that he was not white.

After a moment of struggle, Bambic fell to the ground and died moments later. The attacker, whose clothes were identical to those worn by the man who had shot Tana Smith and Vincent Wollin and whom others identified as J. C. Simon, ran across the street to a gas station where a Cadillac was waiting, with two men inside. The moment he reached it, the Cadillac sped off, and Williams wasn't able to make out the license plate.

When the call came in about Bambic, Sanders half expected it.

"There'd been a pattern of two shootings in one night. But this night just felt bad. Like there was something coming and you couldn't stop it. And I had a feeling that if our theory was right about members of the Nation being involved, the shooting in Berkeley could take things to a whole other level."

Sanders and Gilford were the first inspectors at the scene of the Bambic killing and, as with the Hosler and Moynihan murders, took charge of the investigation. Though they had lent a hand on the two earlier shootings, this crime scene was theirs. They became the inspectors of record, directing the other police in the investigation in matters from securing the area to talking to anyone who, as Sanders puts it, "knows something, thinks they know something, and don't know shit."

"One challenge when you're talking to witnesses is to discern between what you can trust and what you can't. I'm not talking about people deliberately lying, although that happens too. I'm talking about people who just like to hear themselves talk. Sometimes people like that are gold. But sometimes they'll take you places you have no reason to go, just because they *think* they know all the answers."

Sanders and Gilford spent about an hour at the scene, trying to re-create in their minds what happened and looking for clues. Almost all the people they spoke to from the nearby bars had heard the shots. Clues were scarce, but they were able to find two .32-caliber bullet casings that they were certain would match the others.

Then word came of another shooting. And Sanders and Gilford both began to worry that this was a horror that would not stop. They were not alone.

As news of the shootings began to be reported on television and radio, the city became gripped by panic. A sense of fear had grown in San Francisco throughout December, but subsided with the month-long pause in the shootings. People returned to their normal routines, going out, seeing friends, acting as if the streets were safe. Now, bars and restaurants emptied out. Businesses normally open in the evening hours shut down. Cabbies who heard about the shootings stopped driving. Buses were either filled with people hurrying home or utterly empty.

Ron Baker and Roger Kieval, a young gay couple who lived in the Upper Haight, had gone out that evening for dinner at a family restaurant on Potrero Hill. They were nowhere near a radio or TV, so as far as they were concerned, it was just a pleasant night out. Sirens could be heard now and again in the distance, but even when the sirens became more frequent, nothing about the evening seemed particularly unusual or alarming, until their African-American waiter approached them with a stark look on his face.

"You have to go home," he said. "They're killing white people."

Baker and Kieval looked at the man like he was joking. He was not.

"Please," their waiter repeated, imploring them now, "you have to go home."

Jane Holly was washing clothes.

At forty-five, Jane was known for her selflessness. Despite working full-time for Wells Fargo Bank and taking care of her duties as a mother and wife, Jane Holly had spent years working for the Order of the Eastern Star, a Mason-like charitable group that was open to everyone, men and women of all races, rising in the organization to become the leader of her chapter and achieving the title of Worthy Matron. Jane and her husband, George, lived in Silver Terrace, a mixed-race neighborhood on the rolling hills that surround Silver Avenue, overlooking the Bayview and Hunters Point districts. A busy woman, Jane was taking advantage of a quiet Monday night to get caught up on chores, and headed out to a local Laundromat with a hamper full of dirty clothes. In a situation that was typical for Jane, a woman for whom hate and prejudice seemed inconceivable, she was the only white person there.

Anthony Harris sat in the back of Manney's Cadillac as J. C. Simon drove him and Manuel Moore up Silver Avenue. Harris, who claimed not to have actually witnessed any of the shootings, later said he was growing increasingly uneasy about what was going on, and remained quiet while Simon parked the car and checked out the Laundromat at Silver and Brussels. Noticing activity inside, Simon drove off again and parked around the corner. Then he and Moore got out while Harris stayed behind.

Like Harris, the tall, muscular Manuel Moore was born in southern California. He grew up in the San Bernardino area in a large family that included not only six brothers and seven sisters but also a number of white stepbrothers and stepsisters, the children of his white stepmother. Though Moore attended school through the ninth grade, he was functionally illiterate, unable to read or write. While they lived together, J. C. Simon had been trying to do for Moore what none of his teachers seemed to have done, using photocopies of the "Lessons of Elijah Muhammad" to teach him to read. Simon, like other members of the Nation of Islam, kept these in a binder that he had put together, combining them with other teachings and prayers from the Nation's liturgy. Among them was Lesson No. 10, the passage intended as a metaphorical discussion about killing the devil inside the devil: "Mohammad learned that he could not reform the devils, so they had to be murdered." To someone who can barely read, the subtleties of metaphors tend to get lost.

Lonnie Green, a black U.S. Navy serviceman who was washing clothes in the same Laundromat as Jane Holly, watched as a tall, muscular black man who fit Moore's description in every regard walked in, glanced at him, and then continued on toward Jane Holly as she took clothes out of a dryer. Without hesitating, the man pulled a gun from his waistband and pumped two bullets into the unsuspecting Holly's back, then turned around and started out without speaking a word.

The room erupted in pandemonium. People rushed for the door, and Moore seems to have panicked as well, sprinting past them. Eighteen-year-old Denise Norman and her friend, Vera Lang, had just left another Laundromat down the street and were on their way to their car when they heard the shots. Moments later a black man ran from the Laundromat where the shooting took place, bumped into them, and raced over to a Cadillac they saw parked around the corner. The women heard someone in the car say, "Hey, man, come on, let's get out of here." Then the Cadillac pulled out.

Those with Jane Holly, all of whom were African American, did what they could to help her. But it was no use. The two .32-caliber bullets that entered her, one in the left side of her upper back and the other in the rear of her abdomen, killed her within seconds, taking away a life that had been all about giving.

Coreris and Fotinos took the lead on the Holly killing, speeding to the scene the moment word of it reached them. By now, practically the entire SFPD was either involved in the search for the killers or investigating the shootings. Or, in the case of cops like Sanders, Gilford, Coreris, and Fotinos, doing both.

A number of cops back at the Hall of Justice had begun to chart the locations of the killings, coordinating with those on the street to anticipate where the killers might strike next. Sanders and Gilford realized that if you were following a path from south of Market to Silver Terrace, it would either lead into Hunters Point or else up on the 101 Highway. So, making sure other officers kept their crime scene intact, they raced off on the same path they thought the killers were taking, and, along with other cops in patrol cars, followed Coreris and Fotinos to Silver Terrace, figuring they would decide once they got there whether to go into Hunters or onto the 101. Then one more call came in.

According to Anthony Harris, J. C. Simon took off so fast from the Laundromat where Jane Holly had been shot that the lumbering old Cadillac literally went airborne as it sped over the hills, catching so much air that Harris hit his head on the roof. Wild though it may have been, the ride was a short one, because less than a mile and a half later Simon suddenly pulled to stop. They were in the Excelsior area, on Edinburgh Street, just above Silver Terrace. Up ahead of them, a young white couple was obviously in the process of moving house.

Roxanne McMillian was carrying boxes.

At twenty-three, Roxanne McMillian was a pretty young woman who stood at the threshold of a new life, moving with her four-month-old son and husband, Alan, into a new apartment in the Excelsior so that Alan could start a job selling shoes at the nearby Serramonte Mall. She and Alan had been shuttling back and forth from their car to the apartment for about an hour, carrying in all their worldly belongings while they also tried to get the baby to sleep in his new surroundings. It was a difficult process, and Roxanne went out to grab one last box of clothes from the car while Alan began putting things away to establish at least some sense of order.

Roxanne and Alan had been so involved in what they were doing, they hadn't even thought of turning on a TV or radio. So they knew nothing of the panic sweeping the city, and when the tall African-American man in a long coat and a floppy hat walked toward her as she carried the box from her car to her apartment, Roxanne didn't think twice about it. When he said, "Hi," she simply said, "Hi," back and then started up the stairs.

That was when he fired. The bullet hit her in the back and passed through her body. If that had been the only shot he fired, the damage would have been minimal, but it wasn't. He fired a second time, and that bullet hit Roxanne in her spine, causing her to collapse on the stairs and paralyzing her from the waist down — stopping her, literally, right on the threshold.

Anthony Harris, who had been left alone in the car, heard the shots as he sat in the Cadillac. Moments later, Simon and Moore came running back. They jumped in and sped off once again before the police could get anywhere close.

Sanders and Gilford were nearing the Laundromat on Silver Avenue when they got the call about the shooting on Edinburgh, so they raced there instead. By the time they arrived, Sanders knew that whatever chance they had of catching the killers had ended. From Edinburgh the killers could go almost anywhere, heading down Alemany or Mission or Bay Shore, or hopping onto the 101 Freeway and getting anywhere from San Jose to the south or Richmond to the northeast, or any point in between, in under an hour.

Sanders, Gilford, Coreris, Fotinos, and most of the rest of the SFPD worked that night until dawn. Some worked even longer.

Ken Moses, who had to go from one killing to the next, making sure every crime scene had been scrutinized inch by inch and bringing in huge banks of lights to illuminate whole streets when he had to, kept himself steeled against the horrors of the night and worked the way he always did, taking his time, puffing his pipe, and letting no one rush him, knowing that anything in the path of a killer or victim could end up being evidence.

By the time Moses got to Ninth and Howard, where John Bambic's body still lay cordoned off within the crime scene, it was close to midnight. Sanders and Gilford were there, too, having come back from Edinburgh Street to verify that the investigation under their watch was done as close to perfectly as possible. While Ken Moses could keep up a professional detachment, however, Earl Sanders could not.

Even in the cool air, the smell of Bambic's body had begun to ripen, mixing with the booze and urine odors that permeated the skid-row streets south of Market. Sanders took in the stench and the sadness as he gazed at the eighty-four-year-old man whose senseless murder he was trying to solve and who was now splayed out on the concrete, lying on his back, one leg tucked under the other, staring sightlessly up at the dark sky. The insanity of the whole night weighed down on Sanders, and for a moment he was unable to fend off any of the emotions it triggered and that swamped him with a sudden mix of frustration, anger, and dismay.

"When the killing was happening, none of us had time to think about it. It just kept coming, and it was all we could do to keep up. But when it ended, it hit me. Five shot. Four dead. In one night. And no matter what we did, or how fast we drove, or how many of us flooded onto the streets, we couldn't stop it.

"It felt like the gates of hell had opened up and something evil swarmed out. It was a feeling that grabbed your stomach and wouldn't let go. Because as bad as that night was, what made it worse was we didn't have a clue when it would end."

There was one more shooting on the night of January 28, but not in San Francisco. This one happened across the bay in Emeryville. Although it was never officially tied in with the other five, the circumstantial evidence seems persuasive that it was related.

The incident took place around one in the morning, long after the bloody spree had stopped in San Francisco, as Thomas Bates, a twenty-six-year-old from Massachusetts visiting the Bay Area, was hitchhiking at the Emeryville on-ramp leading to the Bay Bridge to catch a ride to the city.

Earlier in the day, J. C. Simon and Manuel Moore had driven to the East Bay for what some investigators believe may have been a meeting to discuss a response to the shooting of Larry Crosby. If that were the case, then it would make sense that Simon and Moore might have returned to the East Bay at the end of the night, for a follow-up to the earlier meeting. If they did, it would be logical for them on their way back to San Francisco to take an on-ramp leading to the Bay Bridge right around one in the morning.

Bates was hopeful when he saw a dark-colored Cadillac with two black men in it pull over as it approached the on-ramp. Instead of opening a door for him, though, one man rolled down the window and, without reason or warning, pointed a gun at him and fired three shots, hitting him in his hip, stomach, and arm. Then the Cadillac raced away, driving up the ramp and disappearing across the bridge, into the night.

Bates staggered to a nearby Holiday Inn. No slugs were found in his body. And no bullet casings were ever found at the scene. But according to the doctor who treated him, the wounds were consistent with what one would expect from the impact of a .32-caliber cartridge.

The headlines the next few days seemed to cry out in ways that the victims never could:

> S.F. Killing Spree.
> Two-Hour Death Drive.
> The City Grows Edgy.

The news that had dominated the press in January — Watergate, Arab terrorism, the oil crisis, even the furor surrounding the movie *The Exorcist* — drowning out all else in the media, suddenly receded. Overnight the murders pushed the .32-Caliber shootings back to center stage. Death, as the saying goes, has a way of focusing the mind. Four dead and one paralyzed in one night made the citizens of San Francisco focused beyond compare.

"They're killing white people, you have to go home": the warning given to the gay couple on Potrero Hill became the shared fear of every white person in San Francisco. The city became a ghost town. No one went out at night. Restaurants, bars, and theaters remained empty. If they could, people stayed home during the day as well. It was like London during the Blitz. Fear gripped San Francisco in a way it never had before, crippling it with a citywide paralysis.

It wasn't just whites who were frozen by fear, either. Nonwhites felt it, too, especially blacks, who worried that revenge attacks by whites might come next, causing the terror to spiral even further out of control.

Herb Caen, the ubiquitous columnist who covered San Francisco for some fifty years, reported in a *San Francisco Chronicle* column soon after the bloody night of January 28 that he had received a call in his office from a man who told him, "You read the paper, right? Five white men dead, right? Tonight, we're goin' out and getting us ten black men. Two for one is about right, don'tcha think??" With that, Caen reported, the man hung up.

The caller got his figures wrong. There were four dead, not five. And one of them was a woman. But even if he was fuzzy on the facts, his sentiment, and the hateful rage that fueled it, was clear.

Sanders vividly recalls the foreboding that the killings created inside the black community.

"People were frightened by how anonymous the killing was. And how mysterious the killers were. And how crazy it all seemed. Blacks might understand rage, but not the kind of insane rage that results in mindless killing. But there was something else, too. Historically, when blacks lashed out with violence, whites came back with even more. And the call Herb Caen got was exactly what people feared."

What is more, in Sanders's opinion, a white backlash was probably exactly what the killers wanted: "If they were what we thought they were, they wanted their rage to create more rage, among blacks and whites. They wanted an uprising, a race war. And if that call was any indication, we were on the verge of giving them exactly what they wanted."

The fear that pervaded the streets of every neighborhood and was made manifest in the headlines did not stop there. It resounded in the hallways and backrooms of the two buildings that rule over San Francisco, City Hall and the Hall of Justice.

Joseph Alioto was a passionate and often impetuous mayor who seemed dominated by two qualities above all others: his love for the city of San Francisco and a willful, stubborn belief that he was always right. Born in what was then the rough-and-tumble Italian immigrant ghetto of North Beach, the young Alioto competed as an amateur boxer, and that training showed in his tough and combative approach to running the city he so loved.

Alioto had been a successful San Francisco lawyer when the sudden death of the man he was then supporting for mayor thrust him into politics. The candidate who died, Eugene McAteer, had been favored to win, and Alioto, a charismatic speaker with a savvy that made up for his lack of political experience, won in his place.

Alioto was a controversial figure from the start. Prone to speaking first and thinking later, he made enemies as quickly as he did coalitions. Although he was a liberal, his relationship with the city's black community was often prickly. When the Officers for Justice was first formed, for instance, Alioto spoke out against it, siding with the old-boys' network that ruled the SFPD and calling the OFJ a "segregationist organization."

Alioto's shoot-from-the-hip approach to running the city, and his unbridled mouth, ruffled the feathers of many over the years. Nevertheless, he was a rising force in Democratic politics. After an impassioned speech introducing Hubert Humphrey at the 1968 Democratic Convention, he became the favorite to be Humphrey's pick for vice president. Then *Look* magazine printed an article that linked Alioto to organized crime, and Humphrey passed him over. Alioto sued *Look* for slander, but the damage was done. Even so, he remained unbowed. As the .32-Caliber shootings flared into a crisis, he was running in the California Democratic primary for governor and once more was among the favorites.

Alioto's first response to the crisis was to give Chief Donald Scott and Chief of Inspectors Charlie Barca, in his capacity as supervisor of all the investigative bureaus, the authority to begin the largest manhunt in the city's history. Then Alioto canceled a trip he had planned to Washington, D.C., so he could maintain hands-on control. The next morning, January 29, Alioto, Scott, and Barca held a press conference at which they were joined by the heads of Homicide and other bureaus, to announce plans for the operation, which was to be code-named "Zebra" because the Z channel on police radios, known as "Z for Zebra," was being dedicated for use by the manhunt.

Charlie Barca took the lead at the press conference, setting forth the plan for the historic task force and underscoring that it was to be comprised of men from every unit in the department. Barca went on to

appeal for help to people in the communities where the killings had occurred. "This is a case where the public will be our best detectives," Barca
said, assuring anonymity to anyone who came forward with information.

Gus Coreris and John Fotinos were put in charge of the new, expanded task force. The involvement of Sanders and Gilford, however,
as the only African-American Homicide inspectors, remained critical.
The killings mostly took place in areas where the killers themselves felt
comfortable, communities that were either African American, like the
Fillmore, or mixed, like Potrero Hill and Silver Terrace, places where
the access available to white police officers could often be limited. Yet
even the access of black officers was fragile, dependent on the broader
relationship between the community and the police force as a whole.

"When a police department burns a community too often," Sanders explains. "It doesn't matter if a cop is black or white. They won't
be trusted. When that happens, you lose those 'best detectives' that
Barca talked about. Because the whole community becomes blind, deaf,
and dumb."

At the start of Operation Zebra, Sanders thought that was a lesson the department understood. In time, however, he would realize he
was wrong.

Something else Barca said during the press conference struck
Sanders at the time and made him question just how honest Barca
really wanted to be with the public. When asked whether or not a radical group or sect might have been responsible for the shootings, Barca
answered, "There is no hard or soft evidence to support such a theory."

No concrete evidence perhaps. But given what Sanders had read
about the shooting of Larry Crosby and the rally for him, along with
the fact that he, Gilford, Fotinos, and others had already discussed a
possible connection between members of the Nation of Islam and the
earlier attacks, the existence of "soft evidence" seemed undeniable.
Barca was obviously holding back information for a reason. As for motive, the department had already theorized the connection between the
shooting of Larry Crosby in the East Bay and the possibility that revenge was at least part of what fueled the shootings the night before —
but Barca didn't mention that either, of course.

Richard Hague, who was still recovering from the attack on him and his wife, gave an interview to the *San Francisco Chronicle* later that day. In it, he outlined what he had been told by some of the higher-ups in the SFPD who were part of the investigation. According to Hague, who was referred to as "Smith" in the article out of fear that the information might cause the perpetrators to come after him in retribution, he was told that some units in the SFPD were working with both state and federal investigators to develop evidence that might conclusively link an unnamed group to the attacks. Hague also said that these investigators saw the attacks as "a very terrifying form of terrorism."

It was the Intelligence Bureau, led by Lieutenant Paul Lawler, that normally had the most contact with federal and state agencies. The involvement of outside agencies in SFPD investigations varied from case to case. In this instance their role was mostly advisory, especially when it came to the FBI, which was distracted at the time by Watergate and by the controversy that arose when its covert intelligence program COINTELPRO, targeting the Nation of Islam among other groups, was exposed to the public. Even so, whether the notion of terrorism applied to the Zebra attacks had been under discussion between higher-ups in the SFPD and outside agencies since the wave of shootings in December. Those in Homicide, including Sanders and Gilford, had their own theories, which they communicated up the chain of command, but they were not always kept abreast of discussions going on between the Intelligence Bureau and outside agencies. Richard Hague's interview was the first time they heard the word *terrorism* used in public to describe the Zebra attacks. Once spoken, the word stuck.

Terrorism. How else could one describe it?

After the January 28 attacks, the collaboration between the SFPD and the state stepped up considerably. Dick Walley, a high-ranking investigator with the California Department of Justice who had been looking into the rash of motiveless killings around the state, began to collaborate not only with the Intelligence Bureau but directly with Homicide, especially Gus Coreris, making available the results of the state's investigation. Working in tandem with Lawler, Walley and other investigators from the Department of Justice arranged for a huge aerial

lens, the kind designed for use by the CIA in spy planes, to be modi-
fied for ground use and attached it to a surveillance camera. Lawler had
a team from his unit then set up the powerful camera at the top of the
Miyako Hotel, on Geary in San Francisco's Japantown. From there
they had an unobstructed view of the Nation of Islam's Temple No. 26,
and they began to monitor activity there around the clock.

The department might not be ready to admit it publicly yet, but
those at the highest levels were drawing the same conclusions that
Sanders, Fotinos, Gilford, and others had about a possible connection
between Zebra and the Nation of Islam. The problem was how to
prove it.

The fear experienced by the citizens of San Francisco was not just an
abstract thing for Sanders. It was as physically and emotionally real to
him as were his wife and his children.

"When fear grips a city, it does the same thing to cops and their
families as it does to everyone else. It's just that the cops can't show it
when they're on the street. But sometimes that makes it even worse.

"I was living and breathing those killings. I'd seen the bodies, I'd
smelled the blood, and I'd heard the sobs of the victims' families. One
of the homicides that Gil and I handled, the nineteen-year-old Moynihan, was holding a teddy bear that he got for his baby sister when he
died. His parents were good people, and they were devastated. Why
shouldn't they be? What had their son ever done? His murder wasn't
just a crime; it was something so vile that it's hard to see how it could
ever be atoned.

"But my job wasn't just to think of the victims. I had to catch the
killers. And to do that, I had to figure out why they killed. From what
I could see, the one thing that seemed to guide every other possible
motive, whether it was to start up a race war or just avenge what they
saw as injustice, was rage. A crazy, insane rage over what they thought
whites had done to blacks. Once you got to that realization, if you were
black, you had to pause. Because the truth was there wasn't a black I
knew who didn't feel at least an inkling of the same thing.

"I don't mean the kind of rage that makes you want to murder.

That's madness. I'm talking about the kind of anger that makes you want to change the world underneath your feet; that makes you want to do away with hate, not add to it. That's a righteous kind of anger, the sort that any black who had to grow up around racism has every right to embrace. But they had taken that righteous anger and twisted it into something evil, and that made me hate the killers almost as much as the killing did. Because I felt violated, too. They had stolen my own righteous anger and turned it into something sick.

"I used to wonder sometimes what would've happened if someone tried to tar me with what those killers were doing. That was a fear a lot of blacks felt — of getting lumped in the same boat with the killers, looked on by whites like we might be capable of that, too. As close as I was to the case, and as hard as I was working at trying to catch those killers, I kept wondering how I'd react if I'd had something like that thrown at me. What kind of rage I'd feel. And what I would do."

The anxiety afflicting the city was ratcheted up a notch when, for the first time in San Francisco's history, the police issued a warning to all residents to stay off the street at night or, if they had to go out, to travel only in twos and threes. One incident that captures just how crazy things became occurred two nights after the assaults of the twenty-eighth. As Sanders recalls:

"A white woman was grabbed by a black guy and dragged into a Cadillac. The guy told her not to worry because he wasn't one of those 'Zebra killers.' Then he raped her. It was sad. But it was also surreal. When rapists reassure women by saying they're not mass murderers, you know things are out of control."

As if the atmosphere in the city wasn't tense enough, the *Chronicle* received a creepy letter that was alleged to be from the Zodiac killer, the first from him in over three years. Bill Armstrong, who along with Dave Toschi was the lead investigator on Zodiac, believed it to be genuine. In Armstrong's opinion, Zodiac was even more interested in publicity than in killing, and the letter was his attempt to steal Zebra's thunder. Apparently, one infamous serial killer had become jealous of the attention being paid to others, and, in an insane mass-murder competition, was trying to wrest the media's spotlight back in his direction.

Then another letter to a news organization, this time KGO-TV, the ABC affiliate in San Francisco, seemed to take credit for the shootings. This one purported to be from the Symbionese Liberation Army, the same group that had claimed responsibility for slaying Marcus Foster. Postmarked on January 30, two days after the attacks, it predicted, "Any day now there will be more killing and more shooting," and went on to call for the release of Joseph Remiro and Russell Little, the men charged with Foster's murder. Nothing in the letter indicated any knowledge of the shootings beyond what one could have read in the newspaper, so in the minds of most investigators there was little reason to think it was anything other than a hoax or an attempt by the SLA to add to their notoriety.

Even so, the seeds were sown in the minds of some that a connection might exist. Although the SLA was unknown before the murder of Marcus Foster, since then they had been using letters and communiqués filled with incendiary rhetoric to gain increased media exposure, joining the legion of other shadowy, secretive groups in the Bay Area like the Weathermen and the Black Liberation Army. Like the latter group, the SLA was believed to be an alliance of black and white radicals. Most in Homicide did not take the letter seriously, but others, especially in the SFPD brass, felt it was worthy of serious consideration.

The inspectors in Homicide, meanwhile, followed their own lines of inquiry. There were numerous witnesses to the January 28 shootings, and the detectives patiently questioned all of them, trying to elicit descriptions of the killers or obtain an ID by showing arrays of photographs of various possible suspects. Nevertheless, they were hindered in the investigation by the very randomness of the crimes. Little in the way of physical evidence ever surfaced, and even as they were dragging out the photographs, everyone knew that the perpetrators were almost certainly not among their lists of usual suspects.

These were not just any homicides, nor were they just a string of serial murders. This was a kind of killing for which there was little precedent in American policing, at least since the early part of the century. As Richard Hague stated so eloquently in the *Chronicle,* this was terrorism, a variety of crime with a uniquely senseless logic to it, and a new way of investigating had to be devised to deal with it.

Recognizing the possible connection between the incident with Larry Crosby and the shootings of January 28, Sanders, Gilford, Coreris, and Fotinos tried to figure out a way to pierce the veil of solidarity surrounding the Nation of Islam and determine whether or not its members might be involved. However, doing so was harder than one might think. Real cops are not movie cops. They cannot act without evidence, warrants, or some sort of probable cause.

Complicating matters was the fact that the Nation of Islam is a religion, and as such protected by a battery of constitutional rights. The first line of the first article of the Bill of Rights reads: "Congress shall make no law respecting an establishment of religion, or prohibiting the free exercise thereof." Doing anything that is seen as contravening those words can bring a gale wind of legal wrath down on a police department.

In this case, the constitutional barrier was reinforced by the insular nature of the Nation of Islam. With most radical groups like the Panthers or prison gangs like the Black Guerilla Family, cops can achieve some degree of access, especially black cops who have established a measure of trust in the community and can use it to get to informers. But not with the Nation of Islam. That organization was simply too tightly wound to be compromised in such a way.

Part of the reason for this insularity was the Nation's combination of politics and faith. Groups that are merely political can be discredited by their results or lack thereof. To the faithful, however, there is no way to debunk a religion. Their truth is their truth, and it is unassailable.

Another part of the reason was the Nation's internal division in the 1960s and '70s and the revenge its leadership had taken against those who had quit. The Nation of Islam made a practice of shunning ex-members. More than that, the fate of many who had left and then dared to speak out against the Nation in those days served to silence potential informants. Malcolm X was the best-known example of the kind of retribution that the Nation could take back then against former members, who were considered apostates. But he was not the only one, and the legacy of violence within the Nation had a chilling effect on many who might otherwise have spoken out against it.

Yet the bloodshed of January 28 made the investigators in Homicide determined to find some sort of avenue into the Nation. Both Sanders and Gilford suspected that a few African-American officers in the SFPD might be members. Not surprisingly, those officers tried their best to keep their membership a secret and were unwilling to speak about it even with other black officers. There was no way they could be used as sources. The only avenue Sanders could think to turn to was a personal one, a friend of his named Ron Hilton.

Sanders and Hilton had been close growing up. They had played football together in high school and hung out on "the 'More," as Fillmore was called by those who frequented it most. Then Hilton was drafted, went to Vietnam, and came back addicted to heroin. Sanders had tried hard to help him beat the drug but was powerless to break his addiction. When Hilton joined the Nation of Islam, they were able to do for him what his friends could not, and Hilton got clean.

"The Nation of Islam is a different organization now than it was then," Sanders explains. "It does wonderful things now, without the secrecy and negativity that often seemed present then. But what Ron went through made me see how positive a force it could be even then. I started to think that if I could talk to Ron, I might be able to convince him to help me get to the bottom of whether or not a connection existed between some rogue element inside the Nation and Zebra. Because if there was, it was a cancer. And it could destroy all the good the Nation did."

Less than a week after the night of January 28, Earl Sanders began to seek out his old friend, determined to find some way to open a window into the Nation of Islam. However, before he or anyone else on the task force could make any progress in that direction, something happened that turned the investigation, and the entire Bay Area, on its head, and stopped them all in their tracks.

Patty Hearst was kidnapped by the SLA.

8

Patty

"ONE YEAR OF WATERGATE IS ENOUGH."

Richard Nixon's message in his 1974 State of the Union address sounded like a plea that he might wake up from a bad dream. But a few days later, the House of Representatives responded by voting to broaden the powers of the Judiciary Committee's impeachment probe, allowing the committee to subpoena anyone of interest to the investigation, including the president. The vote was a resounding 410 to 4, demonstrating overwhelming support for the committee's work investigating Watergate. One year of Watergate, unfortunately for Nixon, would not be enough.

He wasn't the only politician starting off 1974 on the wrong foot. Just a week or so before the tragedy of January 28, Joseph Alioto, locked in a contentious primary battle against Jerry Brown for the Democratic nomination for governor, suddenly found his marriage in shambles and himself blindsided by the frightening meltdown of his wife, Angelina.

At fifty-eight, Angelina Alioto was still strikingly beautiful, elegant, and every bit as willful as her husband. They had always had a tempestuous relationship, but the friction between them combusted when Alioto failed to introduce Angelina, who was sitting by his side, to the adoring crowd at a campaign dinner in Palm Springs. Feeling jealous and ignored, Angelina absconded, running away from home without telling anyone where she was going or what she was doing.

Traveling under the alias Angelina DiPuma, which had been her grandmother's name, the mayor's wife rented a car and began a leisurely eighteen-day tour of the California missions, using her disappearance as a way to get back at her husband. It worked.

Afraid that Angelina might have been kidnapped or even killed, Alioto mobilized the SFPD in an effort to find her, keeping the entire matter far from the public eye and never letting on about his worries to either the press or his opponents in the Democratic primary. Despite the search, Angelina stayed hidden until the SFPD finally went public, issuing an all-points bulletin just six days after the bloody night of January 28. When Angelina heard a report about herself on a Santa Cruz radio station, she decided to come out of hiding and return to both the city and her husband.

The next day, she and Alioto gave a bizarre and oddly embarrassing press conference. Here was the mayor of a city racked by trauma, trying to run what could be the most important political race of his career, airing his marital woes in public, with his wife telling the world that she felt "neglected." When asked whether or not she had ever considered divorcing her husband, Angelina answered in a way that was meant to be ironic but came out as startlingly inappropriate: "Actually, it wasn't dissolution I was thinking of. It was murder."

Given the wave of murders that had just swept across the city, it is understandable that the *San Francisco Chronicle* should describe Alioto as being "unnaturally pale" during the press conference. As bad as he must have felt, however, things were about to get worse.

At nineteen, Patricia Hearst was a rather pampered college sophomore who could have had any advantage she wanted while attending the University of California at Berkeley. Yet, although she was the granddaughter of tycoon William Randolph Hearst, with a mother on the California Board of Regents and a father who was the chairman of one of the largest and most influential media conglomerates in the nation, Patty seemed unaffected by her status, moving across the bay to Berkeley's student ghetto, blending in with classmates and living with her fiancé, Steven Weed, who once taught Patty math at an exclusive girls' school and was now a Ph.D. candidate in philosophy at Cal. Patty appeared to want a taste of the real Berkeley experience, and by all reports from friends and family she was enjoying an idyllic college life. Then, in one harrowing night, Patty Hearst's perfect college idyll ended.

At about 9:15 P.M. on Monday, February 4, one week after San Francisco had been terrorized by a night of bloodshed, a woman and two men knocked on the door of the apartment Patty shared with Steven Weed and then barged in once it was opened, beating, gagging, and blindfolding Weed and dragging off Patty as what they called a "prisoner of war." One of the male kidnappers was Donald DeFreeze, the SLA's African-American leader; the other was Bill Harris, a Caucasian. However, Weed, confused by his beating, reported that both men were black. With the SLA's letter to KGO-TV about Zebra still fresh in their minds, some at the police department made a link between the two events, turning the attention of Chief Scott as well as others in leadership and Mayor Alioto, who had ultimate authority, away from the Nation of Islam and toward the shadowy Symbionese Liberation Army. Many of the investigators who had been concentrating solely on Zebra were now forced to divide their focus.

"Most of us in Homicide never thought the SLA was involved in Zebra," Sanders recalls. "The m.o. of Zebra was different from what the SLA did. But some of the brass got it in their heads that it might be connected, and a lot of our manpower went in that direction. You can't blame them. The daughter of one of the richest men in the city got kidnapped, and everybody, from Alioto on down, wanted to get her back. And get her back *alive*."

There was also a political dimension to the decision. As Sanders explains: "Zebra wasn't just any murder case. It was a case that had the kind of political implications that can define careers, both for the brass inside the department and politicians outside it. People wanted results. And if focusing on the shootings didn't get them, then some people started to think that maybe looking into the Hearst case would."

Nor was it only the SFPD that shifted attention to the kidnapping. Overnight, the saga of Patty and the SLA subsumed all the other radical stories in the media and overwhelmed the Zebra assaults. The press literally camped out on the front lawn of Randolph Hearst's palatial mansion as he began to negotiate in public with the SLA, answering the communiqués they released with press conferences.

"Greetings to the people, and fellow comrades, and brothers and sisters," began one early statement by the SLA. It went on to claim that Patty had been "arrested" for crimes her mother and father had committed, cataloging a laundry list of corporations in which they played a role, and demanding an unrealistic array of "good faith gestures" from the parents to secure Patty's well-being. "Death to the fascist insect that preys upon the life of the people" was the ending for this and most of the other SLA communiqués. Yet no matter how outrageous their demands or insulting their invective, Randolph Hearst would always step up to the microphones that had become semipermanent fixtures on his front lawn and deliver a measured response, trying to reason in the face of violence with the revolutionaries who held his daughter captive.

This colloquy would dominate the newspapers and airwaves for nearly two full months, until, in another headline-grabbing story, Patty declared that she had taken the nom de guerre of Tania, and the resolution to the kidnapping that had seemed so near suddenly melted away.

Meanwhile, the Zebra investigation continued to run into dead ends, despite the string of new cases from the January 28 attacks and the eyewitness accounts of the shootings. Another development complicated matters. Although the gun used on January 28 was a .32, it was different from the one that had been used before. Mike Luksich, the weapons expert, initially couldn't determine whether the new shootings involved multiple guns or not, but eventually he was able to match the markings on all the casings and slugs collected from January 28. Once again, a single gun was used, but the investigators were certain now that there was more than one assailant. As Sanders explains:

"The descriptions the witnesses gave us, both during the December shootings and on the night of January 28, were varied enough that we knew there had to be more than one perpetrator. Even so, they made a habit of using one gun over and over. Professional killers use a gun once and then get rid of it, hoping it won't be traced. This crew was doing just the opposite. They *wanted* us to link the shootings. The bullets were like calling cards, a way of taking credit for each shooting.

That was one more factor that made most of us on Homicide certain a radical group was behind it all, and after that long night of bloodshed we were more determined than ever to find out who it was."

Yet once again their efforts were stymied by a simple fact: the shooters, so tantalizingly close on January 28, seemed to have gone underground, vanishing the way violent winds do, leaving little in the way of evidence apart from the devastation they had spawned. As in December, no one on the street knew anything about who they were or where they might have gone. It was time to reassess.

"When an investigation seems to hit a wall, you try to look at it from every angle possible." Sanders frowns as he thinks back about how the investigation had stalled, as if the frustration still rankles. "One thing you start to do is look at the timeline, especially with multiple or serial killings. When each assault took place, and what came before it. And from looking at the patterns, there always seemed to be some incident that preceded the attacks. The incident with Crosby was an obvious precursor to the shootings of the twenty-eighth. But as Gil and I looked it all over, there seemed to be others, too.

"It had come out in early December that the FBI had been trying to infiltrate the Nation of Islam as part of COINTELPRO. That was followed by the incident in the Federal Building, where an FBI agent shot a young kid from Hunters Point, George Session, in the back. Just a few days later the December shootings began: Dancik, Agnos, Di-Girolamo, Bertuccio, DeMartini, then Moynihan and Hosler.

"But when it became news and we covered the streets in search of the killers, the shootings stopped. For a while, everything was quiet. Then came the Crosby shooting, which was followed by the five attacks in one night. Then the press went wild again, and the killers went silent.

"It was like they were playing a cat-and-mouse game with us. Almost as if they were fighting guerrilla style, getting in licks, then laying low when things got too hot. And then when the time came, striking again."

In the wake of the shootings of January 28, Anthony Harris quit working at Black Self-Help Moving and Storage. Harris later claimed that he had been unnerved by the events of that night, and felt his own life was in danger. Thomas Manney, the owner of Black Self-Help, disputed that, claiming he had fired Harris. Yet Harris may also have been unnerved by something else. The fact that his picture had been printed in the *San Francisco Chronicle* on the day of the shootings did not in itself link him to the assaults. It is easy to see, however, how someone who spent most of his life either in jail or trying to avoid it might feel vulnerable on seeing his image tied so directly to the rally in support of Larry Crosby, knowing, as Harris claimed he did, that the shooting of Crosby was the real motive behind the assaults in which he had been involved as an accomplice at the very least.

Regardless of the reason, Harris moved to Oakland with Deborah, the woman with whom he had been living, and cut himself off from Black Self-Help and the men who worked there. The one exception was Larry Green. With him, Harris still retained a sense of friendship and remained in at least intermittent contact.

In the days that followed January 28, the others from Black Self-Help went about their business with an air of normalcy. Green involved himself in his work with both the temple and Black Self-Help, and also threw himself into his new marriage, devoting time to be with the son to whom he had become a stepfather. J. C. Simon and Manuel Moore made plans for a trip to Chicago at the end of February for the Savior's Day festival, held each year at the temple's headquarters to honor the Nation's founder.

This return to normalcy may have been attributable to survival instinct, given that swarms of police filled the streets in the weeks after the attacks. As Sanders points out, it might also have been a tactical choice.

"You see the same pattern with a lot of terrorist groups. There'll be a surge in violence that creates a wave of fear in the public and makes the police step up their investigation. So the terrorists shut down for a while. Eventually they come back with another surge, and when they do the wave of fear that follows grows exponentially, getting bigger than ever."

Meanwhile, the effort to establish some source within the Nation went nowhere. "I did everything I could to get in touch with Ron Hilton, my old friend who had joined the Nation," Sanders recalls. "I heard he moved back east to New York, but every lead on how to get in touch with him washed out. It was like he disappeared."

Gilford tried to follow a similar avenue by reaching out to Dwight Stallings, whose family he knew well and who by coincidence worked at Black Self-Help. In high school, Gilford had been good friends with Stallings's older brothers, and the much younger Dwight had looked up to Gilford, following him around like a protégé or mascot. As Sanders recounts, "Stallings had big ears like Gilford, who had ears so big as a kid that his mother took to calling him Jughead. Stallings became 'Little Jug.' They were close when Stallings was a kid in the fifties. Even in the sixties they stayed in touch, with Stallings serving as a pretty good source for Gil. But in the late sixties, Stallings hooked up with radical groups, and when he got involved in the Nation, he cut Gil off. It was part of the whole insular nature of the Nation back then. If you weren't a believer, you couldn't be part of it. They created a walled-in world. And without the kind of solid evidence that would allow us to get warrants, there was no way we could tear the walls down."

As February progressed toward March, the Patty Hearst kidnapping continued to merit banner headlines in the local papers, while the Zebra case, with no new shootings, faded from view. With the SFPD brass putting so much emphasis on solving the kidnapping, Sanders and Gilford began to spend more of their time investigating it, tapping their sources in the black and radical communities in both San Francisco and in the East Bay to develop information about where she was, the names of the individuals who had taken her, and what links there might be between her abductors and other radical crimes.

"A lot of the information we gathered had to do with safe houses, the loose network of places radicals stayed when they had to go underground. We checked out endless safe houses on the East Bay, in Berkeley and Oakland."

Their digging may not have uncovered Patty Hearst's whereabouts, but it did take them deep into a political netherworld where radical ideology and crime mixed in ways that made them seem inseparable. One such case involved the Black Guerrilla Family, the organization that George Jackson had started in prison, which tended to function as much like a gang as it did a radical cadre.

"Between Zebra and Patty, the whole Homicide Bureau was at a point where we were literally worked around the clock again," Sanders recalls, "and one night Gil and I got a case tossed at us at about one A.M. A call came in about a white girl who got killed out in Bernal Heights, up above the Mission, first strangled and then shot in the face with a nine-millimeter. Our first worry was it might another Zebra killing, only this time using another gun. But when we did a little digging, we learned the victim was connected to the prison movement.

"What a lot of the groups did, especially the ones based in the prisons, was use girls as couriers, mostly white girls in their twenties who could go pretty much anywhere without being stopped or looked on with suspicion. This girl had been suspected of being an informant by some of the movement guys she worked with, and they killed her, but no one that we talked to knew who her contacts were.

"Then around dawn one of our insurance policies told us she'd been hanging out with a guy named Lawrence Fields, who just got out of Quentin and was staying at a halfway house on Twentieth Street in Oakland. So we went to the East Bay, hooked up with an Oakland cop we knew, and headed over to where he was staying.

"As soon as we got there, we saw him. Lawrence was short, maybe five-six, like a fireplug with legs. And he was right there in front, walking down the porch of the halfway house.

"Well, Lawrence took one look at us, reached in his waistband, and started running. We all took off after him. He kept looking back, with his hand tucked in his pants. But when he got his gun out, he bumped into this woman he didn't see. The two of them went sprawling, and the gun skittered across the sidewalk. I leaped on top of Lawrence, got my own gun out, and told him if he moved, I'd blow his ugly head off. Then Gil picked up the gun. Sure enough, it was a nine-millimeter, and the bullets matched the ones that killed the girl.

"That wasn't the end of it. The girl had a boyfriend who was a lifer in Quentin and a major player in the Black Guerrilla Family. But he loved that girl. When he heard what they did to her, strangling her and then shooting her in the face, he decided to roll on everybody. It's hard to get a source in prison to do something like that, because most times they get killed. But he was so angry he didn't care. He just wanted to get the guys who hurt his girl."

One tip in early March, about a month after Patty had been abducted, sounded like it might be the real deal and lead to a break in Zebra. And once again, it started with a woman.

"There was a character named Shabazz who used to try to stir up stuff in the Fillmore. Shabazz was the name that Malcolm X took before he died, so it became popular among people in the Nation and outside it. This guy was somewhere in between. He'd hung out on the fringes of Temple No. 26, but he was only on the edges of the scene there, spending as much or more time with other groups, like the Panthers and the BLA. In the language of the streets, he was the sort who could 'talk more shit than a Christmas turkey.' You could only believe every other word he said, and that was probably being generous. But he was someone who always wanted to be a mover and shaker.

"Ambition like that drove a lot of the guys who hung out on the radical fringes back then. A decade earlier, some of them would probably just be crooks trying to get over. But one of the best ways to get juice in the seventies was to be a radical, the more extreme the better. That was what Shabazz was trying to do in the Fillmore.

"But like a lot of wannabes, he'd promise one thing and then do another. And a woman who was tired of being lied to came to Gil and me and rolled on him. According to her, Shabazz and his crew had turned an old rooming house at the corner of Fillmore and Fulton into a fort, lining the walls with steel plates, even putting them over the windows and leaving little holes for high-powered rifles. She said they were going to go out at night and shoot at some cops, then lure them back to the rooming house for a shootout, figuring they could kill off a couple dozen from inside with the kind of weapons they had.

"What it sounded like was a ratcheting up of Zebra, taking random shootings and turning it into a full-fledged war. She said Shabazz even had an escape plan. He and his crew dug a hole from the floor of the rooming house all the way down to the sewers, so that after they were done picking off cops, they could just crawl out to safety. The problem was that the fools didn't know the sewers below Fillmore were only thirty-six inches wide, and they'd have to practically be midgets to get out that way."

Sanders and Gilford began investigating the woman's claims, talking to their own informants, and quickly developed enough information for a warrant. With the help of Charlie Ellis and Charlie Barca, they arranged to have a special tactical squad put together. Then Sanders and Gilford prepared to infiltrate Shabazz's group themselves, literally opening the door so the tac squad could rush in.

"We stopped shaving for a day or two, tossed on some black leather jackets and floppy hats, and looked like some pretty bad dudes. The word was that the deal was supposed to go down on a Friday night. So early that evening Gil and I set up the tac squad around the corner from the rooming house, then he and I went up to the front door and knocked. After a minute a guy came to the door and opened it a crack, and I told him that we were there 'about the business.'

"He got a scared look on his face and opened the door some more, saying, 'You gotta get out of here, man, the cops're gonna be coming and—'

"He didn't get any further than that. I put my hand over his mouth and grabbed him around the chest, Gil grabbed his legs, and we picked him up and ran off while the tac squad rushed inside, helmets on and shotguns ready. The guy was trying to warn us about the shootout with the cops, but what he didn't know was that we had twenty right around the corner, waiting to get in."

When they entered the rooming house, Sanders and Gilford found it exactly as their informer had described, with steel plates lining the walls and windows. Shabazz and about a half dozen others were there, along with a stockpile of weapons. A hole really had been dug into the building's foyer that went all the way down to the sewer. But although police examined every inch of the building and interrogated everyone there for hours, nothing was found to tie it to the Zebra shootings.

"We stopped some fools from stirring up a lot of shit," Sanders explains, shaking his head, the frustration seeming as real now as it was thirty years ago. "But as far as Zebra went, it was just one more brick wall."

As winter marched toward spring and the frustration level mounted within the Zebra investigation, the Officers for Justice lawsuit began to stir up tensions again as well. The lawyers heading up the OFJ suit in federal court, Robert Gnaizda, along with his cocounsels William Hastie Jr. and Lois Salisbury, had scored a preliminary victory with the ruling of November 26, 1973. But what seemed like progress had quickly become an example of one step forward and two steps back. The SFPD, apparently complying with Judge Peckham's directive, took initial steps to allow more minorities and women into the department, for example, eliminating the height requirement and bringing both female and minority recruits into the academy. However, in February 1974 they reversed themselves on the height requirement, claiming once again that it was essential for good policing and reinstating it. At the same time, they joined the POA in an effort to chip away at Peckham's 1973 decision through a series of appeals and challenges on specific, narrowly focused issues. Both the department and the POA knew that Peckham's ruling was far too persuasive for a higher court to overturn it on a direct appeal. So instead, their long-term tactic became to eviscerate it, to get Peckham to reverse all of the decision's significant provisions and, in effect, win by way of myriad cuts rather than with one single blow.

In addition to the elimination of the height requirement, the SFPD, the POA, and the Civil Service Commission challenged stipulations having to do with the hiring of women, promotions, testing, and pay, to name just a few. Their multiple attacks created a tremendous burden on the limited resources of the OFJ and Public Advocates, the firm representing them, which could not match in money and manpower the alliance of city attorneys and private firms representing the other side. Outside the courtroom, the SFPD did its best to disqualify the women recruits they had been forced to accept by putting them through an even tougher physical regimen than the men, in an unfair effort to prove that women didn't have the body mass or strength to handle the job.

The department simultaneously tried to sow division among blacks in the SFPD, appealing to African-American officers who hadn't aligned themselves with Officers for Justice to give statements that countered the OFJ's claims of discrimination. The obvious incentive was an expectation of personal advancement. This was a cynical tactic, designed to use the natural desire of all officers for better jobs and plum assignments to divide blacks, undermining the greater good by enticing an ambitious few. Sadly, in some instances it worked.

"It was a painful time for some of us," Sanders says, recalling the tensions. "Some of the blacks who sided with the department in the appeal had been friends of mine. I think some felt that they could gain favor by taking the other side, and that over time it might pay off. The truth was, they were being used, and instead of gaining favor, they were losing friends."

As part of their campaign first to circumvent Judge Peckham's decision and then to gut it through multiple appeals, the department used various other ploys, many far from subtle, including intimidation both of OFJ and their lawyers and of Judge Peckham himself. Once the department filled Peckham's courtroom with more than two hundred white officers, including the entire SFPD Tactical Squad, who arrived wearing helmets and holding billy clubs. The scene was so threatening that Gnaizda asked Peckham to clear the courtroom, asserting that his witnesses didn't have room to sit down. Peckham refused, instead instructing Gnaizda to have his witnesses sit in the jury box and allowing the officers, weapons, helmets, and all, to remain.

One of the SFPD's most deceitful ploys was their attempt to pad the number of minority officers on their rolls, which they did by fabricating ethnic backgrounds for some cops. In the department's initial count of minorities, prior to the preliminary ruling, there were only three Native Americans on the force. As the appeals process began, that number somehow swelled to sixty-three. To Gnaizda, Judge Peckham was a decent man who wanted to do the right thing. However, Gnaizda also knew that Peckham felt tentative when it came to change and preferred to move things along at a snail's pace rather than enable the kind of revolution the OFJ wanted.

Gnaizda understood perfectly well the game the SFPD was playing. So, rather than react with the kind of anger that might put Judge Peckham on edge and possibly prompt him to allow the inflated numbers to stand, he decided on a different tack. Standing before the judge, he began with irony, congratulating the SFPD on having accomplished one of the greatest feats in the history of affirmative action, increasing the numbers of Native Americans by over two thousand percent in only a few months. The SFPD, he said, might now have more Native Americans than could be found in all the other police agencies throughout the state combined, and, most impressive of all, they had accomplished this feat without hiring a single new officer.

The judge scowled at Gnaizda and asked if he was being sarcastic. Gnaizda responded that he was. When Peckham angrily asked him what he wanted to do about the sudden upsurge in the number of Native Americans, Gnaizda pulled out the ace he knew was sitting right there in court.

William Hastie's wife, Cassandra, happened to be the head of the San Francisco office of the Equal Employment Opportunities Commission and had come to court that day to watch the hearing. So Gnaizda told Peckham that he wanted the EEOC to serve as arbiter and have the officers in question appear before the EEOC and affirm that they were, in fact, Native American. Peckham agreed, with the stipulation that not coming in would be a tacit admission that the officer was *not* Native American. Out of the mythical sixty-three, only nine showed up at the EEOC. Then, at a hearing that followed, Gnaizda made the second chess move, asking that Peckham order the nine officers who said they were Native American to go to the Department of Justice and do the same thing under oath. Again, Peckham agreed. This time only three men showed their faces. As Gnaizda would wryly put it later, there had been in court a "slaughter" reminiscent of Wounded Knee, with the scores of Native Americans claimed by the SFPD magically reduced to the original three.

Yet as skillful as the OFJ's defense was, Gnaizda and Hastie could not halt the city's Civil Service Commission from circumventing everything they had gained in court. One of the most important parts of the lawsuit, and one that could ultimately have the most wide-ranging impact on police departments across the country, was the assertion that the whole promotion process was slanted against minorities. When it came to changing the SFPD, promotions were the ultimate battleground. The old-boys' network that ran the department cared about maintaining control over who could join the force as a whole, but what concerned them most was entry into the top brass, and what controlled that were the exams.

Although the exams gave the promotion process a veneer of fairness, the truth was just the opposite. Eventually it was proven that some of the tests given to minorities were statistically more difficult than those given to whites. More important than the tests, though, was the issue of seniority, and the way it was played to determine who was on track to become part of the brass.

At the time of the OFJ lawsuit, no black officer had yet achieved the seniority to become eligible to take the lieutenant's exam. In fact, under the current system, it would be years before any black could take the exam and years more before any might be promoted to lieutenant. Moreover, in a classic instance of catch-22, no blacks could even begin the process of becoming eligible for the captain's exam until they had already made lieutenant. And the obstacles didn't end there. Promotions occurred only when there were openings, which were filled from a list of those who had passed the exams most recently in chronological order. So even if a black did pass the lieutenant's exam, he would have to wait for every single white officer ahead of him to make lieutenant before he even had a shot.

Gnaizda surmised that if the system in place at the time of the lawsuit were allowed to remain, it would be over twenty-five years before an African American could make captain, meaning that no matter what the lawsuit achieved with respect to recruits, the ruling clique of the SFPD would remain white for at least another generation.

Knowing this, Gnaizda and Hastie tried to persuade the judge to enjoin the Civil Service Commission from making any promotions until the courts could decide the issue. Peckham, however, ignored their pleas, and the commission was permitted to forge ahead and fill the ranks of lieutenant and captain for years to come, enabling the all-white men's club that ruled the department to retain the upper hand.

A lot has been written over the years about breaking through the color lines at various institutions. To Sanders, the integration of police forces, which has generally been ignored, was a milestone of far more importance in the fight for civil rights than anyone has ever acknowledged.

"Everybody understands that integrating schools is important because it gives people a chance to better themselves. But people don't think about how important it is to integrate the police. In the same way schools have the potential to help people up, the police have the potential to hold people down.

"I'm not saying all cops are guilty of that. I'm a cop myself, of course. I believe in police. But you're a fool if you don't think they have the potential for it. Gil and I used to talk about how the only guarantee we'll ever have that a police force won't turn into some kind of armed gang holding down this group or that is to make sure that every facet of the community is represented on the force. It's like a built-in system for checks and balances."

Sanders and Gilford were both passionate advocates of the OFJ lawsuit. However, one detail about their situations was different, which made Gilford's advocacy even more intense and more pressing. He was ten years older than Sanders, which meant he had ten years less time to get what he wanted.

Gilford never backed away from confrontation, racial or otherwise. From the moment he came onto the force, he was a figure blacks looked up to and whites respected, at least to his face. If they didn't, they would have to answer to him.

"When Gil and I were in Robbery, back in the very early seventies just before we both got promoted to Homicide, we went in together on a Saturday to put in some overtime," Sanders says, recalling one incident in the Hall of Justice that could have turned tragic. "There were about ten guys there, all white except for us. The inspector sergeant who ran the bureau on weekends dropped a stack of purse snatchings on our desk and said, 'This is the kind of stuff you two can handle.' The point was clear: we weren't good enough to solve a robbery any tougher than that.

"Well, Gil got in his face and they went at it right there in the office, with fists flying. It got so bad that other guys got up to help the sergeant out. That was when I pulled my gun out of my desk drawer and laid it on the table, telling everybody to 'let it play out on its own.'"

Gilford won the fight with the sergeant. But he could not win the fight with time — or with the institutional racism of the SFPD.

If Gnaizda's projection was correct that, failing a radical change, there would not be any blacks at command level in the SFPD for another twenty-five years or more, Gilford was out of luck. That truth made every loss in court not just a setback but something irretrievable, and every professional slight so much salt in a wound that might never heal.

San Francisco has always been a city of extremes. Sometimes, though, even extremes can be taken to extremes.

In March 1974, as the SFPD was taking on the twin terrors of Zebra and the SLA and as Gnaizda, Hastie, and the members of Officers for Justice battled the appeals of their civil rights lawsuit, San Francisco's city workers suddenly decided to go on strike, demanding higher wages and increased benefits. Except for the police and firemen, all of the city's civil servants walked off their jobs en masse.

For nearly two weeks, buses, streetcars, schools, and even the city's sewage treatment plants were shut down, adding transportaton, education, and sanitation to the list of crises. The streets, swollen with commuter cars because of the stalled transit system, became nearly impassable. And a city that was already traumatized was reduced to a state of hysteria. Then came the bombing.

The Weathermen, who now called themselves the Weather Underground, had been operating in the Bay Area since 1970, when a bomb planted in the SFPD's Park Street Station killed Sergeant Brian McDonnell and injured eight others. Other bombings around the area were also linked to the Weather Underground, and just a year before Zebra began, the FBI discovered an abandoned bomb factory they had fashioned in the Fillmore. Now, amid all the chaos, they struck again.

This bomb went off in the early-morning hours of March 7, blowing out a section of wall on the fourth floor of San Francisco's Federal Building, inside the Department of Health, Education, and Welfare. A communiqué declared it a product of the "Women's Brigade" and claimed the blast was a protest against the alleged forced sterilization of poor women in the South. Never ones to be out of fashion, the Weather Underground added a postscript, claiming that it was also an act of solidarity with the SLA.

The SLA had become as controversial among radicals as it was among the rest of America. Most on the left denounced the group for kidnapping Patty Hearst. Perhaps most eloquent was Jerry Rubin, who had been one of the stars of the radical Left in the late 1960s and was a veteran of Berkeley's Free Speech Movement, cofounder of the Yippies, and one of the Chicago Seven, the group tried for inciting the riots at the Democratic Convention of 1968. "When mass movements collapse as ours did in the early 1970s," Rubin wrote in the *San Francisco Chronicle,* "and the problems of oppression remain and even get worse, hopes die and terrorism appears."

Rubin went on to appeal to the SLA to spare the life of Patty Hearst, saying that their tactics had already had a reverse effect, making a sympathetic figure out of the beleaguered Randolph Hearst. "Under no circumstances harm her," Rubin concluded. "That would be a crime outside the boundaries of any revolutionary morality."

Though Rubin's appeal was directed at the SLA, it echoed back to Zebra, and applied to all the victims who had been left bloody, paralyzed, or dead in acts that no argument and no excuse could ever justify.

Despite the appeals of Rubin and others, some groups — the Weather Underground, among others — openly embraced both the SLA and their actions. Bernardine Dohrn wrote a letter of her own to the *Chronicle,* taking a very different tone than Rubin. "The system always holds," she argued, "that its massive violence is legal and that revolutionary violence by the people is illegal and outrageous. It is the opposite that is true." Later in her letter, Dohrn went on to voice a conclusion that was the opposite of Rubin's. Yet like his, it seemed to speak as much to Zebra as it did to Patty: "We must acknowledge that this audacious intervention has carried forward the base public questions and starkly dramatized what many have come to understand through their own experience: it will be necessary to organize and destroy this racist and cruel system."

Dohrn gave voice to a new apocalyptic radicalism, one that longed for an Armageddon-like meltdown of what she termed "the system." Each new act of terror was like another verse of Revelation, with the old world ending by way of bombs, kidnapping, or assassination.

No terror seemed more biblical, however, than Zebra. It was like Revelation 11:8 come to life: "Dead bodies shall lie in the street of the great city."

Terror without end.

Just a few days before the strike began, Randolph Hearst, as part of his effort to win the release of his daughter, started a food giveaway program for the poor that had been demanded by the SLA. The Reverend Cecil Williams, pastor at the Tenderloin's Glide Memorial Church and a well-known figure among Bay Area progressives, agreed to help Hearst organize the multimillion-dollar program, which would hand out cheese, milk, bread, and other staples at various locations around the Bay Area. The program kept going even as the city workers went out on strike, Hearst's private bureaucracy being so well funded that it could function when the city bureaucracy could not.

Though it was greeted with high expectations, and many in the Left began to think that something good might actually come out of the SLA's unforgivable actions, the giveaway degenerated into chaos in short order. So many people showed up at the places where the food was being handed out that riots nearly erupted. By the time the millions were spent, little had been accomplished, and the program seemed to have become a kind of metaphor for the failed hopes and unrealistic expectations of the radical Left. Moreover, Patty was no closer to being free than ever.

But giving wasn't the SLA's only concern. They seemed interested in taking, as well, especially when it came to human beings.

Angela Alioto was the youngest child of Joseph and Angelina Alioto, and their only daughter. In 1968 she married Joseph Veronese, moved with him into a home in Pacific Heights, and started a family. A decade later Angela, a vibrant, dynamic woman who seemed to be cut from the same cloth as her charismatic father, would attend law school and begin a political career of her own. In the mid-1970s, however, she was simply a wife and mother, and when the fighting between Joseph Alioto and Angelina continued to escalate following Angelina's disappearance, Alioto left his own house and moved in with his married daughter.

Angela was happy to have him. They had always been close, and her spacious home could easily accommodate him along with her family. But the move soon had repercussions that neither she nor her famous father could have anticipated.

It started with children playing games.

A little over a month after Patty Hearst had been abducted, and just as the city strike was coming to a close, Angela's two oldest children were playing on the sidewalk in front of the house when a woman stopped to watch them, and then came over to talk. The woman was pretty, with light brown hair, and to a casual observer seemed like many of the twenty-somethings who had grown up during the 1960s and were now drifting through the 1970s, a little vague perhaps, possibly a little directionless, but harmless. In truth, her name was Emily Harris, and she was known as Yolanda by her comrades in the SLA. No one ever found out exactly why she came to Angela's home, but there were only three possible reasons: to kidnap Angela's children, to kidnap Angela, or to kill the mayor.

Harris asked the children if their grandfather lived there. They answered yes, he did. Before any more contact could occur, however, a nanny spied the exchange from a window and came out to whisk the kids away. Later, after Harris had been identified and Joseph Alioto realized that a member of the SLA had come to his daughter's home, he had a dozen or so men from the SFPD Tactical Squad move into Angela's second floor with their riot gear and automatic weapons. Members of the squad would live in her home, day and night, for more than a month.

As far as Joseph Alioto was concerned, the tac squad was there to protect his daughter and grandchildren, not him. The truth was that after having spoken out so strongly against the SLA, Zebra, and the spate of radical violence that had swamped the city, he had turned himself into a prime target for assassination.

As if to prove the point, the same week Emily Harris paid a visit to Angela's home, terrorists in London attacked Queen Elizabeth's daughter, Princess Anne, spraying her limousine with bullets as it approached Buckingham Palace and injuring her bodyguard and others. Back in California, a subcommittee of the legislature felt that the threat of terrorism had become so dire they published a report recommending that citizens begin a series of antiterrorism measures, installing home security systems and establishing neighborhood "intelligence networks," creating a reactionary precursor to neighborhood watch programs to keep each other informed about anything that might seem unusual.

While state and local law enforcement were devoting their assets to the twin purposes of finding Patty Hearst and solving the Zebra murders, seven weeks had gone by since the Patty Hearst kidnapping and more than eight since the last Zebra shooting, with little progress on either front.

"Every tip that came in, every source, every rumor, all of it, went *nowhere*," Sanders says as he thinks back about the bitter frustration that pervaded investigations now. "There were leads we thought were good, both with Patty and Zebra, but when we checked them out we either got there too late, like the safe house on Golden Gate where we learned the SLA had been staying the day they left, or the tips turned out to be about groups that had no connection to either Patty or Zebra, like Shabazz and the other crazies we rounded up in the Fillmore rooming house.

"Yet we knew whoever we were looking for was right there, walking the same streets we were. San Francisco's only forty-nine square miles, seven miles each way in any direction. Berkeley and Oakland aren't much bigger. But it doesn't matter how big a room is when you have to walk through it blind. And that's the way we were starting to feel."

Making them feel even worse was the fact that the SLA kept releasing a stream of communiqués and tape recordings of Patty to the press, advertising how easily they seemed to be evading their pursuers. Some communiqués tried to reach out to other groups like the Weather Underground and the Black Liberation Army, looking to band together in what the SLA saw as the beginning of a revolution. Others, however, were merely childish and arrogant, chiding those involved in the food program and implying that nothing the "pigs" in power do could ever be enough.

The tapes of Patty had a different quality to them than the communiqués. The written documents were generally dry and filled with revolutionary jargon. By contrast, the tapes from Patty seemed plaintive and vulnerable, at least at the beginning. As Sanders recalls, "We would listen to those early tapes in Homicide and, let me tell you, they broke your heart. It was like the hostages you see now in Iraq. You knew Patty was scared, but she was still trying to reassure her friends and family that she was all right. Then the tapes changed. An edge seeped into her voice. It made you wonder what was going on with her. And it frustrated you. Cops protect people. That's our job. But we couldn't do a thing to help Patty.

"Cops are creatures of action. We're at ease when we're in motion. But things had stalled to the point where were starting to feel frozen in place, covering the same leads over and over. Clues are like blood. After a while they dry up and seem of little more use than dust."

9

Flashpoints

"It's hard to say what makes killers kill."

Earl Sanders was not speaking about the psychology of what prompts murders. The emotional underpinnings of some killers may stay shrouded forever, but more often than not, in Sanders's experience, the broad outline of what causes a killer to develop over time becomes clear in the course of an investigation. His point was to question what it is that causes a killer to kill *now*, to choose this day, this hour, this moment.

"When a killing occurs out of passion, or during a robbery, the triggers are clear. But when it's random, like in Zebra, the 'why now?' that triggers the act gets tougher to pin down. It could be something as big as avenging someone's death, or as little as reacting to someone stepping on your shoes."

Or even reading an article in the newspaper.

Duffy Jennings, a reporter for the *Chronicle* who regularly covered homicide throughout the 1970s, developed a two-part feature about Dave Toschi and William Armstrong that centered around a current case they were investigating. It's not surprising he chose to spotlight them. Known as the Zodiac Twins because of their long involvement in that case, Toschi and Armstrong were already recognizable names to the public. But there was another reason that made the choice predictable: Dave Toschi's passion for publicity.

"You couldn't help but like Toschi as a person," Sanders says as he recalls his former colleague. "He was like a character out of the old Rat Pack, smart, funny, stylish, Italian. But he had a thing about seeing his name in the paper. We all knew it. And no how matter how much you might love Dave, if you wanted to play things close to the vest, working with him was a problem. We ended up being teamed a number of times, and on half the cases it seemed like the press would get to the crime scene before we did. I sure as hell didn't call them. But when I looked to Dave, he would throw up his hands like, 'Who, me?' You hate to criticize people unfairly, but unwanted publicity was something that everybody who worked with Dave had to deal with."

Bill Armstrong managed to deal with it for over a decade. Armstrong was more like Toschi's anti-twin than his twin. The two were polar opposites, Armstrong countering lust for publicity with a deeply private nature. He was also as thorough a cop as they come, and possibly too empathic for his own good. Although officially the two of them handled the Quita Hague murder as a team, it really was Armstrong's case. He was the one who responded to the scene and witnessed the unfathomable bloodshed. He was the one who interviewed Richard Hague the next day. And he was the one who kept in touch with Hague, calling to see how he was feeling physically and emotionally, and how the many surgeries he needed to repair his wounds had progressed.

The headline of Jennings's article stated, "They're Tracking Down a Killer." The case he was writing about had nothing to do with Zebra. But with Zebra still so much a part of people's thoughts and fears, the headline seemed to allude to it nonetheless, and the tone of the article was reverential. Cops are not the only ones who like publicity. Killers often have a craving for it too, especially when publicity is a weapon in itself, as it can be with terrorists.

"Nine times out of ten, killers like the ones in Zebra are sociopaths," Sanders observes. "The whole world revolves around them, and anything they do is justified simply because *they* do it. When you're as narcissistic as that, it feeds into everything, including killing. And when you see an article that glorifies the people who are after you, it can act like bait. You want to show you're smarter than them. Better than them. And there's only one way to do it. Kill. And get away with it. Again."

It may never be proven that the article was a trigger for violence, but according to testimony given at the trial by Carolyn Patton (Anthony Harris's ex-wife) and others, some of those involved in the Zebra attacks were acutely aware of the media coverage. Patton recalled, for instance, that after returning home on the night of the attack on the Hagues, Harris turned on the television, curious to see if there were news reports about the assault. After nine weeks of inaction by the killers, the first part of the Jennings article appeared in the morning edition of the *Chronicle* on April 1. When part 2 appeared twenty-four hours later, it would be eclipsed by a far bigger story.

The Zebra killers had struck again.

Throughout the Zebra investigation, Earl Sanders recalls being plagued by a feeling that "the whole world had gone insane."

"It wasn't just in San Francisco. It was everywhere: Washington, the Middle East, Chile, Wounded Knee, there was craziness no matter where you turned. Even when we were stuck spinning our wheels on Patty and Zebra, it still felt like things were moving a mile a minute because the whole world kept blowing up all around us. Like Watergate: I remember Haldeman, Ehrlichman, and the others were indicted at the same time as we were searching for Patty. It was chaos. And no one had a clue when it would end."

As Watergate again dominated the media, the craziness back home in San Francisco took another twist when Sanders and Gilford learned that a handful of white supremacists planned to kidnap the daughter of Belva Davis, the first black TV newswoman in California and one of the most visible African Americans in the Bay Area. According to their informants, their would-be abductors had ties to the Aryan Brotherhood, a racist group that had been formed inside California prisons around the same time as the Black Guerrilla Family. They intended for the kidnapping to "even the score" for what had happened to Patty. Before the attempt could be made, though, Sanders, who was a friend of Davis, put her home under around-the-clock protection. Even so, before long she and her husband, TV news cameraman Bill Monroe, moved out of San Francisco and headed across the Bay to the hills above Berkeley, where they felt they were at least a little farther from harm's way.

Yet even as Belva and Bill fled the madness, Thomas Rainwater and Linda Story, two young people who lived at the center of it in the

Fillmore, appeared barely to notice it. In many ways Thomas and Linda seemed to live in another place and time. This quality lent them a kind of purity, as if they were beyond the madness. But ultimately it couldn't protect them.

At nineteen, Thomas Rainwater was a first-year cadet at the Salvation Army School for Officer Training in San Francisco, one of four regional training schools run by the Salvation Army. Thomas's dream was to do missionary work and help run an orphanage. A natural preacher, he spent much of March in a two-week evangelism campaign with others from the training school, giving sermons before Salvation Army congregations in Arizona. The last sermon he delivered was at a congregation in Phoenix, where he gave a talk entitled "One Life to Live, One Life to Give."

Linda Story was two years older than Rainwater, but her dreams were much the same. Like him, Linda was a first-year cadet, and the two had grown close. On the night of April 1, they had made an innocent date to spend the ninety minutes of their free time between study period and curfew alone together.

It had been raining all day, but there was a slight break in the showers as the young couple left the training school at Laguna and started up Geary in search of a late-night snack at a supermarket on Webster, just a block below Fillmore and Temple No. 26. Fellow cadets passed them on the way; a larger group had gone out earlier and now was heading back. But Rainwater and Linda took their time. The ground was wet, the air was moist and fresh from the rain, and the natural beauty of the city seemed far more real than any of the fears that had been plaguing San Francisco for so long. It had been two months since the last shooting, and the possibility of another seemed remote.

Just as the couple approached Webster, a man came around the corner and passed them but then stopped. Linda turned to say something to Thomas. That's when she saw the man again, and the gun in his hand, held point-blank toward Thomas's back.

Even on a misty Monday night, that area was far from deserted. Both witnesses and police officers were in ample supply. Two plainclothes vice squad officers, Dennis O'Connell and Daniel O'Brien, were standing in a parking garage across the street, so close that they were able to reach Thomas and Linda less than a minute after they heard the shots. Two uniformed officers were also nearby, in a car only a block away. Some people sat by the window, above where the young couple walked. Others drove by in their cars. The officers in the car commented afterward that if the shooter had gone one way instead of another, he would have run right into them. Others who said they saw the shooter could make out only the army jacket and dark trousers that he wore. One woman called to the killer from her upstairs window, asking what happened, not realizing he was the one who had fired the shots. But she, too, couldn't identify him.

Not even Linda was ever able to say exactly what he looked like. Part of the reason was the shadows created by the dense foliage that hung over the narrow sidewalk. But, as Sanders points out, "Sometimes luck is as much a factor in getting away with murder as it is with anything else. And with Zebra, the killers were getting all of the luck."

At the instant Linda turned, the killer pumped two bullets into Thomas Rainwater's back. Then he pivoted toward Linda. She was running when the first two bullets hit her near the waist, sending her sprawling to the ground and causing the third bullet to miss. As she lay in the street, not knowing if she would live or die, the man turned and entered some bushes that bordered an apartment complex, disappearing into the night. After he was gone, Linda realized she could feel her legs. Although two bullets had hit her in the back, both had missed her spine.

If there was any luck to be had, it was in that.

Sanders and Gilford were still at the Hall of Justice when the call came in.

For more than three months, even during the lull in Zebra attacks, there had been no nights except late nights. Sanders kept track of his overtime in the same notebook he used for notes on cases, and a glance at a few days from this period reveals how demanding the work had become:

ZEBRA OT
Sunday	16 hrs
Monday	7 hrs
Tuesday	16 hrs

Sixteen hours of overtime means a twenty-four-hour shift. They had hoped that Monday would not be so harried. But hope and reality are often far apart.

That weekend there had been an escape from San Quentin. George and Larry Stiner, two brothers who had been serving life sentences for killing a couple of Black Panthers in a radical turf war in Los Angeles, had somehow managed to slip through the prison's security. Now they were on the run, and Sanders and Gilford had spent their day checking sources all over the city to try to find some trace of them. Most of the people they talked to thought the Stiners were already long gone, heading for a safe house somewhere down south on their way out of the country. Beyond relaying what they'd heard to cops in L.A., there was little that Sanders and Gilford could do. So they decided to call it a day until they were interrupted.

"Whenever a call about a homicide came in, the first questions asked were whether or not it was a small-caliber weapon, had black male suspects, and had a clear motive," Sanders recalls. "If the answer was yes to the first two questions, and no to the third, it was handed over to the task force to check out."

As the team officially heading up the Zebra task force, Gus Coreris and John Fotinos became the inspectors of record on all the shootings after the night of January 28. With the expansion of the task force after that date and the allocation of more resources before Patty, they had chosen two young inspectors from Burglary, Carl Klotz and Jeff Brosch, to work alongside them and run down any tips or witnesses they wanted checked out. Even so, when it came to the homicides themselves, the division of labor remained largely the same, with Sanders and Gilford, the two inspectors originally detailed to work full-time with Coreris and Fotinos, as well as a few others in the bureau, like Ed Erdelatz, devoting the majority of their time to Zebra work, picking up wherever the Greeks left off.

"At first, Gus and John and Gil and I would trade off, with them taking one case and us the next. Even when all new cases became officially theirs, it was so hectic that if they got caught up with something and a new shooting happened, Gil, me, or one of the others would have their backs and take the lead for a while."

When this call came in, everyone's mind instantly went to the same place: Zebra. As soon as they learned that the new shooting met all the criteria — small-caliber weapon, a black assailant, apparent lack of motive — Sanders and Gilford grabbed their car and sped the two and a half miles to the crime scene, heading up Sixth to Turk and then continuing on Webster. The Fillmore was where Sanders and Gilford grew up, and they knew its streets so well they navigated them without thinking. It was their playground. It was their home. And it was in chaos.

Less than an hour after the shooting, over fifty cops had flooded the streets of the Fillmore. The killer had been seen running into an apartment complex that had originally been built by the longshoreman's union to provide their workers with good, affordable housing. The complex was now open to everyone but remained what the union had wanted, a pleasant place for families to live. Yet despite the fact that the shooting occurred in a location and at a time when there were plenty of witnesses, the shooter had again managed to slip away, leaving no trace except the spent casings of a .32 handgun.

Standing at the murder scene, Sanders couldn't help but notice the yellow brick of Temple No. 26 just a block away, close enough to break one of its circular windows with a rock. Staring at its facade, he weighed the feeling that he and others in Homicide had had about a likely involvement of members of the Nation of Islam in Zebra, before the Hearst kidnapping had taken them in other directions.

"There was still no real evidence," Sanders explains. "But crooks do their 'crookin' where they're comfortable. Even killers. And this was just a block from the temple. So it was one more thing pointing in that direction."

Even with the camera surveillance of Temple No. 26 being conducted from the Miyako Hotel, there was not sufficient evidence for a warrant, and therefore still no way legally to search the temple or any other building associated with the Nation. But standing there and contemplating the institution at the fringe of yet another Zebra crime scene, Sanders came to a realization about the ways in which Zebra, a case of black-on-white terrorism, mirrored and even validated the OFJ lawsuit that Gilford, he, and the others were pursuing at the exact same time.

It struck home: "The only way to break through the silence that surrounds a group as secretive as the one behind Zebra, whether they were from the Nation or not, was to have the kind of presence that would allow you to gather grassroots intelligence, so you can find out who the players are and get some to roll on others. Gil, me, Herman Clark, Nap Hendrix, Willie Johnson, we all had contacts. But we didn't have the numbers you need for something like that. And the reason we didn't was exactly what we were dealing with in the OFJ suit. Racism.

"That's when it hit me. The same thing that sparked the killing was getting in the way of solving it. As hateful as the killers were, it was racism that lit the fire that burned inside them. And it was racism that kept the department so white we didn't have enough black officers to infiltrate a group like the one we were after."

While Coreris and Fotinos oversaw the crime scene, Sanders, Gilford, and the dozens of others who responded to this latest shooting spread out across the Fillmore, searching for clues, going from the clubs to the bars to the little park at Fillmore and Ellis where the dealers and hookers hung out and waited for junkies and tricks to come looking to score one way or the other. Apart from the shell casings collected by criminalists, however, no new evidence was gathered.

Frustrated once again, the SFPD decided to fill the streets with dozens of unmarked cars at night, instituting indefinitely a clandestine Zebra Patrol. The hope was that one of the cars would happen upon a shooting as it was about to take place, or else be close enough to catch the killer or killers as they fled. It was an understandable move. But it was also the beginning of a series of desperate measures that could risk the very thing that the court testimony of both Anthony Harris and the woman Jesse Cooks abducted and raped would ultimately attest the killers were after.

A race war.

For a day and a half Zebra took over the news once more, the gunshots and the terror they aroused echoing in the media and among the public. Local newspapers heralded "Another Senseless Street Slaying" and

"The Walk That Ended in Death," and the *Chronicle* ran a feature about the Linda Story shooting headlined "Anguish of Gun Victim's Mother." On a segment of the national *CBS Evening News* anchored by Roger Mudd, Charlie Barca admitted to his interviewer that the police felt "helpless."

Then an unexpected communiqué from the SLA announced that they might release Patty Hearst soon. Radical lawyer Vincent Hallinan and assemblyman Willie Brown were among those chosen to talk to her once she was freed. As the whole Bay Area anticipated Patty's release, Gilford, who was one of Brown's best friends, was sure the police would make some sort of move against the SLA as soon as she was handed over. Less than twenty-four hours later, a very different communiqué jolted everyone's expectations. Instead of going free, Patty had chosen to join the SLA.

"I have been given the name Tania for a comrade who fought alongside Che in Bolivia for the people of Bolivia," she claimed in a lengthy, rambling statement. Suddenly Patty Hearst, granddaughter of one of the most successful capitalists in the history of the United States, had joined the revolution. "It is in the spirit of Tania that I say, 'PATRIA O MUERTE. VENCEREMOS.'"

The quote, meaning "Homeland or death, we will win," came from the Cuban revolution and was a rallying cry for the Cuban people to rise up and fight. Patty, like her newfound comrades in the SLA, like the Weather Underground and the men behind Zebra, had embraced the apocalyptic Left bent on bringing down white America in a fiery crash in which, as Jesse Lee Cooks had told the woman he abducted and raped back in October, "people were going to be killed and the streets would be lined with blood." Patty's captors, who envisioned a similarly violent future, had convinced her that her parents did not care whether she lived or died. Consequently, she decided, neither did she, and she picked up a rifle, put on a beret, and had her picture taken in a defiant stance of rebellion.

As irrational as that act seemed, Sanders points to sports, not politics, as the real measure of just how senseless and out of control America had become.

"The same week that Rainwater was killed and Patty joined the

SLA, Henry Aaron tied Babe Ruth's record of 714 home runs. A week later, he broke it. And he did it with people threatening to go to games with high-powered rifles and kill him. Not because he had done anything wrong or committed any crimes. They wanted to kill him just because he was a black man breaking a white man's record. This is baseball I'm talking about. *Sports.* And it was on the verge of exploding into a race war the same way Zebra was."

Joseph Alioto was trying to make his own sense out of the madness.

Alioto had been projected as a favorite to win the Democratic nomination for governor. But Jerry Brown, the relatively inexperienced yet charismatic thirty-five-year-old son of former governor Edmund Brown, was proving a more formidable opponent than anyone had expected. One key factor added to Brown's appeal. Besides being young, handsome, and having a keen intelligence, he had succeeded in promoting as a strength the very thing many had thought would prove his greatest weakness: lack of experience. Brown's inexperience gave him the appeal of an outsider, and in the shadow of Watergate that was a plus. Alioto, by contrast, came off as a classic politician. Every morning paper seemed to bring his campaign more bad news.

In the wake of the latest fiasco, with Patty declaring her radicalism only two days after the Zebra killers had struck again, Alioto went public with the idea, long a fixture in the thinking of the SFPD brass, that the cases were linked, saying there was a relationship between the Hearst kidnapping and Zebra and implying that solving one might solve the other. However, he refused to elaborate further, asserting that Randolph Hearst wanted him to defer talking about the connection for now, but that "the moment the Hearst matter is resolved, I am going to have a lot to say on the subject."

The upper echelons of the SFPD and city government had clung to the possibility of such a connection for two months, hoping for a grand solution. But the truth was, they were merely grasping at bad intelligence. Over a year and a half later, after Patty was in custody and the trial of the men arrested for Zebra had begun, Lieutenant Paul Lawler, still head of the SFPD's Intelligence Bureau, asked Patty if there had been any connection. Her answer was a simple "No," the same answer that virtually every man in Homicide would have given Lawler and the mayor as well, if they had been polled in April 1974. Nevertheless, it was Lawler's job to investigate any and all possibilities, no matter how remote. As for the mayor, with an election looming, polls dropping, and an ever-growing need to succeed at something, he had ample reason to look for easy answers and quick solutions.

Members of the Zebra task force paid little attention to the mayor's musings about grand conspiracies. They had enough to deal with in trying to vet the thousands of phone tips being called in and anonymous letters being written, while at the same time following up on whatever clues they had been able to develop about the now seemingly unstoppable, and endlessly vexing, string of murders. Talking to witnesses from the latest shooting and canvassing sporting goods stores where .32-caliber bullets might have been bought, they traced all the lines of inquiry until each led to a similar dead end.

Adding to Sanders and Gilford's workload, another bizarre case now fell into their laps. Initially it was thought a possible Zebra case, as the victim was shot with a small-caliber weapon as well as stabbed and slashed repeatedly with a long, machete-like blade.

"The victim was a Japanese nightclub singer," Sanders explains. "She was a beautiful woman, young and, from what I heard, very talented. We found her body on Bush Street locked in a steamer trunk, shot at close range and hacked up by a long kind of blade. We ruled it out almost right away as being part of Zebra. The bullets were .22s, the blade was a samurai sword, and the killer turned out to be a Caucasian guy who was so nuts about Asian culture that he'd taken a Japanese name. He started stalking the singer, and when she turned down his advances, he killed her."

Two weeks had passed since the shootings on Geary. Other news began to hit the front pages. An Arab terrorist attack in Kiryat Shmona near the Israel/Lebanon border left eighteen dead, and in a rare local act of reprisal, a group of masked men stormed into the Arab Information Center in San Francisco's Ferry Building and vandalized the office while the frightened employees looked on. Though unrelated to Zebra, this incident may be seen in retrospect as one indication that, beneath the unresolved fear plaguing the city, a vengeful sense of rage was building — intimating what was to come.

Ward Anderson and Terry White were waiting for a bus.

It was Easter Sunday, April 14, and though the rains from earlier in the month had long ceased, the night was cool and damp. Eighteen-year-old Ward Anderson was visiting San Francisco from his home in Mesa, Arizona. Though young, Ward already had the rough edges of a grown man. As he sat at the stop on the corner of Fillmore and Hayes, waiting for a bus to take him back to the little hotel where he was staying, he turned to the wiry youth on the bench beside him and asked for a cigarette.

Terry White did not smoke. At fifteen, he was still little more than a kid. Earlier in the day, he had accompanied his family on an Easter picnic in Golden Gate Park. Then he and his brother took the bus to another Easter party across town. Now he was heading back home alone, tired and wishing he was already there. He got up and looked to see if a bus was coming. There wasn't one, so Terry stuck out his thumb to hitch a ride.

Keith Tisdell was also waiting for the bus. Unlike the others, Keith was black, and he sat off to the side, watching Terry try to flag a ride. As he watched, a tall African-American man with a heavy, muscular build turned the corner onto Fillmore and walked by quickly, forcing Keith to move his legs out of the way. Ward Anderson, still yearning for a cigarette, asked the tall black man for one. The man grunted but kept walking. Then, suddenly, he stopped, pulled out a gun, and fired two bullets into Ward's side. As Ward collapsed on the bench, a terrified Keith jumped up and fled, fearing he might be next.

He wasn't. But Terry White was.

Terry heard the shots and turned back to see the man running at him, then firing three times and running on, heading up Fillmore and disappearing around the corner onto Grove. By now, Ward Anderson was screaming, crying out for help and saying he had been shot. Terry thought Ward was mistaken. He didn't realize yet that he too had been shot, since from the sound of the weapon he thought it had just been an air gun. But Ward was upset, so Terry decided to go get help.

In less than a block Terry felt blood dripping from a wound in his arm. Then he felt the blood dripping down his side from where the other bullets had hit. He stopped and lay down in the street while onlookers came, and then paramedics, who lifted him onto a stretcher and rushed him to San Francisco General. Like Ward, Terry was seriously wounded, but also like Ward, he would survive.

Frank Falzon, who was on call that night, was the first Homicide inspector to arrive at the scene. Others arrived soon after, including Sanders and Gilford. They and scores more officers soon covered the area, once again filtering out through the Fillmore in the hope of finding the shooter or clues. Once again, the search was fruitless, with no one able to turn up anything beyond the spent shell casings and a few vague witnesses.

Embarrassed that the shooter had escaped despite the large number of unmarked cars that had been out on the street as part of the Zebra patrol, Charlie Barca's normally composed and confident demeanor began to break down. To the press he acknowledged the "helplessness" that he had talked about before on *CBS News*, saying he would reassess the investigation and "refine" some aspects of the Zebra Patrol, including the numbers he had on the streets. What he didn't say was that by "refine" the numbers, he meant increase. And that what had been a flood of officers patrolling in the Fillmore and south of Market areas was about to grow to a nightly number of anywhere from two to three hundred, creating a police presence so pervasive that it bordered on martial law.

The day after the Anderson and White shootings, another crime occurred in San Francisco that, despite the wave of fear spreading through the city because of what the press dubbed the second double "Zebra-like shooting" in less than two weeks, managed to share the front pages with the latest attacks. It was a bank robbery, at a Hibernia bank out in the Sunset district. What justified such prominent attention was neither the location nor the amount stolen, which was just over ten thousand dollars, but the fact that the robbers were members of the SLA, and included Patty Hearst.

Surveillance cameras clearly showed Patty and four other SLA members robbing the bank at gunpoint. Two onlookers were shot, and warrants were issued for all those involved, including Patty. A debate followed in the media about whether Patty was involved of her own free will or had been brainwashed or was otherwise coerced. Some claimed that a weapon held by one of the others was aimed at Patty, and that she was forced to take part. Others disagreed. Finally, a communiqué from the SLA and Patty decided the issue.

The message was delivered to Inspector Rodney Williams, head of the SFPD's Community Relations Bureau and, along with Sanders and Gilford, one of the leaders of the Officers for Justice. Patty, according to the communiqué, had been a willing participant in the robbery. No one, she said, had pointed a gun at her. Nor would they. The SLA had taken the place of the family she said had failed her. They would take care of her, and protect her.

"I am a soldier in the people's army," she reiterated. "Patria o muerte, venceremos!"

After weeks without a shooting, the Zebra attacks in April provoked a new and more intense wave of fear. Once again, the streets in white areas and black became largely deserted at night. This time, however, the built-up tension was more volatile. The neighborhoods where the shootings occurred were largely African American, and the noticeable increase in the contingent of police who filled areas such as the Fillmore and Potrero Hill each night was starting to create an uneasiness among blacks.

There had long been a concern that revenge attacks against blacks might start to take place, as had been threatened in the anonymous letter to columnist Herb Caen. Now another fear took hold in the black community: a fear of police overreaction. As much as the community hated the Zebra shootings and wanted them to stop, they could not help but feel concerned when swarms of cops, the vast majority of whom were white, in plain clothes and in uniform, began to overwhelm their communities each night, as though they were there not to protect but to repress them, much as would the cops in a police state.

"The department's intent was to catch the bad guys, plain and simple," Sanders explains. "The question was the means, and whether or not that kind of overwhelming police presence was able to accomplish anything except intimidate and provoke the people who lived there. The odds were that seeing a lot of cops on the street would just make the killers lay low for a while. This wasn't a riotlike situation. That's where you want a visible police presence, to keep things under control. But Gil and I were starting to get worried that we really could have a riot if things got any hotter. The killings had made people in the ghetto uneasy for months, and they were starting to have crazy reactions.

"One rumor we heard on the streets was that the Zebra killers were really white cops masquerading as blacks. And that it was the *cops* who were trying to create a race war. That's how crazy things were getting."

The "heat" Sanders spoke of was not limited to the streets. It had also begun to spread to the offices of the Hall of Justice. The rumors there were not unlike the ones in the ghetto, except that instead of white cops being involved somehow, inside the Hall of Justice the talk was that black cops might be part of Zebra.

"It wasn't something that made its way into the task force," Sanders recalls. "The people who were actually working on the investigation would never spread that kind of bullshit. But there were others in the department, pissed off over the OFJ suit, saying things like the only way the killers could be so good at avoiding capture was if black cops were tipping them off about where the Zebra patrols would be. Gil and I were the only black cops who knew what the patrols would be doing, so we took that shit personally. No one ever said anything to our face, but if they had, there would have been fists flying. We were out there busting our ass every night, putting our lives in danger to try to protect white people from black radicals, and if some on the force wanted to question our loyalty, we would have had the argument with knuckles, not words."

The city seemed to be nearing a flashpoint. Then, only a day after

Patty Hearst was photographed robbing a bank, and only two days after Ward Anderson and Terry White were shot down while waiting for a bus, came yet another incident to bring that flashpoint closer.

Nelson Shields was trying to help a friend.

Shields, whose full name was Nelson T. Shields IV but who was called Nick by all who knew him well, had arrived in the Bay Area at the beginning of April, visiting some friends who lived on a houseboat in Sausalito. Shields was at a crossroads in his life. At twenty-three, he had left Hobart College in New York after his sophomore year, taking time off to work as a ski instructor near Denver. The son of a prominent DuPont executive, Shields had already spent some time away from school contemplating his future. Now he decided to pursue his love of photography instead of a liberal arts education. He applied to a prestigious school in New York, the Rochester Institute of Technology, and then drove out to California to do some work on his friends' houseboat while waiting to hear if he'd been accepted.

A natural athlete, Shields was a top lacrosse player in school, and earlier in the day he and another friend, Jonathan May, who also played lacrosse, had gotten together to practice at the Golden Gate Lacrosse Club near the Marina. After the workout they shared a couple of beers, and then Shields offered to help his friend pick up a rug he was buying and drove out with May to the rug dealer's home in Ingleside, a mixed-race, middle-class residential neighborhood at the southern edge of San Francisco's city limits, just north of Daly City.

It was about 9:30 P.M. when they arrived in Ingleside. As May went to up to the front door of the dealer's home, Shields rearranged the athletic equipment in the back of his station wagon so there would be room for the rug.

This part of Ingleside happened to be an area well known to the men who worked at Black Self-Help Moving and Storage. Michael Armstrong, a junkie and part-time fence whom Gilford sometimes used as an informant, and who would later be shown to be the source for the handguns used in Zebra, lived not far from there, as did friends of Armstrong's with whom they were also familiar. In addition, Greta Burgess, whom J. C. Simon began dating after he broke up with his wife, Ada, lived just around the corner.

Around 9:15, the rug dealer had looked out the window to see if the two young men she was expecting had arrived yet and saw instead two African Americans in their twenties in a car parked on the street outside her house. She didn't recognize them, but realized they weren't the men she was expecting and went on about her business. By the time Shields and May arrived some fifteen minutes later, the men who had been sitting inside the car were gone.

No one saw the shots, but many heard them.

From the rug dealer's front door, May turned in response to the detonations, and saw his friend already lying in the street.

One witness said he saw a black man running after the shots were fired and gave a description that could have matched either J. C. Simon or Manuel Moore. Another witness who saw a man running gave a description that, although they did not think of it at the time, Sanders and Gilford later realized seemed to match the young man they had stopped back in December, Larry Green. According to that witness, a fair-skinned African-American man ran to the house where the friends of Michael Armstrong lived, knocked on the door, and yelled to be let in. The witness claimed that he entered the house, but the people who lived there denied it, and no one matching the witness's description was there by the time the police arrived.

Regardless of who fired the shots, or where he or they ran, two things were certain. The three bullets that did the damage were identical to the ones fired at every Zebra victim since January 28. And Nelson Shields, for whom helping people seemed as natural an act as breathing, was dead.

10

Another South Africa

IN THE EARLY-MORNING HOURS of the day that Shields was shot, a small army of Oakland and Berkeley police officers raided the Oakland headquarters of the Black Panther Party. Fourteen people were arrested and taken into custody, along with a small cache of drugs and a not-so-small arsenal of weapons. Among the confiscated items were some two dozen semiautomatic rifles and full-size shotguns, several sawed-off shotguns, one fully automatic rifle, a hand grenade, handguns, numerous boxes of ammunition, bulletproof vests, gas masks, radio equipment to monitor police calls, and a bloody baseball bat that had been used to beat the person who, in street parlance, had "dropped a dime" on the weapons cache, a twenty-one-year-old Berkeley man named Michael Foster. Yet despite the number of people rounded up and an array of weapons capable of starting a small insurrection, the attention the raid received in the press was minimal. From now on nothing could compare to Zebra.

The moment he heard about Shields's death, Sanders had a feeling its impact could be greater than that of any attack before it. There were a number of reasons, including the cumulative effect of all the previous attacks, but the most important factor, and the one that would have a multiplying effect, was location.

"This was the first Zebra shooting in a neighborhood that was still as much white as it was black. Ingleside had been changing since the 1950s, when blacks started to move in and there began a smattering of what they called 'white flight.' But in seventy-four it was still about fifty-fifty. Especially where Shields was shot."

Sanders recalls talking about Ingleside with his partner as they drove to the crime scene.

"Ingleside had personal meaning to Gil and me. It was where my wife, Espy, lived when we first started courting. And until Gil broke up with his first wife, Pat, he lived there with her and their kids, a half mile from where Shields was shot. The same thing struck us both. People got along in Ingleside. Now you had blacks shooting whites in a place where they live side by side. And both of us were scared it might make the tensions explode, tearing people apart all over the city, even there."

They saw their fears begin to play out before their eyes that very night.

"Gus and John ran things at the crime scene, and Gil and I did whatever we could to help out, everything from taking statements to making sure the crime scene stayed pure. And as I looked at people there, it hit me: usually, if a crowd formed in Ingleside it was mixed, but not that night. The crowd around the crime scene was as separate as day and night, whites in their groups and blacks in theirs. But they kept eyeing each other, blacks eyeing whites and whites eyeing blacks. Wary. Like they were waiting for someone to make some kind of move.

"I don't think either Gil or I slept that night. We kept talking about it after we left the scene. If things were like that in Ingleside, what would happen if a crowd formed in the Fillmore, or Hunters, and someone did make a move, white against black or black against white? The whole place could go up in smoke."

Gus Coreris and John Fotinos were unflappable when it came to investigating murders. With over fifty years of experience and other high-profile cases between them, they had quite literally seen almost everything, but neither had seen anything like this. It wasn't the tension on the street that was getting to them, or the political implications of Zebra. Those were things they put aside, keeping them out of mind and out of the way so they could focus on the only thing that mattered to them: catching killers.

What was gnawing at them was that months had gone by, and

they didn't feel they were any closer to doing that than they had been at the very start. And the killers kept on killing.

Like Sanders and Gilford, both suspected that members of the Nation of Islam might be involved. However, they, too, had been unable to develop any solid leads that could take them in that direction, so they had no way to pursue it. An even greater source of frustration was the lack of a solid description from any of the witnesses. Scores of people had seen the shootings. Yet no one witness had a clear enough recollection of a killer's face for them to feel comfortable with a sketch artist making a drawing from that person's memory.

"Witnesses are valuable commodities in a murder case," Sanders explains. "But their worth is determined by the accuracy of what they remember. If a witness goes into a lineup and names somebody, it'd be a positive ID. But if that same witness worked with a sketch artist, and the drawing that got produced didn't look like the person they named, the ID could be called into question."

Neither Coreris nor Fotinos wanted to run that risk. Coreris, however, had been considering another option. What if he and Fotinos worked with the sketch artist? They knew all the descriptions, either from listening the witnesses themselves or else by reading the descriptions that had been taken down by others. The more Coreris thought about it, the more he was certain it could work.

There was only one problem. If they got it wrong and the killer they arrested looked nothing like the sketch, they could be even worse off than if the sketch had come from a witness. A good defense lawyer could take a fact like that and twist it into "exculpatory evidence," showing that even in the minds of the investigative officers the killer looked like someone other than their client.

Ultimately, the Greeks felt they had no choice but take a chance. So, acting on their own, afraid to involve too many people in case the effort blew up in their face, they phoned Hobart Nelson, the Homicide inspector who doubled as the bureau's sketch artist, and called him in for a late-night session. The sooner they could release a drawing or drawings of at least one of the killers, the better their chances of a break in the case.

Coreris and Fotinos weren't the only ones up late on the night of

April 17, seeking some way to confront their frustrations over Zebra. Chief Donald Scott, Chief of Detectives Charlie Barca, and Bunky Cummings, the department's chief of operations, were all joined in a crisis meeting with Mayor Joseph Alioto.

Alioto was the ultimate hands-on leader. In the wake of the latest Zebra killings, he wanted something done fast. A huge task force had been assembled, and unmarked cars were flooding the streets, but no matter what the police did, the killings continued. So he made his mandate to the SFPD brass unmistakably clear: Do what you have to do to make the killings stop. Do it *now*. The consequences of not succeeding were incalculable, both for their careers and for the city.

Some believe that Alioto decided to clamp down on Zebra as a campaign ploy, a way to look tough to bolster his flagging numbers in the primary. Yet talking to those close to him at the time makes clear that another motive was uppermost in his mind: his desire to protect the city he loved. One can, and probably should, doubt the wisdom of how Alioto chose to handle Zebra. But it is impossible to doubt his concern.

When the SFPD brass presented their plan the following morning to the officers leading the task force, they spoke of "extreme measures." Sanders described the meeting:

"It was in a conference room on the fifth floor of the Hall of Justice, where the chiefs' offices are. The meeting was mainly for the brass. Coreris and Fotinos were there, of course, along with Gil and me. But other than us, it was just lieutenants, captains, the chief, and Alioto. Needless to say, Gil and I were the only blacks. Chief Scott started things off. Then Charlie Barca stood up and started to explain the new measures we were supposed to take."

What Barca laid out was a plan for one of the biggest dragnets in U.S. history. It was also a plan for one of the broadest and most expansive cases ever of racial profiling, though of course the term wasn't in use yet. Starting immediately, all the available cops were to patrol the streets at night, stopping, questioning, and searching every black male who was out after dark anywhere in the city, but with the focus primarily on the Fillmore and south of Market. The assumption was that the vague descriptions they had from witnesses were ample justification for the stops, discounting any notion that they might be unconstitutional. But that wasn't all. Sanders explains what followed.

"After Barca was done talking about the sweeps and how hundreds of cops would be on the street stopping every black male they saw, Bunky Cummings got up and put a box of cards down on the lectern in front of him."

Cummings, setting forth a policy that sounded straight out of the apartheid regime in South Africa, held up a "Zebra card," as he termed it, and told the group that these identification cards were to be handed out to blacks who had been searched. With so many cops on the street, chances were some "suspects" might get stopped repeatedly. But, Cummings explained, with a Zebra card, all an individual had to do was show the document to the next officer to stop him, and the suspect would be waved on.

"Gil and I couldn't believe it. I mean, this was the United States of America, and they were telling us we're going to issue identification cards based on *race*. It was crazy. Not to mention illegal. We both stood up and tried to say something, pointing out that it wouldn't work. And that we'd alienate the very community we were trying to get information from. We'd seen the tensions in Ingleside. The city was a powder keg, and this was just the sort of thing that could set it off. But Bunky just told us to sit down and shut up. This was how it was going to be, and that was that. They wouldn't even let us talk.

"Gil and I looked around for some sort of support, figuring somebody else had to see how crazy it was. Gus and John were there next to us, but they wouldn't give us any more support than the brass. Charlie Ellis was there, too. Nobody spoke up. That hurt. And it pissed Gil off. They were talking about turning San Francisco into another South Africa, and we were the only ones standing up and saying it's wrong. It felt like we were back tackling that robbery suspect after the Officers for Justice hearing. We were on our own, with no 'buddies' out there."

Sanders and Gilford stood up and walked out. They were, as sworn police officers, willing to do whatever they were ordered to do, but they weren't going to sit at that meeting and, in Sanders's words, "listen to that bullshit."

Sanders would soon find out just how personal that "bullshit" would become.

Thursday, April 18, was to be the first night of Joseph Alioto's Zebra sweeps. The department issued a vague array of criteria by which to stop men who were loosely being termed "suspects." They were adult black males, twenty to thirty years old, although they could be older than thirty. They were anywhere from five-nine to six feet. They were of slender to medium build. They "may" have a small mustache on their upper lip, although it was also noted that the mustache "may" extend down the corners of the mouth and therefore not be small at all. In practice, this description would prove so elastic as to provide almost no limit at all to the officers' discretion, giving the police the license to stop virtually any African-American male they saw.

There was a joke among black cops that the parameters of the sweeps were "eight to eighty, blind, crippled, or crazy." Sanders was neither blind, nor crippled, nor crazy, but looking in his rearview mirror as he drove, he could see in himself one of the thousands of African-American males who fit the search criteria perfectly.

Sanders was heading east on the Central Freeway, making his way to the off-ramp that would take him to the Hall of Justice. He was on his way back from a quick trip home. Espanola had had to stay late at the Security Pacific Bank to train a new teller, so Sanders, who had been putting in so many hours that he figured his children were starting to forget what he looked like, agreed to help out, hoping to ease the growing tensions at home by picking up their son Marcus from school and taking him to an aunt's house, where he could be looked after, along with his younger sister. Now Sanders was returning to work, where he would be required to take part in a policy he believed was both unconstitutional and counterproductive.

Then he heard the siren. He looked at his speedometer: he wasn't speeding. For a moment the Zebra sweeps went through his mind, and he wondered if he was being stopped as part of that. But it wasn't an SFPD car behind him. It was the Highway Patrol.

"The California Highway Patrol was known for having some of the most racist cops in the state back then," Sanders explains. "When they stopped African Americans in those days, more often than not it was for 'DWB,' driving while black. That's what it was with me. Because there was no other reason to pull me over."

Sanders was being racially profiled.

It had started to rain lightly after nightfall, so the road was slick as he pulled onto the highway's soft shoulder, just a stone's throw from where he would have turned off. Two patrolmen approached, one on his left and one on his right. Both had their guns pulled. It was Sanders's car, so there was no radio in it, and no way for them to know he was a cop except his badge. Which was in the wallet he had tucked in his right back pocket.

Just behind the gun he had holstered on his right side.

"I rolled down my window, and the patrolman on my left asked for my license. But I could see the other patrolman in my side mirror, taking a position just behind me on my right, holding his gun in both hands. I knew if I reached for my wallet, that guy would see my gun and think I was reaching for that instead. And I'd be dead. So instead of getting my wallet, I put my hands up on the steering wheel and said that I was a police officer. But with the rain coming down and traffic zooming by, the patrolman I was talking to couldn't hear me. So he yelled again for my license, and I yelled again I was a cop, and it kept going like that, both of us getting louder, until I just called out as loud as I could, 'I'm a police officer, goddamn it!' Finally, he heard me. And they lowered their guns."

Allowing Sanders to start breathing again.

When Sanders told Gilford about the incident later that night, Gilford was furious, wanting to call the CHP and file a complaint. But with the OFJ suit, the Zebra investigation, and the sweeps about to begin, Sanders felt they had enough on their plate without taking on one more war to wage.

Usually it was Gilford who counseled Sanders, telling him when to just "be cool, School, you got to know when to pick your fights and when to walk away." However, during Zebra, a number of factors affecting him began to shift the dynamics in his relationship with the younger man. Part of it was his divorce, which was making him lonelier than Sanders had expected.

"It wasn't the sort of thing Gil would talk about. But you could tell in the way he always wanted to keep on working or talking, anything to not be alone. Midlife crises don't just happen at home, they happen on the job, too. And the lawsuit was going slow. Peckham's first decision was handed down around Thanksgiving. Now here it was April, and Gnaizda still had to go to court to force the department to follow through on even the judge's preliminary decrees, let alone get anything more. It was clear that if change was going to come, it would take years."

Gilford was the highest-ranking African American on the force, and when it suited the department they treated him almost as if he were a lieutenant, putting him in a position of authority, as they did with Zebra, knowing that other black officers would follow his lead. But when the brass felt that Gilford was getting in their way with his demands, he became "just an inspector" again as they put him in his place.

"That was what they were doing with the sweeps," Sanders says as he talks about his and Gilford's reaction to the massive manhunt. "Gil tried to tell them that it would have the opposite effect from what they wanted. The odds of catching anybody would be slim to none. But it was a sure bet that they'd piss off the black community and alienate the very people we were trying to get to help us. And that was the best-case scenario. The worst case would be if something happened and some innocent guy got hurt by an overzealous cop. Then there was no telling where it would end.

"But they wouldn't listen. And since they didn't want to hear it, Gil became 'just an inspector' again. There was nothing he could do, except try to take his anger and put it somewhere useful."

The same day that Alioto and the police brass made the announcement about the sweeps, the sketches that Hobart "Hobie" Nelson drew for Gus Coreris and John Fotinos were published in both the *Chronicle* and the *Examiner*. Copies were printed up and handed out to every cop taking part in the sweeps, who placed them on the dashboard of their cars. The drawings became ubiquitous overnight. Storeowners taped copies cut from newspapers onto storefront windows, and super- markets posted them on neighborhood bulletin boards. Businessmen carried them in coat pockets to check passersby. No matter where you looked, there they were, two young African-American faces, gaunt, sad- eyed, and with downturned mouths, staring out from a background of white.

Various claims were made about the original sources for the sketches. Sometimes the descriptions used were said to have come from Terry White and Ward Anderson, identified as "Victim 1" and "Victim 2." At other times the sketches were characterized as "composite draw- ings" put together from previous drawings based on the descriptions given by various witnesses and survivors. The truth is that while Hobie Nelson had sat down with many witnesses over the course of the inves- tigation, none of his earlier attempts had generated a sketch that was deemed usable. The real sources for these images were Gus Coreris and John Fotinos.

By now, the leaders of the task force believed that a number of people were involved, with some acting as shooters and others as ob- servers. They also believed that disguises were used, with the killers trading hats, coats, and even wigs. So Coreris and Fotinos had focused on the most common characteristics recollected by witnesses. The re- sults were two portraits they considered to be of a single individual. They did not mind, though, that some saw the drawings as being of two different people. The idea was to cast as wide a net as possible to flush out the killers.

Not even Coreris and Fotinos could have anticipated how wide that net would become.

"We're going to stop a lot of people," Joseph Alioto had told the press when he announced the "extreme measures" on April 18, in what could be one of the greatest understatements of his career. He went on to try to reassure blacks, asserting that it was not "a racial issue": "With this police action, as with other things," Alioto argued, "all we are try- ing to do in this life is hold tragedy to a minimum."

Dr. Washington Garner, the only African American on the Police Commission and one of the few leaders in the black community who supported the sweeps, called for blacks to be understanding. "Many black people will be stopped, and they will be searched, and they will get angry," Garner predicted, adding, "If you are stopped, we ask you, don't resent it."

Chief Scott was more direct: "We're not going to stop very young blacks or big fat blacks. We're not going to stop seven-foot blacks or four-foot blacks."

Subtlety was never Scott's strong suit. Many thought him a poor leader. Dianne Feinstein, then a San Francisco supervisor and later the mayor, and now the most senior of California's U.S. senators, had a number of run-ins with him during her career in city politics, questioning the way he ran the department and eventually calling for his resignation. In some ways, though, it was Scott who issued the most accurate statement. Preteen African Americans, obese African Americans, midget African Americans, and African Americans who had a shot at being centers in the NBA were safe. All others were fair game.

"When Gil and I got out on the street that night, it was like nothing I'd ever seen. Only eight percent of the SFPD were minorities, and only six percent were black. That was what the OFJ suit was about, so I knew the facts. But even I was surprised by what I saw. There were cops out in cars, on horses, on foot. They're everywhere you look, and with only a few exceptions, they're white. But everybody they stop is black.

"We kept moving that first night, heading all over. All we'd do was talk to people we passed on the street. That was it. We wouldn't stop people, and we wouldn't hand out Zebra cards. See, the cards weren't just used as IDs. The department kept a running file on everybody they stopped, using the cards to do it. Gil and I didn't want any part of that."

In fact, the SFPD didn't publicize this, but the cards were comprised of two parts, one of which was a copy for the police to keep. It contained personal information about the "suspect" — name, date of birth, driver's license number, social security number, and the date, time, and place he was stopped — and would be turned in at the end of the shift, to be collated and kept as part of a growing database.

The one thing Gilford and Sanders made sure they did do was keep an eye on other cops.

"The sweeps gave cops a license to do whatever they wanted, and every stop was a situation that could end in disaster. I don't think most cops realized how outraged people were. And we kept hearing reports of shootings all night, with cops rushing this way and that. Each time it was a false alarm.

"I remember Gil and I looked at each other, and all I said was, 'How long, man?' I didn't have to say anything more than that. He knew what I meant. How long can it go? How many more nights before it all blows up? Gil just shook his head and said, 'Not long, School. Not long.'"

Later that night, Sanders and Gilford tracked down some of their usual sources to gauge what effect the sweeps might have on their ability to develop information on the murders. Everywhere they went, they heard the same thing.

"What the fuck is goin' on?"

People in the black community, the vast majority of whom wanted to be helpful in catching the Zebra killers, thought they were being turned into targets. They felt betrayed.

Well over one hundred African-American men were stopped and searched by police that night, with each man being issued a Zebra card and then allowed to continue on. According to police reports, there were no "incidents."

But it was only the first night. The next night, Friday, the SFPD decided, the sweeps would be expanded across an even wider area that included Bayview, Ingleside, and Hunters Point in addition to the Fillmore and south of Market — all black or mixed neighborhoods and, apart from Hunters Point, all areas where shootings had occurred. To achieve the wider coverage, even more cops would take to the street, reaching upward of two hundred officers. The chiefs were determined to get results, one way or another.

After the first night of the manhunt, the political fighting over the Zebra sweeps became as volatile as the sweeps themselves. San Francisco's

Board of Supervisors, led by its president, Dianne Feinstein, held a public meeting over their efficacy, questioning whether the SFPD's actions were more hurtful than helpful.

They weren't alone. Both the NAACP and the ACLU came out against the sweeps. So did Black Panther Party leader Bobby Seale, whose offices had been raided in Oakland just days earlier. Said Seale, the sweeps placed "every black man in the Bay Area in jeopardy of losing his life," and they were both "vicious and racist."

Alioto, meanwhile, called a meeting of black leaders who supported his action. Rather than help defuse the situation, the meeting only added to the tension, underscoring a rift within the black community and leading some of those who were unhappy with the sweeps to brand those who supported it as traitors. Dr. Carlton Goodlett, publisher of San Francisco's largest black newspaper, the *Sun-Reporter,* went so far as to dub the African-American leaders who sided with Alioto "trained seals."

Yet in all the debate over the sweeps, what may have been the most important new twist in the search for the Zebra killers went unnoticed by many. A tiny article on the *Chronicle's* front page, set far down at the bottom, announced a "Zebra Reward" of $30,000 offered by the city of San Francisco to anyone who could provide information leading to the arrest and conviction of the killers.

One person who did not miss it was Anthony Harris.

Harris and Deborah had been having an increasingly tough time in Oakland, with Harris rarely able to earn the money they and their new baby needed to survive. Months before, Harris had been unnerved when he saw his photo in the *Chronicle* on the very same day as the bloodshed of January 28. Now, as he would later tell investigators, the sight of the Zebra sketches had a similar effect. Anthony Harris felt they looked exactly like him.

Like the person depicted in the drawings, Harris was lean, thin-faced, and often wore a mustache much like the one shown in one of the sketches. Harris was so convinced they looked like him that one wonders whether he worried that he had actually been "made" by the police and that the photograph in the *Chronicle* had served as part of their inspiration. In that case, his conclusion would have to be that he was the SFPD's target. When the *Chronicle* printed the sketches again on April 19, the morning after the first day of the sweeps, they became seemingly ubiquitous. Wherever Harris looked, images that he believed were his own stared back at him, tacitly naming him to all and sundry as the killer. Within the Bay Area, there was nowhere to escape.

Unless a means of doing so had been printed in the same paper that published the sketches, in the tiny article at the bottom of its front page, promising the reward.

The tensions of the first night increased dramatically on the second night of the sweeps. As promised by the SFPD brass, even more cops filled the streets, but other promises they made were broken. Chief Scott stated that the officers making stops were interested only in evidence having to do with the Zebra attacks, and that lesser offenses would be ignored. As Sanders recalls, when the sweeps grew, restraint went out the window.

"Cops began to act like they had a license to do anything. Instead of just stopping people and questioning them, they were spread-eagling them against walls and busting them for anything they found: a joint, a penknife that was too long, even unpaid traffic tickets. It got to the point where Gil and I had to get into it with some of the cops, telling them to back off for fear they'd start something they couldn't stop."

Carl Williams was a young lawyer working at a large firm in San Francisco's financial district when the Zebra sweeps began. Fresh out of law school, Carl was recently married and struggling to make ends meet. Rather than spend money on a second car, he rode the streetcar from downtown to the apartment in the Sunset district where he lived with his wife. Bright, well educated, and law-abiding, Carl was as upstanding a young man as one could imagine. But he was also African American. That meant he was a Zebra suspect.

Night was just starting to fall as Carl stood at a downtown corner of Market Street waiting for the bus that would take him home. He was dressed in the office attire he usually wore to work, a suit and tie, and had a briefcase by his side. His mind was on other things as he waited for his ride, going back over cases he had worked on during the day.

Like many African Americans his age, Carl actively followed politics and was passionate about civil rights. He was not naive, but he tried to embrace a positive vision and refused to give ground to despair or cynicism, no matter how dire things might seem. It was a vision he had spent years nurturing, beginning when he was growing up in the heart of the segregated South, in Jacksonville, Alabama. Yet it took only a few minutes to turn that vision upside down, and it didn't happen during the days of Jim Crow or below the Mason-Dixon line.

Carl never even saw the patrol car coming. Suddenly it was just there, nearly mounting the curb as it screeched to a stop. Two uniformed cops jumped out, guns drawn. Growing up under Jim Crow had schooled Carl on what to do next. He dropped his briefcase and raised his arms, not in the air but straight out from his body, as far away from his sides as possible to make sure the cops could see that he had no weapon and posed no threat. What Carl didn't realize yet was that as far as these cops were concerned, he posed a threat just because of his color.

They shoved him against the patrol car and spread-eagled him as they patted him down. They looked at his wallet and checked his ID. Then they opened his briefcase and riffled through his papers.

People stopped and stared, and the public nature of the search added to Carl's humiliation. As strident as the racism was down South, nothing had prepared him for the fear or sense of helplessness that took hold of him as he stood spread-eagled against the patrol car, feeling that if he made a wrong move he could end up dead.

When they were done searching him, they wrote him up a Zebra card. They gave one copy to Carl, for him to present when other cops stopped him, and kept one copy for themselves, to become part of the ever-growing file of Zebra suspects.

As surprised as Carl was by the fear that he had felt, he was even less prepared for the rush of anger that followed.

In the days after his search, Carl took to leaving the office before it grew dark, believing now that it was safer for blacks to travel in San Francisco during daylight hours. Even more disturbing, however, was the effect the stop had on his vision of race relations. His carefully nurtured optimism for what lay ahead dimmed. He began to wonder what he would do if he were stopped again, doubting that he could endure the fear and anger a second time without fighting back. Friends of his in college, instead of going the establishment route as he did, had joined the Black Panthers. Now Carl began to think that their choice was the more sensible one, not his.

The same night Carl was stopped, Douglas Blake was detained while walking on Haight. The police took Douglas to Park Station and interrogated him for over an hour, accusing him of being a Zebra killer, making claims that lacked even the vaguest grounding in reality, and trying to bully him into a confession. Eventually they let him go. No one ever explained why they brought him in or appeared so certain he was one of the killers.

As the sweeps expanded, so did the net they cast across the city. African-American males of all shapes, sizes, shades, and ages were stopped, searched, and interrogated, with little if any regard for civil rights or the supposed parameters of the manhunt. Even someone like Bill Monroe, an African-American cameraman and the husband of Belva Davis, who knew scores of cops from his work with TV news crews, felt unsafe on the streets and made a point of staying out of the city after dark unless he absolutely had to be there.

Perhaps the most ill-advised stop the police made on the second night of the Zebra sweeps was one that belied the very notion the police were following any criteria at all except one: being black.

Joseph B. Williams had taken part in two great African-American migrations. Born in South Carolina in 1912, he had moved north with his parents to Philadelphia soon after World War I. Years later Williams participated in the second black migration, heading west to San Francisco after World War II. Although he had dropped out of school as a youth, Williams eventually got a law degree and joined the California Bar in 1956. By 1974 Williams had spent eighteen years working as a civil rights lawyer, partnering with men like Terry Francoise and both John and Phil Burton, arguing scores of cases for the NAACP. Joe Williams had at least one other significant attribute in 1974. He was sixty-two years old.

That made him more than thirty years older than the parameters called for by the Zebra sweeps. Nevertheless, like every other black man out that night, Joe Williams was stopped, questioned, searched, and classified as a Zebra suspect.

Many African Americans reacted to being stopped by simply swallowing their anger and outrage and never saying a word about it to anyone.

"When you live in a world where humiliation is part of your daily routine, you learn to put it aside," Sanders explains. "It's not that it doesn't affect you. It's that you feel powerless to fight it. So people learn to just let injustice slide by."

Not Joe Williams. Williams had spent a lifetime breaking color lines and tackling injustice, and he was not about to stop now. Determined to follow the same course of action he had dozens of times before, he brought a federal lawsuit against Alioto, the SFPD, and the city of San Francisco to end what he viewed as oppression.

As the manhunt resumed for a third night and continued to expand, other African-American leaders in the Bay Area became more vocal in their opposition. Among them was the Reverend Cecil Williams, who had played an important role in the response to the Hearst kidnapping by overseeing the food giveaway program. Like the other African-American critics of the sweeps, Cecil Williams acknowledged that he wanted the killers caught. However, the manhunt, he warned, and the manner in which the police were conducting it, put the black community under the equivalent of a "police state" that "creates the possibility of a racial war."

That such a war might be brewing was suggested by the unrest on the streets. Protestors from numerous groups began to assemble around both City Hall and the Hall of Justice, including the NAACP, a multiracial student group called the Committee Against Racism, the Urban League, the Vietnam Veterans Against the War, and others, carrying placards and shouting out slogans against what they termed racist police actions. In response, brownshirted and helmet-wearing Nazis joined with other white supremacy groups in counterdemonstrations, offering to help the police round up blacks and getting into shouting matches with the other demonstrators. The confrontations forced cops who had stayed up all night implementing the sweeps to do double duty, stopping fights and trying to stave off violence.

Inside the Hall of Justice, Jesse Byrd, president of Officers for Justice at the time, lodged a formal complaint about the sweeps, referring to them as "Gestapo-like tactics" that could only be viewed as "another form of harassment." Other blacks within the police department also came out publicly against them. Meanwhile, the edginess and anger felt by black officers ran headlong into contrary emotions among the white officers. Rumors had already circulated that black cops might have been tipping off the killers to help them evade detection. Now, with so many black officers criticizing the department, whites rallying behind the sweeps were tempted to retaliate. Emotions in the Hall of Justice reached the breaking point.

"The tension got so thick in there you could cut it with a knife," Sanders recalls. "Homicide was a haven for Gil and me. Most people accepted us there. They welcomed us. But outside Room 450 was another story. There were walls in that building that were covered in racist graffiti. Some people were just itching to get into it with the black officers, and more than once the only thing that stopped a fight was black cops just walking away. But even though fights never broke out in the hall, people took that same hostility out on the street."

And that was where the situation finally began to combust.

By Sunday night, April 21, the fourth night of the Zebra sweeps, more cops were added to the numbers out on the street. Many fresh officers replaced those who had been out on previous evenings and had gone without sleep for three nights running, and others besides regular SFPD officers helped augment the total number patrolling the city. Though never formally counted, it was generally estimated that by now from over 200 to as many as 350 cops at any given time had the sole duty of stopping and questioning African-American males who happened to be out after dark. Among the new officers on the Zebra patrols were volunteers from other agencies, such as the Sheriff's Department, and some 150 reserve officers whose duties were usually

restricted to crowd control at parades. Now, despite their limited training, they were given almost unlimited powers.

"Gil and I began spending most of our time on the street just trying to quiet things down. People were starting to fight back against
the sweeps. A white Pacific Gas and Electric repairman out at Hunters
Point on a job had to take cover when he got shot at from an apartment
building.

"That same night, cops saw a guy driving the wrong way up Nob
Hill, and when they tried to stop him, he took off. He wasn't even
black. But the cops were in plain clothes, so he didn't know who was
after him and got so scared he tried to run one down. All hell broke
loose. They chased the guy for over twenty minutes and got in a running gun battle with him before he finally crashed and got caught.

"Then in the Fillmore this old black guy was out walking by himself. One of the cops patrolling the area, a Filipino dressed in plain
clothes, called out for him to stop. The old black guy kept walking. So
the cop took after him yelling, 'Stop! Police!' Instead of stopping, the
old guy raised a pistol and started firing. Well, that was it. All the cops
there opened up on him. He took six bullets before he went down. The
cops had .357s. Those things have so much force that unless they hit
bone they pass clean through. But the old guy lived, and he told Gil
and me that he took the gun because with all the talk about Zebra, he
was scared of reprisals, and since the cops were in plain clothes he
didn't know whether they were really cops or just guys out to get him."

The incident that nearly sucked both Sanders and Gilford into
the vortex of violence happened just south of Market, when all they
were trying to do was help.

"What had happened was exactly the sort of thing we were afraid
of," Sanders recalls. "Some blacks who got stopped tried to resist, and
a fight broke out between them and the white cops who'd stopped
them. We got a call for assistance, and were able to calm the situation
pretty fast. But just when we thought it was over, a squad car came tearing around the corner, and two more cops rushed out and began laying
into the black guys with their billy clubs, starting an even bigger fight
than the one we'd just stopped.

"Gil lost it. He started to throw down with the cops who drove up. The original cops on the scene and I had to get in between Gil and the other guys, just to stop it from being cop vs. cop right there on the street."

Charlie Walker, who at the time of the Zebra sweeps owned businesses in both the Fillmore and Hunters Point, watched both communities nearly explode under the pressure.

"People were pissed. It was like we were sitting on a bomb with a short fuse, and every time somebody got stopped, it sent off a spark. You knew if it got big enough, the place would blow. And the only reason it didn't, in my opinion, was because of Sanders and Gilford.

"I saw it time and again, in Fillmore and Hunters Point, people ready to start something and those two stepping in to calm things down. Not just any black cop could do what they did. Those two didn't get into bullshit, and they didn't take it either. So they had respect. When something happened and they told you to back off, you did. Because you knew they weren't just there to keep you down. They were trying to help you rise up. Even if you didn't always agree with how they were trying to do it."

No matter what anyone did, though, the furor over Zebra kept spiraling out of control. Protestors began to follow Alioto around, hounding him with placards that accused him of leading a race war. When that Monday, after a series of meetings on Zebra, Alioto left for a waiting limousine, protestors surrounded him, refusing to let him pass. Some shouted at him. Others spat. Then one man began beating Alioto on the head with the sign he was holding, until the mayor's aides stepped in and shoved the man away, helping Alioto push through the crowd to his car. Once he was inside, the protestors surrounded the limousine, pounding on it as the mayor's driver sped away.

While Alioto was being assaulted on the steps of City Hall, the Black Liberation Army took advantage of the outrage over the police response to Zebra to promote its own revolutionary agenda, sending a communiqué to the FM rock station KSAN that called for a massive uprising of all radical groups. The BLA urged the creation of a "People's Army" to support the "struggle" being waged in San Francisco by groups like themselves, the SLA, the Weather Underground, and the group behind Zebra.

Radicals weren't the only ones whose sought to use the passions aroused by Zebra to their advantage. Incredibly, a black assailant who killed a twenty-five-year-old white Safeway worker and then raped his wife during the sweeps actually claimed to be a Zebra killer, an assertion the police followed up until they determined there was no connection.

Meanwhile, letters began arriving at the Hall of Justice from people who claimed to know the identity of the Zebra killers. Tourists wrote on hotel stationery about suspicious black men they had noticed on the street. A landlady claimed that a black man renting from her resembled the police sketches and that she couldn't always account for his whereabouts at the times when the killings took place. One of the strangest tips may have been a handwritten slip of paper sent to the SFPD inside a tiny two-by-four-inch envelope. The person who wrote the note did so with a trembling hand, using block lettering, beginning with the word ZEBRA and then telling the police only a man's name along with the words POLK ST., BLACK, MAKEUP, and GAY. It was as if all the fears and dreads of the city were being shuffled together and tied up in the neat unifying bow of race.

The suit Joseph B. Williams filed challenging the constitutionality of the sweeps moved quickly through the courts. Hearings began almost immediately, and within a few days it was clear that the case was going against the mayor, the city, and the police department. Though the Officers for Justice had no formal involvement in the lawsuit, William Hastie Jr., one of the main lawyers representing the OFJ, was also one of the lawyers arguing Williams's Zebra case.

Some in the department kept on struggling to find ways to defend the sweeps, going so far as to point out that crime had gone down during the period. It was an argument that, as Carl Williams pointed out when he was interviewed for this book, was like saying that slavery was an answer to unemployment.

One thing that those who supported the sweeps could not claim, however, was that it had led to progress in the investigation. Charlie Barca was honest enough to acknowledge that. Unlike the rest of the brass, Barca didn't try to hedge the truth when he was called to testify during Joe Williams's suit. Asked if the sweeps had actually accomplished anything, Barca admitted they had not, and characterized them as "ineffective and unproductive," a claim he repeated as a source for an ABC-TV news report by Harry Reasoner.

Behind the scenes, Gilford continued to lobby against the sweeps as he had from the day they began, using what influence he possessed to find an alternative to a tactic that was manifestly ripping the city apart.

"Gil hated the sweeps for a lot of reasons," Sanders recalls. "He used to say it reminded him of being back in Willis, Texas, where if you were black and went out on the street at night you were taking your life in your hands. But what he objected to more than anything was that it was bad policing. It didn't lead to information, or clues, or anything except ill will. So he started thinking about better ways to get the job done, and came up with idea of forming a plainclothed investigative team made up entirely of minority officers, a group that could work seamlessly inside the community and, if need be, go undercover as well. Then he took the idea to Charlie Barca."

Gilford had a decent rapport with Barca, but the fact that Barca had been one of the front men on the sweeps made him uncertain how his proposal would be received. To his surprise, Barca liked the idea.

"Looking back, it was clear why," Sanders explains. "Charlie was smart. Sometimes when you're the number-two or -three man in an administration, you spend a lot of time trying to make something good out of other people's bad ideas. Charlie knew the sweeps didn't work. The problem was, the mayor and the chief had a lot invested in them, and Charlie had to march in step. But he was looking for a better way, too. And Gil's idea made sense."

Joseph Alioto was far less inclined to admit being wrong than Charlie Barca. Even as the trial began, Alioto remained committed to the sweeps, refusing to acknowledge how disastrous they were turning out to be. Since San Francisco is a city where the police chief serves at the pleasure of the mayor, what the mayor wants is almost always what the SFPD wants, as well. The sweeps were the horse Alioto had hitched his wagon to, and he was stubbornly sticking with it.

However, when it became impossible to ignore the evidence that U.S. district judge Alfonso J. Zirpoli would issue a decision in favor of Williams, Alioto was forced to consider alternatives. During meetings that weekend, he agreed to let Barca put Gilford's plan into action simultaneously with the sweeps. Days later, on April 25, Alioto would finally give up on the sweeps entirely, bowing to Zirpoli's overwhelming condemnation. In what may be one of the first uses of the word "profile" in such matters, Zirpoli forbade the SFPD to stop and search anyone simply because they might resemble, in Zirpoli's words, a broad "profile" the department had prepared about the killer. Going even further, he declared the entire Zebra manhunt to be illegal and proscribed by the Fourth Amendment of the Constitution, which protected citizens from unfair search and seizure.

Before Judge Zirpoli issued his decision, though, a telephone call during the middle of the sweeps would turn the case on its axis and provide the break that everyone had been waiting for.

11

Real Cops After All

WITH THE ZEBRA SWEEPS severely straining racial relations in the department as well as the city, the SFPD brass counted on Gilford's leadership to help set things right among black officers. Given the go-ahead by Chief Scott and Captain Barca, Gilford assembled a thirty-man force that comprised twenty-eight blacks, one Latino, and one white. He would direct the unit, and Sanders would serve as his second-in-command. The plan was for the Zebra squad to function as a plain-clothes force working in areas of the city where they were comfortable and accepted, giving them a chance to develop information at a grass-roots level.

"Most of the sources we used on a regular basis shut down on us because of the sweeps," Sanders explains. "Gil thought if people on the streets saw that we were using tactics which tried to involve the community rather than just overwhelm it, our sources might open up to us again, giving us the kind of support that would lead to some solid information."

The other tactic Gilford intended was to infiltrate the insular group behind the Zebra attacks. Like Sanders, he understood that, because of the racism in the department, black cops hadn't had either the numbers or the operational presence needed to get inside the kind of group they were dealing with, and his hope was that the Zebra squad could remedy that and maybe even create a major breakthrough.

Among the blacks Gilford brought into the Zebra squad was Billye Morrow, a narcotics officer who was one of the best the department ever had at undercover work.

"Morrow was a legend," Sanders recalls. "He was in my academy class, but he had already been a sworn officer for years, working undercover busting junkies before he even went to the academy. Then he went back undercover, and was one of the few cops who successfully took on the drug trade in the Haight, sometimes busting the same people he'd busted years earlier. Nobody was smoother at undercover work than Billye Morrow."

Gilford wanted Morrow to run the undercover operations within the Zebra squad, using some officers who were still relatively unknown in the black community to attempt to penetrate the radical groups most likely behind Zebra, particularly the Nation of Islam. Gilford and Sanders, along with Coreris and Fotinos, still considered rogue members of the Nation among the best candidates to be the perpetrators. At the same time, Gilford hoped he would now have more credibility to pursue another avenue to gain insight into the Nation: securing the trust of the few black officers thought to be members.

"The one most commonly thought of as being involved in the Nation back then was Jesse Byrd, who was president of Officers for Justice at the time," says Sanders. "But Jesse was never open to talking about the Nation, and we knew that as long as he wouldn't talk about his own involvement, everything else would be off-limits, too."

Gilford didn't believe Byrd had knowledge of anything directly related to Zebra. He simply hoped his fellow officer would recognize the value of a minority-based investigative unit and allow himself to be persuaded to help the squad gain access to sources. Yet before he could make that appeal, came the telephone call that changed everything. Not long afterward, Gilford learned that Byrd would almost certainly have rejected his overture.

The phone rang in Room 450 of the Hall of Justice at 4:30 in the afternoon of April 22.

Since the sketches were published and the sweeps began, the offices of the Homicide Bureau had been at the center of a whirlwind. Everything about the case got funneled through there one way or another: the reports from the patrols taking part in the sweeps, the police copies of the Zebra cards, the preliminary work by Gilford's Zebra squad, whatever leads might come from the Intelligence Bureau and their collaboration with both the state and federal Justice Departments, not to mention the ongoing efforts of the squad of inspectors and officers whose work was being coordinated by Coreris and Fotinos.

But nothing added to the tumult inside Homicide more than the number of tips, which had multiplied exponentially the day the sketches hit the papers. Letters, postcards, anonymous notes, and a deluge of calls poured in, with the phones ringing almost nonstop. In the twelve weeks since the official start of Operation Zebra at the end of January, more than five thousand tips had been phoned in, coming at a rate of nearly one every twenty minutes. Almost without exception, they were all worthless.

It got to the point where almost no one wanted to take the calls anymore. When this one came in, it was Ed Erdelatz's turn to answer.

Along with Earl Sanders, Edward Erdelatz Jr. was one of the two youngest inspectors in Homicide. Like Sanders, Erdelatz was considered a rising star in the department, someone who had made inspector in a remarkably short amount of time and seemed to have a lot going for him in terms of both ability and potential. There, however, was where the similarities ended.

While Sanders had faced hardship growing up, Erdelatz had been relatively privileged. The son of college football legend Eddie Erdelatz, one of the most successful coaches in the history of the Naval Academy's famed football program, Erdelatz had a military mien, with a crew cut and a conservative outlook that was night and day from the more liberal attitudes of both Gilford and Sanders. In Sanders's mind, he was also pointedly insensitive when it came to racial matters.

"Erdelatz had the kind of sense of humor where he either didn't know when to stop or else just didn't want to. I remember, one time around Zebra, he came in the office after Gil had the natural he wore back then blown out, and Erdelatz walked up behind him and put his hands right on Gil's natural, like he was petting it. Gil got so angry I had to stop him from going after Erdelatz right there in Homicide.

And Erdelatz acted like he didn't mean anything, but at the same time he was smiling, because you knew he wanted to get Gil's goat. And he did. More than once."

The friction that sometimes entered into the working relationship between Erdelatz and both Sanders and Gilford was surprisingly absent during Zebra. Though racial tensions were on a hair-trigger in much of the SFPD at the time, the inspectors in Homicide found the situation too serious to allow anything that smacked of being even slightly trivial get in the way of the work.

Neither Sanders nor Gilford was there when Erdelatz answered the phone and listened to the man who identified himself as Anthony Cornelius Harris. Coreris and Fotinos were out as well, running down leads on the recent killings, leaving the office about as quiet as it had been in days and allowing those who were still there to think they might have an early night at last.

Unlike most of those who called in tips, Harris refused to give Erdelatz the information he claimed to have over the phone, demanding instead that officers come interview him. That meant driving across the Bay Bridge to Oakland in the middle of rush hour, something Erdelatz did not relish. However, someone had to check out the lead, no matter how iffy, so Erdelatz handed the job to Carl Klotz and Jeff Brosch, the Burglary inspectors who had been detailed to Homicide to assist on the task force. Figuring they were on a wild goose chase, Klotz and Brosch headed to Oakland.

When Klotz and Brosch met Harris on the Oakland Parkway, where he had said he would be, he was wearing a black tuxedo, tennis shoes, and a fezlike hat and acting paranoid, going on about how dangerous the guys behind Zebra were. Klotz suspected he was, in his words, "a sack of nuts." That changed when Harris started talking about having first met the Zebra killers in San Quentin and how they were all Muslim.

Neither Brosch nor Klotz was aware of the theory shared by the leaders of the Zebra team that members of the Nation of Islam were behind the attacks. However, Brosch had worked on a burglary case a year earlier in which he had recovered stolen property from the warehouse of Black Self-Help Moving and Storage, the same company where Harris said he and the Zebra killers had worked. Intrigued, they took Harris, who was still afraid they were all being watched, back to the Hall of Justice to interview him there. When they arrived in Homicide, they were the only ones there. Not long after they began their interview, Gilford and Sanders returned from a Zebra squad operation. Much of what Harris said jibed with information that had not yet been released to the public, so, leaving Harris by himself in the interrogation room, Klotz and Brosch went over the interview with Sanders and Gilford. Both immediately recognized one of the names Harris had mentioned: Larry Green.

"The moment we heard Green's name, a kind of electric shock went through Gil and me," Sanders recalls. "It was like all the tumblers in a lock coming together again. Harris talked about the Hagues being attacked, about Erakat, about Dancik, the five-in-one night — all of it. We'd been knocking on this door for so long, and now, finally, it seemed like maybe, just maybe, it was starting to open. And it actually made you feel a little shaky. Like you had to catch your breath."

Gilford immediately called Charlie Ellis and informed him about what Harris seemed to know. Ellis told him to call in *everybody*. Coreris and Fotinos conducted a formal interview with Harris later that evening, with Gilford also taking part. As the interview progressed, others on the task force began to search for information on some of those whom Harris said were involved.

One name among those mentioned by Harris deeply affected Gilford: Dwight Stallings, who as a kid had been "Little Jug" to Gilford's "Jughead." Recalls Sanders, "Gil said Stallings was a good kid, but after King was killed, he let his anger get to him, drifting into the whole separatist thing, trying to match hate with hate. When you do that, you're lost."

What Gilford heard in that first interview, and what emerged in greater detail in subsequent interviews that Harris had with Coreris, Fotinos, Gilford, and others, was a profoundly unsettling account of horror. Harris's recollections were not always clear or consistent. In addition, as he had no guarantee of immunity at first and was already on parole for other crimes, which meant he could be tossed back in prison if he was found in violation, he almost certainly couched much of what he said in such a way as to minimize his own guilt. Even so, the cumulative effect was overwhelming when it came to establishing the conspiracy behind the crimes and the guilt of the conspirators in the six months of terror that had become known as the Zebra murders.

Harris began with his release from San Quentin the previous summer and his meeting with Larry Green at Temple No. 26. When Green took him under his wing and helped him find work at Black Self-Help Moving and Storage, he met J. C. Simon, Jesse Cooks, Thomas Manney, Clarence Jamerson, Dwight Stallings, and Douglas Burton, among others, becoming part of a group that spent time together after work at the Market Street warehouse listening to lectures as well as in more private gatherings at Simon's apartment on Grove Street. It was there, during meetings in October of 1973, that Simon referred to crimes committed by whites against blacks to justify the need for blacks to "destroy the enemy," asking Harris if his mind was "together enough" to do so and quoting the Nation of Islam's Lesson No. 10 as the rationale for "killing devils." According to Harris, Simon had a case containing handguns that he intended to use for that purpose, including a .32-caliber automatic.

Harris named Jesse Cooks as the instigator for the kidnapping of and machete attack on the Hagues later that same month, detailing how it was carried out by Cooks, Green, and himself. The details in his account of that harrowing crime were what first convinced the investigators of his veracity. Harris recognized a photograph of Quita Hague, and he knew the color and make of van in which she and her husband Richard were abducted, the places and times where both the kidnapping and the assaults had occurred, and what items of theirs had been stolen. He even revealed the fact that immediately after he and the others had forced the Hagues into the van, an SFPD patrol car stopped alongside to inquire whether anything was wrong. The two officers, Marovich and McAlister, remained in the car and never got out. Instead, while Harris stood by the van's door and Green stayed where he was in the driver's seat, Cooks approached the cruiser and assured the officers that everything was all right, they were merely changing a tire. After the police left, Cooks and Harris got back in the van, and Green drove to the railroad tracks below Potrero Hill, where the assaults on the Hagues occured.

The clincher, though, was Harris's knowledge of what took place that night before the Hagues were abducted: he recounted how he and the others had trolled the Ingleside area for victims and tried to kidnap a group of schoolchildren. They nearly succeeded, pulling a gun on two girls and a boy and corralling them toward the van, until the boy yelled, "Cops!" and distracted their would-be abductors, allowing the children to run away. As Sanders recalls: "Nothing about the kids in Ingleside had been printed yet in the press. The only way for Harris to know about it was to have heard it from one of the killers, or to have been there himself. That was the detail that made everyone certain he was the real deal."

Yet that was just the beginning. Harris went on to relate how, in November, after Cooks had been arrested for the murder of Frances Rose, Manuel Moore was released from San Quentin and became part of the group at Black Self-Help. On November 25, 1973, the Sunday before Thanksgiving, J. C. Simon picked Harris up outside a YMCA in the Tenderloin. There was talk of going to hear the former soul singer Joe Tex, who had changed his name to Yusaff Hazzizz and become a minister with the Nation of Islam, speak at the Scottish Rite Memorial Temple. Instead, Simon stopped outside the mom-and-pop grocery store on Larkin owned by Saleem Erakat. Simon said something to Harris about wanting to make a "sting" and posted Harris to keep watch outside, according to Harris. Then he went into the store and committed the robbery, shooting the grocer in the head.

Less than two weeks later, at around 9:00 P.M. on the night of December 11, Harris was waiting for a bus in the Fillmore when J. C. Simon and Manuel Moore pulled up in a black Cadillac that Harris believed belonged to Tom Manney. He got in the back, and Simon, who was at the wheel, drove to the nearby projects on Haight Street and parked, telling Harris to wait as he and Moore got out. Moore then ran into some bushes by a telephone booth where Paul Dancik stood making a call. Simon approached the booth from a different angle. Harris heard gunshots, then Simon and Moore ran back to the car, and Simon sped off past Dancik's body, which lay on the sidewalk. Simon stopped about two blocks away, and he and Moore got out again to speak with two men inside another Cadillac, which Harris believed was owned by Clarence Jamerson. Harris couldn't see who the other men were, but when Simon came back to the car, he told Harris that he'd have to take a bus after all.

Two nights later, on December 13, Harris was again driving around with Simon and Moore in the black Cadillac when Simon parked on Potrero Hill, at Wisconsin Street and Twenty-second. He watched as the other two men got out and walked across the street, each shadowing the other as they made their way toward a group of people who were dispersing. Among them was Art Agnos. Again Harris heard gunshots before Simon and Moore ran back to the car, but he claimed not to have witnessed Agnos's shooting. In his statements, he never made any mention of the Marietta DiGirolamo shooting, which took place about an hour and twenty minutes later. DiGirolamo was shot by a black man whom witnesses described as similar in some ways to both Simon and Moore.

Harris could give no information about the shootings of Ilario Bertuccio and Theresa DeMartini a week later, on December 20. Witness descriptions would allow the investigators to tie Manuel Moore to the Bertuccio murder, and a car similar to Larry Green's Dodge Dart was spotted near the scenes of both crimes. Nor was Harris present when Neil Moynihan and Mildred Hosler were slain on December 22 by men whose descriptions would later be matched to Moore and Green respectively.

Although he claimed to have no knowledge of how the victim known as Unknown Body #169 died, Harris did admit that in late December, around the same time as the shootings of Hosler and Moynihan, Larry Green asked him to help dispose of what he realized from its look and smell was a body wrapped in plastic. The two men retrieved it from the Black Self-Help warehouse and carried it to Green's van, then drove out to the Great Highway and dumped it on Ocean Beach.

Harris's account of the night of January 28 has been incorporated into the narrative of chapter 7. Having driven with J. C. Simon and Manuel Moore to the Fruit of Islam House, about a block or so from

Temple No. 26, he was standing outside, waiting for them to return to the car, when he heard gunshots at a time that corresponded exactly to the killing of Tana Smith at the corner of Geary and Divisadero. Harris was high on barbiturates that evening, and his memory of what followed was vague and at times inconsistent. In some tellings he claimed to continue riding with Simon and Moore, while in others he described riding for a time in a second car with two African-American men he said he didn't know. In both versions, though, he watched Simon and Moore go on a spree of unprecedented mayhem. Minutes after the murder of Tana Smith, Vincent Wollin was shot dead on Scott Street, just a few blocks away. Then John Bambic was shot and killed at Ninth and Howard, south of Market. Harris did not see this murder, but witnesses reported seeing an African-American man run from the crime scene to a Cadillac like the one owned by Clarence Jamerson.

Later, around 9:45, Harris recalled being in the black Cadillac with Simon and Moore, and watching as they got out of the car and went toward the Laundromat on Silver Avenue where Jane Holly was murdered. Harris heard gunshots and saw Simon and Moore return at a run, one of them bumping into two young women before they jumped in the car and sped off. Less than two miles away they stopped again, at Edinburgh Street, where Simon and Moore got out as Harris stayed behind. He heard the shots but did not witness the attack on Roxanne McMillian that left her paralyzed.

After this night, Harris broke with the group at Black Self-Help and moved across the bay to Oakland. He had no knowledge of subsequent crimes considered part of the Zebra murders. However, on the night he turned himself in, Harris did make claims about other crimes. One was a stabbing in Berkeley that Harris said had been committed by Larry Green before the attack on the Hagues. There had indeed been a killing similar to what Harris described on about the same date he told the police, but the authorities never felt there was enough evidence to tie it to the Zebra murders or to bring charges against Green.

While making his statement, Harris spoke of a group in the Nation of Islam called the "Death Angels," whose members, according to him, killed white people to amass points and gain entry into the hierarchy of their exclusive secret society. For many, Harris's story of the

Death Angels came to define the Zebra killings. However, it wasn't this that convinced investigators his claims were true, but what he said about the crimes themselves.

Around ten o'clock, Klotz and Brosch, accompanied by Gilford, drove Harris back to Oakland. Gilford was concerned about letting him go, fearing he would be in jeopardy if any of the men he had named learned that he had gone to the police, but Harris insisted on going home to his family. When they left him, he seemed safe.

Later that night, Harris called Coreris and Fotinos from an Oakland police station, claiming he had talked to Green, who had told him that people knew what he had done and that a contract had been taken out on his life. He asked for protection for himself, Deborah, and their child. So Coreris and Fotinos drove out to Oakland again and brought Harris and his family back to San Francisco, to the Holiday Inn at Market and Eighth, not far from the Hall of Justice. What followed was a tragicomedy of errors that began that night. It might have been funny if not for the danger involved and the bloodshed that had gone before. Harris escaped custody, somehow giving his guards the slip. This continued for weeks. Sometimes he would disappear for days and then call up and once more ask for protection.

Even when witnesses are more predictable than the wildly erratic Anthony Harris, knowledge of their whereabouts is privileged information. With a case like Zebra, stamped with wanton violence and murder, secrecy was absolutely necessary, not only for Harris's sake but also for the sake of the investigation, which at that point hinged on his testimony. So Gus Coreris was taken aback when an SFPD officer who had nothing to do with the case came to the Homicide Bureau and asked straight out where Harris was being held. When Gilford and Sanders learned about it, they were surprised too, although not by the name of the officer who had asked.

It was Jesse Byrd. According to Gus Coreris, Byrd said he was making the inquiry on behalf of the Nation of Islam. Coreris, of course, refused to tell him anything, adding that if he didn't stop trying to discover Harris's whereabouts, he would report him. Though neither Gilford nor Sanders ever spoke to Byrd about the incident, both were deeply disappointed. Sanders explains, "Jesse and I had run-ins more than once, over a number of issues. But I never expected anything like that from him. To this day I don't believe that Jesse intended any harm to come to Harris. From what I understand, Jesse's involvement with the Nation of Islam was just beginning at that time, and when you're a recent convert to something, you often try to please those above you, believing things that might be better viewed with a critical eye. It's more than possible that someone with the Nation told him they were afraid Harris was being held against his will, and that all they wanted to do was 'talk to him.'

"Talk was hardly where it would have ended, if you ask me. But I wouldn't be surprised if Jesse believed that the information would do nothing to endanger Harris — even though we all felt sure it would."

Part of what so disappointed Sanders about Byrd's request was that while his job as a police officer was first to protect the public, he seemed to be putting another priority, and another loyalty, above that. What is more, his behavior gave an opening to racists.

"Remember, there were cops on that force who were slandering black officers, trying to make it seem like we didn't care. And here Jesse was giving them fodder. We had real battles to fight, and real injustice to put an end to. Jesse knew that. He was as much a part of the Officers for Justice suit as anyone. Hell, he was the president of OFJ back then. But Harris came in on his own. Period. And you have to know when you've got a real fight worth winning, and when you're just wrong."

Ultimately, information about where Harris was staying did leak, but not from anyone on the police force. It came from Harris's girlfriend. "For some reason Deborah, the woman he was with, started talking to Carolyn, the woman he *used* to be with," Sanders says, shaking his head at the bizarreness of it all. "And then Carolyn leaked out word they were at the Holiday Inn."

Soon people from the Nation and Black Self-Help began showing up in the lobby, forcing Klotz and Brosch to spirit Harris and his family out the back and install them at another hotel.

Later Harris took off on his own again, going to Berkeley to see the mother of Larry Green, hoping she might talk her son into confessing to his role in Zebra. Upset by Harris's tale of bloodshed, Mrs. Green asked him to come back and speak with her husband about it.

So Harris returned later that evening and went through his story again for Green's father. Afterward, his mother called Green in San Francisco and confronted him about Harris's account. Green told her to put Harris on the phone, then began to yell at him, ordering Harris to get out of his house and threatening him with violence if he ever returned.

Harris left and soon was back under the protection of the SFPD. Except in court, he would never again see the young man with whom he had once been so close, and who had first brought him inside the walls of Black Self-Help.

Though the SFPD had Harris, they did not have the alleged perpetrators. By his own account, Harris was an accomplice, and as such all his claims had to be corroborated by another source to have the weight of proof in a court of law. Otherwise, the task force would have nothing.

By April 24, with the sweeps still going on, the task force began to set up round-the-clock surveillance of the men Harris had named. Gilford, Sanders, and the rest of the Zebra squad conducted part of that work. New surveillance units were brought in as well. Code-named the Rainbow, Yellow, and Eagle commands, they were assembled from officers in the Narcotics, Sex, and Missing Persons details. Setting up in the Bradmar Apartments at 1651 Market Street, which were separated from Black Self-Help only by a narrow alley, the crews kept watch 24/7. The officers in the Bradmar had warrants not only to take photographs of Black Self-Help but also to use the latest audio surveillance equipment to record what was said there. In addition, they were equipped with enough mobile units to maintain a constant watch on every single individual involved, no matter where they went.

Greg Corrales, the narcotics officer who had busted Zebra victim Paul Dancik in a violent confrontation just a week before he was killed, was one of those assigned to the surveillance squads. Known as someone bold enough to do almost anything, Corrales offered to put himself in harm's way as a potential victim, suggesting he walk alone along darkened streets in areas that were deemed the most dangerous in the hope of drawing the killers out. The offer was turned down as too risky, even for Greg Corrales.

Napoleon Hendrix, who years later became Sanders's last partner in Homicide, also did surveillance on Zebra, working inside the apartment that looked directly down at the parking area behind Black Self-Help.

Nothing Green, J. C. Simon, or the others did or said was directly incriminating, but the crews soon became aware that they were using slang as code words to talk about the terrorism that was clearly still their goal. Although Hendrix worked on the visual surveillance, not audio, he recalls some of the terms they deciphered. Going "rolling" meant to go searching for victims to attack, while to "sting" meant to do the deed itself.

"Nap and the others could tell they were getting ready to go out 'rolling' again, as they called it," Sanders recalls. "They knew that panic was high, and they wanted to time the next shooting in a way to maximize its impact. And its terror."

Tension rose even more when members of Sacramento's Nation of Islam temple were arrested the afternoon of April 24 for what was described as the "random slaying" of a twenty-five-year-old white man, who was killed by a shotgun blast through a picture window. Another member of the temple was accused of shooting an off-duty Sacramento cop. The arrests created a temporary lockdown of the black community in Sacramento that went even beyond the severity of the sweeps in San Francisco, with a large portion of the ghetto being cordoned off for over six hours while the police searched for suspects. Two other motiveless shootings were said to have occurred in Sacramento since the Zebra sweeps began, and the sheriff told the press he thought they had been "fostered" by the Zebra attacks.

"By this point, word had spread among cops throughout the region that members of the Nation could be involved in Zebra," Sanders explains. "And when the shootings in Sacramento happened, the connection became pretty much an open secret."

Despite the arrests in Sacramento, and the fact that the men of Black Self-Help knew Anthony Harris had made contact with the

SFPD, they continued to talk about going "rolling" again soon. It was as if they felt they were invisible — or invincible.

Though under constant watch, Harris escaped custody again and again, slipping out through windows, back doors, and service elevators.

"Harris was not exactly an ideal witness," Sanders says with more than a touch of irony. "He had a record that practically went back to when he learned to crawl, he had drug problems, and he was prone to overstatements and delusions of grandeur. Plus he had a habit of slipping out of custody just when you needed him most. He even did it after the trial started, picking up and taking off without anybody realizing it. I'm talking about a material witness; lose him, and you don't have a case. The U.S. marshals were guarding him then, and Klotz and Brosch had to go search him out. Fortunately they found him down in L.A., or else God knows what would have happened."

In this instance Harris had gone off to find a lawyer. He was getting nervous, and he wanted to be assured that he would get the reward, as well as immunity. What is more, he wanted the promise of both to come from none other than Joseph Alioto.

Alioto didn't know anything about Harris until the lawyer who claimed to represent Harris approached him at a fund-raiser for his gubernatorial campaign. At first, Alioto wasn't sure what to think. When he found out that what Harris's lawyer had told him was true and learned from the SFPD that they no longer knew where their potential star witness was, he responded with profane eloquence, suggesting in no uncertain terms that they should locate him, fast.

Klotz and Brosch were soon back at Harris's apartment in Oakland, hoping they would find him there. Instead, they found a man lying in wait for him. It was Dwight Stallings.

"Gil and I were trying to track down information on Tom Manney, who owned Black Self-Help and who Harris also named as being involved," Sanders remembers. "So I was with Gil when he heard about Stallings waiting there for Harris. He had been holding out hope that Stallings wasn't as involved as Harris said he was. But that was it. Gil gave up on the kid then, and it hit him pretty hard.

"The Nation of Islam used to refer to African Americans as the 'Lost-Found Tribe of Shabazz.' But the deeper we dug, the more we began to feel that these guys, at least, were just lost. With no way to ever get back to being 'found.'"

Eventually the Oakland police picked Harris up, and Klotz and Brosch went to collect him once again. This time, however, he refused to cooperate until he talked to Alioto. So the leaders of the task force met to decide whether or not there really was enough to what Harris said to put it all before the mayor. Everyone agreed: there was.

"None of us had any doubt but that Harris was for real," Sanders confirms. "I'm not saying he made us comfortable. Anthony was too squirrelly to make anybody comfortable. And there was a lot to question when it came to what he said about motive, but not about who was involved. Those claims we all felt certain were legit."

Alioto was on a campaign trip to southern California when he got word from Gus Coreris that the only way Anthony Harris would go on talking to the police was if he talked to the mayor first. Alioto immediately canceled all the appearances he had scheduled and returned to San Francisco that same night, arriving at three in the morning. At 3:30 A.M. the mayor met with Harris, Harris's lawyers, Charlie Barca, and Walter Giubbini, the chief assistant district attorney. Coreris, Fotinos, Klotz, and Brosch were also there. Absent, however, were Sanders and Gilford. It was one of the first important meetings on Zebra to which neither Sanders nor, more significantly, Gilford was invited.

Alioto listened to Harris's story, paying attention as Coreris and others made sure that Harris gave the mayor the details that he needed to make a decision. Normally, plea deals are left up to the district attorney's office. Not in this instance, however. If any deal was to be made with Anthony Harris, it would be up to the mayor.

Alioto only had one stipulation. Being an accessory to murder is one thing; being a murderer is another. He would not grant immunity to anyone who had actually killed someone. Harris, as he had insisted all along, assured Alioto that he had not. With that, the deal was done. Immunity was his, and the reward would be as well, if his evidence led to a conviction.

The problem was, deal or no deal, Harris's evidence still wasn't evidence until they got corroboration.

Bill Armstrong had remained close to Richard Hague since the night some six months earlier when both Hague's face and his life were slashed wide open by the cruel blows of a machete. Armstrong had confronted losses of his own over the years, but what Hague had endured seemed inconceivable to him. What impressed Armstrong most of all was not Hague's patience with the damage to his body and the pain of repeated surgeries and healing; it was the resilience he showed when it came to the damage to his soul. To Armstrong's ongoing amazement, Hague remained a positive young man despite all he had endured, not harboring an ounce of bitterness and blaming no one for what happened to him except the three individuals who had done it.

Those three men were the reason Armstrong went to see Hague on the morning after Alioto's meeting with Harris. If Hague could identify them, it would be an important step in getting the corroboration they needed. Hague was in the hospital, preparing to go through yet another operation to repair his face, and Armstrong showed up carrying an envelope filled with photographs. Armstrong laid a phalanx of pictures before Hague, showing him a dozen or so all at once.

Armstrong expected Hague to have to mull over the faces and work at recalling them. Instead, Hague picked out the three men who had abducted him and his wife without even a moment of hesitation.

"Him, him, and him," Armstrong remembers Hague saying, pointing to each.

The three "hims" he pointed to were Jesse Cooks, Anthony Harris, and Larry Green.

Armstrong returned to the Hall of Justice to report his conversation with Hague to Chief Scott. However, Scott was in a meeting with Alioto and the district attorney, John Jay Ferdon, so Armstrong told Scott's secretary he would come back. Before he could leave, Scott opened his office door and called Armstrong inside.

With Scott, Alioto, and Ferdon all listening intently, Armstrong described his meeting with Hague and the positive IDs. Thrilled, Alioto wanted to make a statement to the press right away. Ferdon disagreed. He was glad they finally had corroboration, but while it seemed to validate Harris's credibility in general, it spoke substantively only to the crimes against the Hagues, and it would help them convict only two men: Cooks, already in prison for the murder of Frances Rose, and Green.

Both Ferdon and Alioto knew that the surveillance teams assigned to Black Self-Help had reported that the conversations about "rolling" had become more urgent. The feeling was that another Zebra hit would come, and come soon. Alioto had only just extended immunity to Harris, having met with him the night before. In Ferdon's mind, the investigation was still young, and like the men in surveillance, he wanted to wait and be certain they could bring everyone to justice before making any move at all. Alioto, who had been up all night, displayed little patience with Ferdon, and the disagreement turned into an argument. Then, as Armstrong watched, the argument turned into a fight, with Alioto and Ferdon shouting at the top of their lungs at each other, both trying to browbeat the other into agreement.

"From the standpoint of policing, Ferdon was right," Sanders says now. "The key to a conviction is holding off your arrest until it's absolutely necessary, and giving yourself time to amass as much evidence as possible. But the key words are 'absolutely necessary.' Alioto wasn't a prosecutor. Or a cop. He was a mayor. And he had a city on his hands that was in a state of terror.

"The information the guys on surveillance had gathered about another possible hit had to scare him. Because if it turned out that we couldn't stop them in time and another innocent person died, there's no telling what that city would have done. Moving fast might've seemed wrong to a cop or a DA, but it might've seemed absolutely necessary if you were mayor."

The next day, April 29, determined to calm the fears and put a stop to the killing, Joseph Alioto held a press conference to lay out what he believed he knew about Zebra. Never one to do anything halfway, he didn't limit his comments to the attacks in San Francisco. Rather, he laid out a huge collection of speculative intelligence, claiming that more than eighty killings across the state going back to 1971 could be linked to Zebra, and implying that those responsible for all the crimes might be tied to the Nation of Islam.

Irrespective of Alioto's claims, which were highly debated at the time and have been speculated on ever since, one thing is sure. Saying what he said, when he said it, tipped off those responsible for the crimes as to just how close on their trail the SFPD really was. And while doing this may have avoided further tragedy, it probably also allowed at least some of the guilty to go free.

"The guys on surveillance felt sure we could have had the goods on everyone Harris named if they were given more time," Sanders says now, weighing the effects of Alioto's decision. "The Zebra squad was part of the group that kept tabs on the building where Larry Green and J. C. Simon lived during those final days, and Gil and I felt the same way. It didn't seem to matter to them that Harris had gone to the cops. But when Alioto went public, everything changed. There was a price paid by going public that soon."

Yet, with fears of a potential race war still in the air, an indication of how high the price of inaction might have been came just two nights after Alioto's press conference. The incident, which in retrospect supports Alioto's decision to go public, occurred at about 9:00 P.M., as two young African-American men driving east toward North Beach were entering the Broadway Tunnel. Theodore Gooden, an eighteen-year-old student who had just arrived in the Bay Area, was at the wheel and noticed that a white man driving a pickup seemed to be following him and his companion, Specialist 4 James Cook, an army medic stationed at the Presidio's Letterman Hospital. About midway through the tunnel, the truck suddenly sped up and pulled alongside Gooden's car on the right. Another white man with long hair leaned out across the driver and pointed a gun at them through the truck's window, firing three times before speeding off into the night. Gooden was hit in the hand and looked to see his friend collapsed beside him. Pulling to a stop as soon as he could, he ran to a bar where he called the police, but it was too late. His friend was dead by the time the police arrived at the scene.

Hobart Nelson, the same inspector who drew the Zebra sketches, investigated the killing along with his partner, John McKenna. They were never able to solve it, a failure that disturbed Nelson at the time and gnaws at him to this day. But although the "who" of the killing never became clear, Nelson recalls that the "why" was obvious to him and everyone else involved in the investigation from the moment the shooting ended: revenge for Zebra.

The madness that the letter writer to Herb Caen spoke of had finally happened.

Alioto held another press conference the next day and announced that one of the .32-caliber handguns used in the Zebra killings had been found, discovered by a child in a neighbor's backyard just around the corner from where the last Zebra victim, Nick Shields, had been shot. It had apparently been tossed there as the killer ran away. No traceable prints were found on the weapon. Even so, Mitch Luksich was able to match the firing marks caused by the handgun with those on the shell casings and bullets found from all the victims since January 28.

The discovery was important. However, the blowback caused by the mayor's comments of the day before was already coming his way. California attorney general Evelle J. Younger told the press that there was "no evidence" to link Zebra to killings elsewhere in the state, adding that similarities are one thing, but an "evidentiary connection," as Younger put it, is something else.

Informed of Younger's comments, Alioto refused to back off, telling reporters he would hold another press conference the following day and list all eighty killings he thought were Zebra-related, letting the public decide if there was an "evidentiary connection." He concluded by promising that "things will be a lot clearer tomorrow."

What he didn't say, though, was why. At the same time as he was lecturing the press, the entire Zebra task force was being mobilized for a massive assault early the following morning to arrest the seven men who had been fingered by Harris as being involved in the killings.

"It felt like the night before D-Day," Sanders says, recalling the preparations. "I trained for years in the military, and you learn how to prepare for battle. That's what it was like. There were seven suspects, and they were spread out all the way down to San Jose. Plus we had

Black Self-Help to go into, secure, and try to collect whatever evidence we could. We had to do it fast, to make sure no one got wind of what was going down and took off on the run. On top of everything else, Harris had said that there was no way these guys would be taken alive. So we were afraid of a huge shootout.

"But as intense as the preparations were, one thing was disconcerting, especially for Gil. We'd been involved in Zebra since the start, and Gil in particular had been in a supervisory position. Gus and John were the number-one and -two inspectors; there was no doubt about that. But we'd been right there with them all the way. Now that it was getting near the end, we couldn't help but feel like we were being pushed back.

"Gil especially felt that way. Zebra became personal for him. Not just because of Stallings. He and I looked up to Malcolm X and believed there was a lot of good the Nation had done. But to see something we loved, like the struggle for civil rights, turned into something evil pained us in ways you can't describe. Being a cop isn't just about going after what's wrong. It's about keeping things right, too. That's part of what Zebra became about for us: setting right something that had gone more wrong than we ever thought possible. But when it came time to make the arrests, we got pushed to the rear.

"I don't mean by Gus and John. They were the lead inspectors and had the right to collar whoever they wanted. But there were others who took the lead, as well, and made arrests. Gil never got to make even one.

"If you're a cop, collars are how you keep score. And that hurt Gil. I was still young. I felt like there was no end to the chances I would get. But it was different for Gil. He wanted to be up there in front, the way he'd been all along, as one of the leaders. Instead, Gil, me, and the other black cops were part of what gets listed in an arrest card as '& posse.'

"Gil felt that a big part of the reason for that was his involvement in Officers for Justice. Being made '& posse' felt like payback."

Hundreds of cops around the city prepared to descend on the suspects. Many, including Sanders and Gilford, had not slept for days, and it was still dark on the morning of May 1 when they assembled with the others who had been detailed to 844 Grove, the building where

Larry Green and J. C. Simon lived, in the heart of the Fillmore. It was a large complex, and the plan was to occupy the entire building, going in with a squad large enough to match any firepower and make sure no escape was possible.

Sanders recalls a rookie female officer, one of the few women the SFPD had at the time, who had been made part of the tac squad in case there were any women to be searched. She turned to Sanders with a look of fear before the raid and asked, "What do we do if they start shooting?"

"I just looked at her," Sanders recalls, "then smiled and pointed at her weapon. I said, 'See that gun you got? Well, what I suggest is that you take it out and shoot back. And don't stop until it's empty.' She smiled, which was what I wanted. Moments like that, if you're not scared you're probably not breathing. But you still have to find a way to get the job done."

The raids went like clockwork. Despite Harris's warnings, none of the suspects resisted arrest. Only one, Manuel Moore, was even preparing to flee. The others seemed oddly complacent, as if they had succeeded in outwitting the police for so long that they expected to do so in court as well. The raids, which began at dawn, were completed by the time the sun had fully risen.

Lineups were scheduled for the same day, and because of the choice Alioto had made to tip the hands of the police before they could fully corroborate Harris's claims, they were critical. Richard Hague had already made positive identifications in his case. However, it was through photos, so he was coming in to make sure he could do the same thing in person. Beyond his case, there were a score more that still had no corroboration at all.

Both the police and prosecutors knew what the hurdles were. If a suspect could be identified, he would almost certainly be charged and tried. But if he was not identified by at least one of the dozens of victims and witnesses brought in to view the lineup, then the odds of the suspect being successfully charged became exceedingly slim.

The room where lineups were held inside the Hall of Justice looked like an old-fashioned movie theater, with a raked house filled with about 250 seats facing a raised wooden stage. The suspects were placed among other men selected from the city jail, which was also in the Hall of Justice, and were held backstage before being trotted out with their groups in front of a curtain and, with a numbered card held in their hands at waist level, paraded before the audience.

Herman Clark, who had been part of the Zebra squad and at the arrests at 844 Grove earlier that morning, was one of two officers running the lineups, responsible for picking the various groups and then sending them out on stage one after another. Gilford stayed backstage most of the time, along with Coreris and Fotinos, keeping a watch on the suspects. Among them was Dwight Stallings, who could barely meet Gilford's eyes.

Sanders kept in motion throughout the lineups, moving from the audience to backstage, keeping an eye on security in both places. When in the audience, he sat up front to be sure he could get between the suspects and the witnesses if he had to, and when backstage, he always stood close to the suspects, ready in case some muscle, or more, was needed.

"I'd never seen tension like that before in a lineup," Sanders says as he thinks about that day. "We had cops all over that room for security. Most of us hadn't slept for days. And it wasn't just us who felt the tension. There were victims there, and witnesses, people whose lives had been torn up. And here we were finally facing the guys who we believed had been terrorizing the city.

"I remember sitting there thinking about all the cases. About the brutal wounds on Quita Hague as she lay spread out on the autopsy table. About Dancik covered in broken glass and Moynihan with his teddy bear, Hosler lying in a sea of blood, and old man Bambic staring up at the sky down on skid row. And I thought about the body on the beach, nameless and faceless, somebody's son or lover or friend, lost forever and never found.

"You try to keep your head about you when you work. To never get too close. But there was no way to keep this job at arm's length anymore. There was too much sorrow. Too much pain. Too much blood.

"It really hit me when I went backstage. Herman Clark was getting the group that Larry Green was part of ready to go out. Stallings was in that group, too, along with six other guys we pulled from the jail. As Herman handed out numbers, Green started talking to him, calling him a 'Tom,' saying he'd pay for what he was doing, and telling him that he knew where Herman and his family lived.

"When I heard that, I lost it. I grabbed Green out of the line and threw him against the wall backstage. It was like everything we went through, the terror, the fear, the righteous anger he and the others stole from me and every black in the city, turning it into something sick and evil, came out all at once.

"I pinned him to that wall, stared at his hazel eyes and pale skin, and said, 'Let me tell you something, you high-yaller motherfucker!' This was back when there was no death penalty in California, so he and the rest knew that the worst they could get was life. But I held him there and told him, 'If your friends ever get near the families of these officers in here, you're going to *wish* there was a death penalty in this state, because I don't care where they send you or what shit-hole you end up in, I'll make it my personal business to search you out and kick your motherfucking ass!'

"After that, he stopped talking."

There seemed a stark disconnect between the Larry Green that his family and friends from Berkeley knew and the angry, hate-filled, arrogant young radical that Sanders saw when he and Gilford stopped him soon after the Hosler and Moynihan shootings in December and then witnessed again backstage during the lineups. Art Agnos, who had been shot by one of the Zebra killers while leaving a community meeting in Potrero Hill, and who some fifteen years later would be elected mayor of San Francisco, experienced that disconnect in a curious but revealing way.

Sitting in the audience, Agnos looked at the lineup that Green was in and leaned over to a cousin who had come with him, pointing to Green and whispering that he was sure he was a plant. Boyish and innocent-looking, Green struck Agnos as too middle-class to be involved in Zebra, and more likely an employee from the Hall of Justice who had been grabbed to help fill out the lineups. On the other side of Agnos, however, sat Richard Hague, his face still scarred and slowly healing from yet another operation. Later, Agnos would learn that Green was anything but a plant and that, as unlikely as it may have seemed, he was one of the men who had abducted and so cruelly scarred the gentle, unassuming man beside him.

Some who were close to Green, especially his family, later argued that it was impossible to reconcile those two realities, and that their impression of him as a caring, sensitive young man ruled out all other notions. In an article published in the *Chronicle* after the arrests, Green's younger sister asserted that he had never been in trouble and that it was obvious he was innocent. "All he ever wanted to be is a man," she told the reporter. In the same article, Green's father said that Green had "never in his life made any kind of derogatory remarks about anyone's race." His mother added that her son was "incapable of hate."

Yet at a parole hearing nearly thirty years later, when speaking about what it was like to let go of the beliefs of the Nation of Islam after it disbanded in the late 1970s and to change his mindset so he could embrace the beliefs of traditional Islam, Green acknowledged that the transition was like going "from one extreme to another." He went on to explain that he went from thinking "the white man was a devil" during the time of Zebra to thinking that "the white man was just like everybody else" a few years later, when he converted to mainstream Islam.

Those statements are by no means an admission of any crime, and in the same parole hearings he denied being involved in the Zebra attacks. On the other hand, they do suggest that the person his family knew during the time of Zebra was not the same one who walked the streets outside his parents' home.

"You'd probably hear the same thing if you talked to the parents of any violent radical from back then," Sanders says, commenting on what seemed to be Green's divided nature. "But their truth doesn't rule out the truth of the victims whose lives those same people destroyed. I'm sure the people who spoke well of Green saw what they say they saw in him. But I also know what I saw. And when I weigh the two, I have no doubt about his guilt. None."

Seven men were arrested during the raids. At the lineup only three could be positively identified: Larry Green, J. C. Simon, and Manuel Moore. All three were charged with multiple counts of murder. Four others whom Harris had said were part of the conspiracy — Thomas Manney, who owned Black Self-Help, Dwight Stallings, who had once been Gilford's surrogate little brother, Clarence Jamerson, who worked as a mechanic at Black Self-Help, and Douglas Burton, who also worked there — all went free.

The police continued the surveillance of Black Self-Help for months. Some officers, frustrated by their inability to bring to justice men they felt sure were guilty, tried to pressure them into doing something foolish by slashing the tires on some of the moving trucks at Black Self-Help and even destroying one truck in a fiery blaze. Nothing worked. There was no more talk of "rolling" or "stings." And none of the four who was released was ever charged with any crime connected to the Zebra slayings.

"There are some facts we had nailed," Sanders says as he considers the fate of those who were never charged. "We knew Tom Manney bought at least one of the weapons that was used in Zebra from Michael Armstrong, the junkie that Gil knew from Ingleside. We knew Stallings bought ammunition that was used, and later that he was lying in wait for Harris. According to Harris, Jamerson and Burton were at meetings where the crimes had been planned. But even with things like Stallings buying ammunition or lying in wait, there was no way to prove that he knew what the ammunition would be used for or that he meant to harm Harris. So none of it was enough to bring charges, and without more evidence, they have to be thought of as innocent."

What many feared would happen, did. By going public prematurely, Alioto had made certain that some suspects went free. But only a day after the grand jury hearings ended with the indictments of Green, Simon, Moore, and Cooks and the release of Manney, Stallings, Burton, and Jamerson, there was an example of what could have happened had Alioto not made the decision to move quickly. The incident took place in Los Angeles, as Zebra and the SLA continued to shadow each other in a terrorist pas de deux.

Up until the Zebra arrests, members of the SLA had been holed away on Golden Gate Avenue, just off Divisadero and not far from where Green and Simon lived. Nervous because of all the police activity, the SLA finally cleared out, moving from the San Francisco ghetto of the Fillmore to L.A.'s South Central. There, on May 17, the LAPD and the SLA engaged in a furious gun battle, trading shots for over an hour as America watched on live TV and stopping only when everyone who had been in the hideout was dead.

"The shootout in L.A. was terrifying," Sanders recalls. "If that had happened in the Fillmore, with the city gripped by fear and the black community outraged over the sweeps, it would've been like tossing a grenade into an armory. One house burned down in L.A. because of that shootout. Here it wouldn't have stopped at one."

Even though some of the guilty may have gone unpunished, in Earl Sanders's mind Alioto made the right choice.

In the aftermath of the indictments, the police work remaining on Zebra was largely a matter of preparing for the prosecution, and for the most part was done by Coreris, Fotinos, Klotz, and Brosch, with a few others, such as Bill Armstrong, joining in on cases that were specific to them. Even so, it was far from being just mop-up work.

Despite the positive identifications, the prosecution had begun to fear that unless the weapon the SFPD had in their possession, the .32 automatic found in Ingleside near where Shields had been shot, could be directly tied to one of the defendants, the charges against all four of them might have to be dropped. That prospect sent a shudder through everyone who had participated in the task force and evoked the fear that six months of the most intense police work of their lives might be rendered completely valueless and men they considered dangerous killers might go free.

To ensure that didn't happen, they began the tortuous and somewhat desperate job of trying to trace the weapon's chain of possession. Michael Armstrong, the junkie and sometime fence who had long been one of Gilford's sources, claimed to have sold the gun to Tom Manney, giving the SFPD the final piece of the puzzle they needed to connect the killers to the weapon, providing they could prove that Armstrong had had possession of it. This was a job easier said than done. Traveling to the Pacific Northwest, SFPD inspectors were able to establish that the gun, a .32-caliber Beretta, had been purchased in 1968 at a Penney's in Tacoma, and eventually made its way to San Francisco, where it traded hands as payment for a bet. The .32 was then sold, then stolen, then sold twice more until it ended up in San Francisco in the hands of a Samoan named Moo Moo Tooa. Tooa, the SFPD was able to prove, then sold the .32 to Michael Armstrong. With Armstrong willing to testify that he sold it to Manney, the puzzle was complete.

Even though Gilford had long been familiar with Armstrong, he and Sanders played little part in this evidentiary work. Despite being two of the four investigators first detailed full-time to the .32-Caliber shootings, despite being principals throughout the Zebra investigation, and despite Gilford's leadership role in the Zebra squad, neither he nor Sanders was ever called to testify in a trial that lasted over a year and produced a transcript of more than 40,000 pages.

For Sanders, being left out was a disappointment. For Gilford it was far more significant.

"Gil could talk about Zebra for hours," Sanders says of his friend and mentor, who passed away in 1998. "But the only time he talked about feeling like he was left out was after the indictments. Gil was an old football man, and he said not helping to take Zebra to trial felt like helping to carry a football ninety-eight yards up a gridiron, then having your coach call you to the bench so he can send in somebody else with the play that takes it in for a touchdown.

"It wasn't about Gus or John or Klotz or Brosch or any of the guys who handled things during the trial. Gil respected them. It was about the machine, the old-boys' club that used to run things. Gil once told me that what he loved about the SFPD wasn't the way it was, it was the idea of what it could be. He always had a sense of hope about things. But every now and then hope would get hard for him to hang on to. And that was one of those times."

Equally testing for Gilford was the lack of progress in the Officers for Justice lawsuit and the unceasing struggle against it by the SFPD, the POA, and the Civil Service Commission. Since the moment Judge Peckham had first ruled in favor of Officers for Justice five months earlier, Gerald Crowley and POA had been raising money to mount their campaign against it. Funds continued to flow in from all over the country, mostly from unnamed sources, and were substantial. Though officially earmarked for the POA's own appeals, in effect the money served as a financial buttress for the SFPD as well, allowing the department to join with the POA in numerous actions and thus prolong the suit into the indefinite future.

What had once seemed a victory nearly in hand was slowly but surely being pushed further and further away. Then, in May 1974, the Civil Service Commission succeeded in doing what Bob Gnaizda and the lawyers for Public Advocates had been trying to prevent, circumventing the freeze Peckham had ordered on command-level promotions by jamming through a list of newly promoted captains from the current eligibility rolls, filling that rank for years to come. Gilford, who was nearing fifty, and had just had to swallow being deprived of due credit for his work on Zebra, now had to face the fact that any chance he had to achieve a command-level position would be severely limited. The rank of chief was appointed by the mayor, and as such was open to any officer of the SFPD. Anything short of that, however, would forever be out of Gilford's reach

"That," according to Sanders, "was when Gil showed what he was made of. There were a lot of things he wanted in his career. A few years after all this, George Moscone promised to make Gil the first black chief but backed down because of politics. If anybody deserved to be the first, it was Gil. At a certain point, though, he knew it would never happen. But he never stopped fighting to make sure it could happen for someone else. After Zebra he pushed aside the disappointment he felt and threw himself into the Officers for Justice suit, fighting to make things better, knowing that it didn't matter if you lost this battle or that, as long as you won the war."

In many ways, that was one of the most important lessons Gilford ever gave Sanders, schooling "School" not only on the ways of policing but also on what it took to fight for change in the world around you.

"It didn't matter how many disappointments Gil faced, he kept fighting to make things right, even when he knew he wouldn't be the one to reap the benefits from it. It's not that he was selfless. I took care of Gil during the last week of his life. I can count the dreams he had, and I can count the sorrows. But I also know that when it was all said and done, what mattered most to him was the world he left behind."

In 1998, when Earl Sanders, then assistant chief of the SFPD, spoke at the hearing that declared at last complete the long process that began twenty-five years earlier with the filing of the Officers for Justice lawsuit, he began by thanking all the "unsung heroes and heroines" who had given up so much to make that day possible. The first person he mentioned was his late friend, partner, and teacher, Rotea Gilford, who had died less than five months earlier.

"It's kind of like Moses," Sanders says now. "Gil may not have gotten into the Promised Land, but he was the one who led the way."

Epilogue

Finding the Truth in a True Story

"To explain is not to excuse, and to understand is not to forgive."

With that axiom, Earl Sanders set out what he hoped would serve as the guidelines for this book. He had no desire to either excuse or forgive crimes that he believed were unconscionable and inhuman. At the same time, he felt an obligation to explain and, even more importantly, to understand those crimes and the response they elicited — to remember the past so as not to repeat it.

"If we don't try to explain what happened with Zebra and understand the reasons why, there's no way we can learn from it. I believe there are lessons in what happened that can help us deal with our problems today and guide us in making choices about what we might face in the future. But the only way you can get at those lessons is to learn what really happened. Otherwise, it's like going in a room and turning off the lights the moment you step inside. You don't know how to move forward without tripping over every obstacle in your way. But if you turn on the lights and see where the obstacles are, then you might have a chance of getting somewhere."

One way to understand both Zebra and the Officers for Justice lawsuit for Earl Sanders is to recognize how deeply interrelated they were, not merely in chronology but also in the fabric that made them, the weaving together of race and rage that can either turn into a positive struggle for something better or else become twisted and violent — a hunger for justice or a desire for revenge.

*　　*　　*

Buoyed by the money from the Police Officers Association, the POA and SFPD appeals against the Officers for Justice lawsuit dragged on for six years in all. As well as in the courts, the POA and SFPD continued to pursue their agenda on the bureaucratic battlefield, which was often the site of the bitterest fights. One such example is the war waged over the notion of "like work, like pay."

"Like work, like pay" is the commonsense concept of paying someone commensurately with the work they are actually doing. If someone who is not a captain, for instance, is doing work that is the equivalent of what a captain would do, he or she should receive a pay equal to what a captain would make.

Following the maneuvers of the Civil Service Commission, the SFPD used the promotions of whites to create a civil service logjam intended to bar the way for minorities for years. If white officers had seniority, minority officers would have to wait. The principal of "like work, like pay" gave the Officers for Justice a way around that logjam, offering minorities access to command-level jobs and command-level pay they would not otherwise have. Although a black officer might not have enough seniority to be in position for promotion to captain's rank, he could be appointed to a position that was equivalent to that rank.

This rankled POA leader Gerald Crowley. Commenting on the example of Rodney Williams, who earned captain's-grade pay for heading the Community Relations Bureau, Crowley labeled his remuneration a product of "influential friends," and insisted that it was he himself who was really fighting for equal opportunity. Yet the truth was that, although an inspector, Rodney Williams had earned his position by first helping to establish the bureau and then working his way up to a supervisory role, in which he exercised responsibility and performed work equal to that of any captain. The fact that he hadn't achieved that rank was attributable to the institutional racism of the department.

During the long struggle of the initial trial and the appeals, Robert Gnaizda constantly pushed Judge Peckham to widen rather than constrict the scope of the Officers for Justice lawsuit, and turned the appeals process on its head, in the end using it to get more rather than less. Though relatively unknown among the general public, Robert Gnaizda is one of the most deft and successful civil rights attorneys in the United States, having served as chief counsel on over a hundred civil rights class action lawsuits over the past forty years. He managed to turn what began largely as a complaint by African-American officers into an all-inclusive case covering race, sex, and sexual orientation, creating a template of diversity for the modern police force. Even so, when the first set of trials came to an end in 1979, and Judge Peckham filed his consent decree, he concluded, "Blacks, Hispanics, and Asians were and continue to be substantially underrepresented." To right those and other wrongs, he ordered a phalanx of remedies that related to every facet of the department, from the recruitment of officers to the selection of applicants, assignments once officers were hired, and all promotions and nonpermanent appointments thereafter, creating a twenty-year review process to make sure that the remedies were carried out.

Perhaps even greater than its effect on the SFPD itself was the impact that the groundbreaking Officers for Justice lawsuit had on police departments across the nation. In 1975, two years after the filing of the suit, a coalition of groups led by the National Black Police Association used it as their guide and model to bring their own lawsuit, aimed at cutting off the federal financing for any police department in the country found guilty of discrimination. More lawsuits followed, and when the OFJ suit was decided in 1979, it became what could be called the *Brown v. Education* for policing, serving as the standard by which all police departments in the United States would be measured, and setting a level for minority representation that all police departments knew they had to meet if they were to pass federal muster.

Jesse Cooks, Larry Green, Manuel Moore, and J. C. Simon were indicted by the grand jury on numerous counts, including conspiracy to commit murder between October 20, 1973, and April 30, 1974. Cooks and Green were also indicted for the kidnapping, robbery, and murder of Quita Hague, as well as the kidnapping and assault with a deadly weapon of Richard Hague. Moore and Simon were both accused of the murders of Tana Smith and Jane Holly on January 28, 1974, as well as the assault with a deadly weapon on Roxanne McMillian that same night. Moore was also charged with assault with a deadly weapon against Ward Anderson and Terry White on April 14. Although evidence was presented regarding the murders of Saleem Erakat, Marietta Di-Girolamo, Ilario Bertuccio, Neal Moynihan, Mildred Hosler, Unknown Body #169, Vincent Wollin, John Bambic, and Nelson Shields IV, as well as the assaults on Art Agnos and Theresa DeMartini, no indictments were brought on those crimes other than the charges of conspiracy.

The jury trial in the Zebra case finally got under way in March 1975, almost a full year after the grand jury indictments, and it lasted for another twelve months, until March 1976. The jury found the defendants guilty on all counts, resulting in multiple life sentences for each. Although the testimony by Anthony Harris was by no means the only factor leading to the convictions, it formed the foundation of the prosecution's case.

Yet the volatility Harris had displayed after turning himself in to the police persisted in the days before the trial. He disappeared so often that eventually he had to be kept in protective custody so rigorous it was prisonlike. One particularly unnerving pretrial twist for the prosecution came when he wrote a letter recanting all the claims he had made about Zebra and mailed it to everyone from President Ford to Minister John Muhammad of Temple No. 26. Harris subsequently recanted his recantation, claiming that the reason he had written the letter was that he had not yet been given an attorney to represent him. Once his complaint was addressed, Harris reaffirmed his original statements, and the prosecution was able to resume building its case.

Harris's antics were not limited to the preparatory stages of the trial. On the day he was to testify about the murders of Quita Hague and others and name Cooks, Green, Simon, and Moore as coconspirators, he arrived in court wearing a Nehru jacket and with his hands folded in prayer, as if he was about to perform a holy act. After the trial, even one of the jurors characterized his manner as "flaky." Besides that, it has to be admitted that Harris's version of the events was if anything self-serving, which made him vulnerable to the defense, as did the fact that his testimony was contingent on the quid pro quo of immunity and the reward. Harris's account conveniently exculpated him from the worst of the crimes, namely murder, even in the case of Quita Hague, in which he admitted to being at the very least a willing participant in her and her husband's abduction, and after which his fiancée at the time, Carolyn Patton, claimed he was covered in blood. She testified that he had watched television for news accounts of the Hague attack, telling her, according to Patton, that he had been "out killing devils."

Another discrepancy in Harris's testimony arose regarding the murder of Saleem Erakat. In his initial statements to the police and during his grand jury testimony, Harris claimed he had remained outside the store during the robbery and murder. Later, at the trial, it came out that a palm print found *inside* the store, and whose substance was formed with nothing less than Erakat's blood, was his. Needless to say, Harris was forced to reverse himself, explaining that the reason he initially denied being inside the store was that he feared having his parole revoked.

Regardless, Harris and the prosecution were able to parry questions about both his credibility and his truthfulness. Despite his eccentric behavior, the testimony Harris gave was convincing when it came to the details of the crimes, and created a foundation of guilt for the accused that their defense lawyers could never dismantle.

As convincing as Harris was when it came to the criminal activities that led to guilty verdicts, his words were far less persuasive, both in retrospect and to many at the time, including Earl Sanders and others, when it came to the motives for the crimes and the underlying cause that he claimed set in motion all the violence.

To get a murder conviction, one has to prove the facts of what went on beyond a reasonable doubt. However, one does not have to prove motive at all. All that is needed when it comes to demonstrating motive is that the possibility of one be established. Because Anthony Harris was an accomplice in the Zebra murders, anything he said about the facts of the case had to be corroborated to be admissible as evidence. What he said about motive did not. Nevertheless, some of his statements about the motives of the Zebra defendants, such as their hating whites and objectifying them as "devils" or trying to start a race war, were corroborated by others both in the course of the trial and in the years since. During the trial, as mentioned earlier, the woman Cooks raped two nights after the Hague assault testified that among his ranting remarks were predictions of indiscriminate slaughter, that "people are going to be killed and the streets would be lined with blood." In addition, Harris testified that Manuel Moore had wanted to be taught kung fu so he could kill whites in just such a struggle. Harris also told the court that J. C. Simon spoke repeatedly about killing whites in a variety of ways, using the Nation of Islam's Lesson No. 10 as his justification.

Although Simon denied Harris's claims that he wanted to start a race war in his own testimony during the trial, his denials were fraught with statements so bizarre that they seemed to beg the question of his sanity. He claimed under cross-examination that he had come to California from Texas not by way of car or bus or train, but by riding "a snake" halfway and "a tornado" the rest. Then, when asked by the prosecution about the binder that he had in his possession at the time of his arrest, which contained Lesson No. 10 among its contents, he claimed that he had received the material "from Allah" in 1971 at a park in San Francisco's Fillmore district. More than twenty-five years later, both Green and Cooks would confirm during separate parole hearings that they had embraced a doctrine of hate toward whites during the time of the Zebra murders, which took them years to get beyond. Yet perhaps the most chilling evidence that they viewed the killings as part of a longer, ongoing struggle came from a statement that Cooks, after the verdicts were handed down, made to someone involved in the investigation, who was so unnerved by the threat that he still wishes not to be named. In a voice quiet enough that the judge couldn't hear but firm enough to be frightening, Cooks said simply, "This isn't over."

However, one key element not corroborated at trial or ever thereafter was Harris's description of the group he called the Death Angels, the supposed secret clique within the Nation of Islam. According to what Harris told both the police and the court, membership in the Death Angels was the primary motive for the attacks.

This is not to say that there was no conspiracy. There was, and those involved were indeed members of the organization of that time known as the Nation of Islam, a group vastly different from the Nation of Islam of today. The Zebra conspirators were revolutionaries. They were true believers. And they were murderers, guilty of the crimes with which they were charged. But there is no proof other than Harris's own statements that they belonged to any such group as the Death Angels, or that any of the details Harris provided about that organization have any basis in reality.

No police investigator who worked on Zebra has ever heard the Death Angels mentioned by anyone other than Anthony Harris — not one. That is true, too, of the lawyers who worked on Zebra, both for the prosecution and the defense.

Among Harris's claims about the Death Angels was that pins affixed with wings were given out to those who became members. Not one such pin has ever been found, nor has a photograph of one ever emerged. Harris also purported that Jesse Lee Cooks was high up in the Death Angels, and that this was the reason he could shave his head. Yet shaved heads had absolutely no relation to status inside the Nation of Islam. Roger Pierucci, Cooks's lawyer in the Zebra trial, who once it was over had no doubt about his client's guilt, discounts the shaved-head story as absurd. Harris claimed that photographs of victims were taken to document each kill for the purpose of getting credit for it with the Death Angels, but not a single such photograph has ever been found. Harris also asserted that there were scores and possibly hundreds of Death Angels in groups located across the nation, yet in over thirty years not one of these supposed members has ever come forward in the hope of trading information about this infamous group as a way to curry favor in an arrest or prosecution.

Harris's most lurid and sensational claims revolved around the notion that there was a point system for gaining membership in the Death Angels. According to him, a prospective member had to kill at least nine white males, or five white women, or four white children. He offered the Nation of Islam's Lesson No. 10 about killing the devil within the devil as proof of this assertion. While it is possible to construe Lesson No. 10 as encouraging the killing of whites, as Harris claimed that Simon did, the language of the lesson makes no distinction between men, women, or children and says absolutely nothing about "points" or the relative value of one white person versus another.

Perhaps the most powerful refutation of some of Harris's claims came in a parole hearing for Jesse Cooks that was held in 1999. In that hearing, Cooks confessed to all the crimes he was convicted of in Zebra: the abduction of Richard and Quita Hague and the murder of Quita. He also confirmed that Larry Green was one of those involved in the crimes against Richard and Quita Hague. In addition, he admitted to other misdeeds and transgressions that he had committed in life, including the abduction and rape of a woman two days after the assault on the Hagues, and the abduction and murder of Frances Rose. Throughout the hearing, Cooks seemed to hold nothing back.

However, when asked about his motive in the attack on the Hagues, there was no talk of Death Angels or points. The killings, Cooks said, were a response to the radical "rhetoric" of the time. That, of course, is no excuse. But it was the motive, according to Cooks. When asked why he and the others had tried to abduct children before happening on the Hagues, he claimed it was "a spur-of-the-moment thing," done randomly. There was no mention of children or women having any more value than men. Going after the children, like going after the Hagues, was what Cooks called "a racial thing," a monstrous, unforgivable effort to create terror, but not part of an effort to achieve Death Angel membership.

"When the arrests were made," recalls Sanders, "the Death Angel stories seemed a little crazy to me. But like most people, I figured that because what Anthony said about the crimes checked out so well, what he said about the Death Angels must be accurate too. But I spent another twenty years in Homicide after Zebra and about thirty more years overall on the force, and I never once heard anyone ever mention the group again. Not *once*.

"It's one thing to say that people were scared to talk at the time. But not after years go by. And you can't say that the Nation of Islam stopped people from talking about the Death Angels, because after Elijah Muhammad died in 1975, the Nation disbanded. So there was nothing to stop people. But I never heard a thing. And after years of talking to people, and digging, and investigating, I haven't found one person who can tell me they heard about the Death Angels from any source other than Harris."

Sanders also discounts claims that tie the Death Angels to scores of other killings across the state. "There had been talk of black-on-white motiveless killings as far back as 1971, but up until Harris began to talk, there had never once been any mention of a group called the Death Angels. From what I have been able to tell, every mention of them since has used Harris's statements as the sole source. What had been discussed prior to Zebra in regard to the motiveless killings was that those involved might be connected to the Nation of Islam some-how. But even with that, there was never any proof. The Zebra killers were involved in the Nation, but all the rest is conjecture. It may be that some of the unsolved motiveless killings followed a pattern similar to that of Zebra. But it may also be that there's no connection at all."

Sanders has tried to understand why Harris would fabricate, with a fair amount of detail, the story of the Death Angels, as he clearly seems to have done. Part of the answer may lie in a desire to ensure that he didn't implicate himself in such a way that he would appear equal in guilt to the others. In yet another peculiar twist to this tragic case, to accomplish that, he may have taken a clue from the police themselves.

Three days after the bloody night of January 28, when five victims were shot down in cold blood on the streets of San Francisco, and three days after a photo of Anthony Harris was published in the *Chronicle,* showing him about to enter a rally for injured Nation of Islam member Larry Crosby, the *Chronicle* published an article stating that the police were "convinced of the existence of a fanatical black sect whose requirement for membership is the slaying of a white." By creating the Death Angels, Harris was giving the police information that was consistent with their own theories.

Harris may have calculated that, if he merely said a rogue element within the Nation of Islam was responsible for Zebra, he would not differentiate himself sufficiently from the others. However, if he laid Zebra at the feet of a group like the Death Angels, in which he could say he hadn't yet gained membership, this would allow him both to distance himself from the crimes and to place the blame more squarely on those he alleged were either further along in gaining membership, like Larry Green and J. C. Simon, or else already full members, like Jesse Cooks.

Supporting the notion that Harris took at least some clues about how to couch his activities from news articles is a statement he made in his meeting with Alioto, in which he claimed that he had met Patty Hearst and Donald DeFreeze at Temple No. 26. No one has ever given much, if any, credence to this claim. But it is revealing that he made it to Alioto, who more than once stated publicly that he believed there was a connection between the SLA and Zebra.

Sanders points to another motive that might have led Harris to create a group like the Death Angels: the need to aggrandize himself and exaggerate his own importance.

"Most times, when guys roll on each other, it's a combination of three things: fear, anger, and greed. We know he felt fear when he saw the sketches. And a $30,000 reward was like a fortune to Harris, so the greed was there, too. The element that's not as clear was the anger. But I think that's where the Death Angels come in.

"Like a lot of these guys, Harris wanted to be a big deal in the Nation. He wanted to be important. You see it in the way he talked about himself, overstating some of the things he did, like teaching martial arts, talking as if he was the only one to teach it at the temple when he was just one of many who did.

"He never became the big deal he wanted. So he made himself big this way, revealing something that sounded huge. The irony is, it *was* huge. Because of the people who were killed, and what that did to the city and everyone in it. Zebra didn't need a group called the Death Angels to make it big, or terrifying, or evil. But I think Harris needed it to make himself feel important."

Proof of what Sanders says can be found in the way Harris described the group in one of his written statements. It is repeated here the way he wrote it, with his spelling and punctuation as well as his sentiment intact.

> I thought it would be best to write these few lines now be-for it is to late, for I feel a very string type of unknown power to mankind slowly pusessing my physical mind, and forceing me to reviel that which has never befor now been reviel, it is so stingering to the imagination! That I can not

live with it alond, you may life, grin, or smil, or even make marker, but it is you to who are living within a very dark cage of fear. And now it to is your turn to learn of the secrets of what is now known as a very secretty orginuzation called THE DEATH____ ANGELES____.

Debunking Harris's story of the Death Angels is in no way exculpatory, for it in no way diminishes the evidence against the Zebra killers. However, if belonging to the Death Angels was not the primary motive behind the Zebra attacks, then what was? For Earl Sanders the answer lies in the radical politics of the era.

"People have come to see Zebra as some sort of exception to what else was going on at the time. But it wasn't. It was just a more extreme example. You look at the things that Patty Hearst said once she joined the SLA, or what Bernardine Dohrn said, and you'll see the same sort of anger, the same sort of destructiveness. The only thing that set Zebra apart as something different was adding religion into the mix. That helped add to the fanaticism. And the fanaticism added to the horror of it all. But it still was part of the same puzzle. And it was driven by the same passions.

"When people talk about Zebra, it's usually as a serial killing. That may be technically true, but the most accurate description of what Zebra was is terrorism, plain and simple."

One indication of this can be found in a written statement Harris gave to police before the start of the trial, in which he characterizes what took place on the night of January 28 as "revenge for the shootting [*sic*] of Larry 3X." By "Larry 3X" Harris meant Larry Crosby, who had been shot by Berkeley police a few days earlier.

Random acts of revenge were intended to create terror among whites in what killers saw as an ongoing struggle. Other assaults also had possible triggers motivating revenge. Just prior to the attack on the Hagues in October, members of the Black Liberation Army were convicted for the murder of SFPD sergeant John Young. Just before the shootings in December, an FBI agent shot a young black man, George Session, in the back in San Francisco's Federal Building soon after the

Chronicle reported that the FBI had been trying to infiltrate the Nation of Islam. The very day of the attacks on Thomas Rainwater and Linda Story in April, the *Chronicle* began a two-part story praising the work of the SFPD's Homicide Bureau.

What is the point, one might ask, of reinterpreting the motives behind Zebra? Is it just a matter of setting the record straight? For Sanders, the purpose goes far beyond that.

"I see history as being a little like a murder case. You begin at the end, with a set of results. Maybe someone won an election. Or some country won a war. Or some sorry son of a bitch just got himself killed. But no matter what it is, history or homicide, the process is the same. You trace your way back to see how it all happened, and why. You start with a true story, those end results that you know took place. Then you try to find the truth that lies hidden inside that true story, because that's where the real meaning lies. And you have to figure that out to be able to move forward. With a murder case, moving forward means bringing the killer to justice. But with history it means a whole lot of things, from the way we live our lives in the present to the choices we make in the future."

To Earl Sanders, what makes the Zebra murders important is not just the horror that was felt at the time but also the parallels that exist up to this day.

"It doesn't take a genius to see that ever since 9/11, we've been caught up in a cycle of terrorism, both abroad and at home. Just like then, the whole world seems to be going crazy, with bombings and insurgencies and a feeling that every time you step outside there'll probably be one cataclysm or another going on."

In San Francisco in 1974, the campaign of terror involved not bombs but random shootings, but the political response to what had become a crisis — a case of murder and mayhem unequaled in the history of the city, with a total of twenty-three known attacks and fifteen deaths by unknown and apparently unstoppable killers — has resonance today. The desire to calm the public at a time of runaway fear surely lay behind the decision to adopt such a radical, if wrongheaded and ultimately unconstitutional, approach to policing as the Zebra sweeps. Any politician, and any government, faced with a similar set of circumstances would probably feel impelled to err in the same direction as Alioto did, although some might not succumb to that impulse. As Sanders elaborates:

"Politicians are leaders, or at least they should be. Part of how they function is akin to a general in war, making sure their troops feel secure. But there's another function politicians have that's not just about instilling confidence or appealing to your base constituency: it's about doing what's right and what effects the greater good.

"The temptation in a situation like Zebra is to do whatever seems to get the quickest results. The government can respond to the public's panic by panicking itself, and acting more to stem that panic than to solve the problem at hand. That seemed to be what happened after the subway bombings in London in July 2005, where Scotland Yard's shoot-on-sight policy nearly made the situation spin out of control.

"It was the same with Zebra. To this day I believe that the sweeps would have made it blow up in our face if Joe Williams's lawsuit hadn't pulled us back from the brink.

"But parallels aren't just in the problems. They're in the solutions, too. And the lack of them. Again, this really came home during the terrorist bombings in London. One of the London police officials went on TV soon afterward and appealed to the public for help, saying that although one in every ten Londoners was Muslim, they only had about three hundred Muslim officers in Scotland Yard, which was a fraction of what they felt they needed. My first thought was, 'Why didn't you say that five years earlier?' It's the same situation we were in during Zebra. If you don't have a solid corps of people with access into communities that might prove volatile, there's no way to anticipate problems before they happen. All you can do is react afterward.

"That's when I began to think back to Zebra, and it struck me again how it wasn't just a coincidence that the Officers for Justice lawsuit and Zebra were going on at the same time. The truth is, they were connected. And by more than just time and circumstance. We had great cops working on Zebra. Not just good ones, great ones. But even though we had suspicions that members of the Nation of Islam might be involved, we couldn't get the kind of access we needed to develop the information we had to have to act. So all we could do was react, like in London, after the fact.

"That's where OFJ comes in. If we'd had more blacks on the force, we would've had more of a presence in the community the killers came out of, and a better chance to gain access to the group that harbored them. There's no guarantee we could've stopped anything from happening. But the odds would have been so much better.

"That's what people don't understand about the OFJ lawsuit. Integrating a police force is not about doing what's 'fair.' It's about good policing. The reason the SFPD tried the sweeps was because they felt they couldn't police the black community from the inside. So they tried to impose their will on it from the outside. That might fly in a dictatorship, but not in a democracy. When people are free, the only way to police their community is from within. And the only way to do that is to have a force that's representative of that community, one that makes people feel they're included rather than excluded.

"That's when people start to feel like they've got something worth protecting. And they'll do all they can to help a police force, because they feel like they have a piece of the pie, too. And, man, let me tell you something: when you got your piece, you want to protect the whole goddamn pie."

Sanders pauses for a moment as he talks, considering the lessons to be learned from Zebra and from the link with the Officers for Justice lawsuit.

"I think many people feel that the time could come when we'll face another situation like Zebra. Not from members of the Nation of Islam. That organization is miles apart from the organization back then, having been taken apart and rebuilt in a way that transformed it and reformed it in every way imaginable. Tomorrow's threat may not come from any Islamic group, although most people would probably assume that's the likely choice. The truth is that we don't know where it will come from. But we do know this:

"The only way we'll have a chance of protecting ourselves, and anticipating terrorism before it takes place, is if the community it comes from has already been made to feel included in the whole of society. Part of that is economic. It's about jobs. About opportunity. About having that piece of the pie.

"But part of it is also about having that community be represented among the officers who are supposed to police it. Since you can never be sure where that next Zebra will come from, the only solution is to do exactly what the OFJ suit called for, and make sure that every community has a place among our police. Every race and ethnicity, every sex and sexuality, every religion and every creed.

"The easy thing to say is that we need more Arab Americans and more Muslim Americans on our police forces. And we do. But it can't stop there. In a democracy, the only way to have a truly effective police force is to get to the point where your police look like your people, and your people look like your police. I'm not saying that we can only have blacks policing blacks or Asians policing Asians. I'm saying that we need our communities, *all* our communities, to feel that their police forces include them, and understand both who they are and what they're about.

"We need to have trust. That's why looking at the relationship over the years between our police and the black community is so illustrative of the problem. And why Zebra is so illustrative of the dangers. Because of the legacy of slavery, and Jim Crow, and the racism that continues to this day, the trust between the black community and our police is not what it should be. But I believe it's possible for us to build it. If I didn't, I wouldn't have devoted my life to being a cop. But the importance of that trust is not limited to the black community. Because the way in which it's built can serve as a roadmap for building trust with every community and group that feels outside society, or disenfranchised in any way."

There are lessons to be learned from everything in life. But the lessons drawn from crime all too often come at simply too high a price, even for those who are not the direct victims. Everyone who was touched by the fear inspired by Zebra, whether from the specter of the killers or the threat of the sweeps, paid at least a measure of that price. However, for some the burden was greater than many could realize. This was the case for the family of Larry Green.

Anyone who got to know Green's family quickly realized that they were good and caring people. Even some of the officers in the investigation, who had little feeling for Larry Green himself, still ask about his family when their names come up today, thirty years later, and wish them the best. None of these officers was aware of what the Greens had gone through in the aftermath of Zebra, of the death threats his parents received, or of how deep was the trauma they endured.

Green came up for a parole while Art Agnos was mayor of San Francisco, and Green's mother called him to ask if he would speak on her son's behalf at the hearing. The heartfelt pleas of Mrs. Green, who has since passed away, moved Agnos. However, they couldn't change his feelings when it came to her son, or his belief in Larry Green's guilt. The fact is, despite his mother's sorrow, Larry Green has never even once expressed remorse. Without that, there cannot even be the beginning of forgiveness.

As someone who has seen terror as a both victim and as a policy maker responsible for dealing with it, Art Agnos, who spent over a year of his life recovering from his wounds and in some ways will never get over them, has what can only be called a unique understanding of the issue. Like Richard Hague, he was able to navigate the emotional aftermath of his assault without blaming blacks as a group for the actions of an individual. Nor did the injustice he experienced as a victim of terrorism do anything to lessen his concern over injustices done to blacks, or diminish his determination to right them.

At the same time, no matter how aware Agnos is of the social problems that nurtured Zebra, he never forgets the victims, and the families of victims, whose lives were torn apart by its random and cruel violence, and who had something taken from them that no person or court can ever return.

That sad truth is something that Earl Sanders is aware of, as well.

"When I think of Zebra, I don't just think of the dead. I think of families and friends, of grandchildren never met, dreams never realized, and all the lives that were affected in all the ways imaginable.

"Quita Hague. Frances Rose. Saleem Erakat. Paul Dancik. Marietta DiGirolamo. Ilario Bertuccio. Neal Moynihan. The poor unnamed soul we found at the beach. Tana Smith. Vincent Wollin. John Bambic. Jane Holly. Thomas Rainwater. Nick Shields.

"And the victims who were wounded, but still lost worlds of their own: Art Agnos. Teri DeMartini. Roxanne McMillian. Linda Story. Terry White. Ward Anderson.

"Nothing learned from Zebra can ever pay back what was taken from those people, or their friends and families. But at the same time, if we don't try to learn from Zebra, don't find out what really happened, and why, then we're not honoring the victims in the way they truly deserve.

"After Nick Shields was killed, his parents gave up everything they were doing and devoted their lives to fighting for gun control. They responded to their son's death by trying to figure out a way to help heal the world. If you ask me, that's the best way to mourn that I can think of. Following in their footsteps is the best way that anyone could ever respond to Zebra — not just fighting for gun control, but trying to learn all the lessons. And doing everything you can to make sure that for everyone's sake, on every side of the equation, there are no more Zebras."

Thirty years have passed since the Zebra killers were brought to trial. The four who were convicted, Jesse Cooks, Larry Green, J. C. Simon, and Manuel Moore, remain in prison, still serving out their multiple life sentences. Whenever any of them comes up for parole hearings, many of the victims who survived the attacks and the families of those who did not make a point of having their voices heard, retelling their stories with an eloquence that is both moving and persuasive. Each and every time, parole has been denied. Given the horror of the crimes, that is as it should be.

The thirty years that have elapsed since the attacks have created one new mystery. Anthony Harris, whose testimony was so critical to the killers' convictions, has disappeared. There was talk during the trial that he was being given a new identity by federal authorities, along with a new place to live and a job. Yet if he did take another identity, many believe that, like everything in Harris's peripatetic life, it was temporary, and that he returned to using his original name. Although he was constantly in need of funds before and during the trial, he did collect on the thirty-thousand-dollar reward once it was over. There are several rumors about his life in the years following Zebra. One had him back living a life of petty crime in southern California, and possibly using drugs again, though no one has found reports of such in any police records. Another rumor claimed that his last known residence was a homeless shelter in Los Angeles. Yet another asserted that he had left California and moved to Texas. But the source that may be most reliable claims to have heard through the prison grapevine that Anthony Harris is dead, having fallen prey to what Earl Sanders says is a common end for anyone who, in one way or another, embraces murder.

"It doesn't matter whether it's radicalism or just the rackets, you'll wind up with one of two possible ends: an old age in jail, or no old age at all."

Just as no one who lived in San Francisco during Zebra could fail to be affected by it, the cops who worked day and night to find the killers and stop the bloodshed all view it as one of the defining episodes of their lives and careers. Paul Lawler, who wrestled with the limitations of his Intelligence Bureau as he sought a way to pierce the seal surrounding the world of the killers, speculates to this day about the things the SFPD might have done differently in their efforts to save lives, his voice still tinged with sorrow for the ones that were lost. He is not alone. Gus Coreris, John Fotinos, Carl Klotz, Jeff Brosch, William Armstrong, Hobart Nelson, Herman Clark, Napoleon Hendrix, Greg Corrales, Ken Moses, and scores of others carry with them the burden of memory and sorrow for a time when the world appeared to go insane, and there seemed so little they could do to stop it.

However, they did their best. And in doing that much, they saved the lives of people whose names we will never know, the random souls who would have been next.

The same can be said for two other men for whom Zebra became a defining experience: Rotea Gilford and Earl Sanders. Both went on to achieve much in the aftermath of Zebra. Although Gilford was frustrated in his desire to become chief, George Moscone brought him into the mayor's office, making Gilford chairman of his Council on Criminal Justice. When Dianne Feinstein took office as mayor in 1978, she appointed him deputy mayor. He became one of her closest and most valued advisers, and would go on to work in various capacities for every San Francisco mayor until his death in 1998.

Earl Sanders, the young Homicide inspector who even at the time saw Zebra as a pivotal event in our nation's history, both in terms of race relations and in regard to domestic terrorism and how we respond to it, would go on to become not only one of the most successful Homicide investigators in the department's history, but also the person with whom the Officers for Justice lawsuit was most closely associated. With his colleagues in the OFJ and their superb team of lawyers, he would successfully help to steer the suit to the consent decree that became an equal rights model for every police department across the nation, forever changing the face of policing in America.

And if, as Sanders says, Gilford was like Moses, leading the way to the Promised Land but dying before he could go in, then Sanders was like Joshua, not only crossing over but going on to become the first African-American chief of police in the history of the SFPD.

Sometimes there is justice. Even in the Hall of Justice.

Acknowledgments

THIS BOOK IS A tribute to all the courageous men and women in the Officers for Justice and on the Zebra task force, as well as to fair-minded police officers everywhere who did their jobs in difficult times, coming together to bring wrongdoers to justice while at the same time taking giant steps in the professional growth of law enforcement by introducing a new diversity into the ranks.

The authors were surprised to learn that after more than thirty years, some remain reluctant to talk about the Zebra murders, finding the subject either too charged or too tendentious to be aired, preferring, one imagines, that the story disappear much as the San Francisco coastline does at times, vanishing into a fog, in this case the fog of history. Yet for all those who balked, far more were willing to share what they knew. Many people offered their help in the writing of this work. It is inevitable that some will go unmentioned here. To them, we apologize. Among the current and former members of the SFPD to whom the authors wish to express their gratitude and thanks are Gus Coreris, John Fotinos, Carl Klotz, Jeff Brosch, Frank Falzon, Jack Cleary, Ed Erdelatz, Ken Manley, Ken Moses, Shoji Horikoshi, Paul Lawler, Herman Clark, Napoleon Hendrix, Greg Corrales, Kelly Waterfield, Troy Dangerfield, Hans Anderson, Rodney Williams, Arlene Drummer, Joyce Watkins, Andrew Citizen, Johnny Monroe, and Cornelius Johnson. We would also like to thank the lawyers who took part in the Zebra trial for their invaluable help, including Roger Pierucci, Robert Podesta, Judge Robert Dondero, and Walter Giubbini.

Additionally, we would like to thank attorney Robert Gnaizda, who headed up the Officers for Justice lawsuit; San Francisco's former mayor, Art Agnos; the late Dr. Boyd Stephens, San Francisco's longtime medical examiner; attorney Angela Alioto; newswoman Belva Davis-Moore and her husband, TV cameraman Bill Moore; the Reverend Amos Brown, pastor of the Third Baptist Church; community activist Jim Queen; Bayview community leader Charles Walker; Judge John Dearman; civil rights attorney Peter Cohn; attorney and civil rights leader Joseph Williams; attorney Carl Williams; and Pierre Jacomet.

There are others who also need to be mentioned: Percy Pinkney, longtime aide to supervisor, mayor, and now senator Dianne Feinstein; Dr. Daniel Collins, mentor to Earl Sanders; Judy and Patricia Gilford; Richard Washington; attorney Robert Granucci; Robert Pinkard; Gary Fong of the *San Francisco Chronicle;* John Gollin of the *San Francisco Examiner;* John and Marie Duggan, owners of San Francisco's Original Joe's Restaurant; Jimmy and Esther Terry; Errol Hall; attorney Ben James; Marguerite Donaldson; Elizabeth Brown; and Kevin Brady.

The authors wish to offer thanks to Calvert Barksdale, the value of whose editing and counseling has been immeasurable; publishers Richard and Jeannette Seaver, who have shown both support for and faith in this work; Jessica Kaye; Kevin Mills; and the one who was there at this book's inception, Edit Villarreal.

Finally, the authors wish to thank all the men and women of the Officers for Justice, past and present.